READING WRITING

JULIEN GRACQ

TURTLE POINT PRESS

NEW YORK

READING WRITING

TRANSLATED BY

JEANINE HERMAN

EN LISANT EN ÉCRIVANT

Copyright © 1980 Librairie José Corti

ISBN 10: 1-933527-02-1

ISBN 13: 978-1-933527-02-4

LCCN: 2006900893

Design and composition by Jeff Clark
at Wilsted & Taylor Publishing Services

CONTENTS

LITERATURE AND PAINTING

We know of hardly any painters who are born to their art already armed head to toe with their own technique, masters of their palette, touch, impasto, glazes. All of them seem to have arrived at their craft, which constitutes their signature, gradually, slowly, sometimes even in the public eye. Because writing and editing are the foundations of the scholarly institution, literature reveals an entirely different picture: a number of writers, beginning with their very first book, already write the way they will write their entire life. It is in their homework and school essays, from grammar school to high school to college, that one must seek the progressive maturation, which has remained private, and that, with their public debut, has placed them in possession of a complete instrument. But there is also a whole category of writers, not necessarily inferior ones, who emerge in public while still immature, and whose formation is completed, sometimes rather laboriously, under the eye of readers, the way the gestation of a marsupial is completed in the open air and in a ventral pouch. Eminent examples of writers of the first sort: Claudel, Valéry, Stendhal, Montherlant; of the second: Chateaubriand, Rimbaud (who represents the extreme case of a literary *premature baby*), Proust, Mauriac.

There is a price to pay for this delay in development, which is to leave a part of one's published works in the state of rough drafts and exercises, even to drag around with oneself for a long time the remnants of an incubating cocoon. There is also a privilege to be had, which is to conserve in one's writing the vibration that is inseparable from the effort toward distinct form, a vibration that writers who have received the gift of an impeccable line of *ready-to-wear* do not know.

*

It is the *slowness* of the art of writing, in its mechanical execution, that for years now has at times repelled and discouraged me: the wasted time of a writer throwing words on the page, like a musician throwing notes on a staff. The work of a transcriber and copyist—sometimes as sobering as a splash of cold water—is interjected between the heated agitation of the mind and the material arrangement of the work. What I envy painters and sculptors, what makes their work so sensually jubilant and consistent (at least I imagine it this way), is the complete absence of these lulls, however minor they may be; it is the miracle of economy, the instant feedback of the brushstroke or the blow of the chisel that in a single movement creates, establishes, and corrects at once; it is the circuit, animated and tangible from end to end, uniting in them the brain, which conceives and enjoins, to the hand, which not only produces and establishes but, in return and indivisibly, rectifies, nuances, and suggests —a circulation without any lulls at all, at times arterial, at times venous, that seems at each moment to convey a sort of spirit of the material toward the brain and a materiality of thought toward the hand.

*

Every now and then I am consumed by the desire to write against the contemporary adulation of the visual arts, and, most particularly, painting. On the market, the preeminence of painting over all the other arts is paraded, crushingly. Without saying so expressly, and without writing about it, Breton in fact half-recognized this. Malraux, in *L'homme précaire et la Littérature*, treats it as a *fata morgana* that comes to shimmer belatedly, fleetingly, on the very old background of sculpture and rock carving.[1]

It would not be inconsequential to ask oneself why, in

this unending trial between word and image, the great monotheistic religions, of Israel as well as Islam, have thrown Images into the fire and kept only the Book. The word is an awakening, a call to excess; the figure a freezing, a fascination. The book opens a distant horizon to life, while the image bewitches and immobilizes it. One, in fairly clear fashion, refers invariably to immanence, the other to transcendence (this is particularly true of post-medieval literature, and, singularly, of the novel, which is its supremely "Faustian" aspect. Greek tragedy, meanwhile, the literary emblem of antiquity operating rigorously in a closed circuit, tends only toward a final silence that petrifies it, and whose symbol is either Oedipus with gouged eyes or Prometheus with the vulture— in both cases, a perfect statue).

When I visit a museum, particularly when the canvases are arranged by school and in chronological order, what intrigues me is the aspect, the essentially terminal significance, of the masterpieces it assembles; by exalting them, they impose an obsolescence (in the most noble sense) on the moments of history that produced them, leaving them all inexpressibly dated. What a century deposits and bequeaths in its painting are its imaginary archives—its most dazzling archives, but archives

4

nonetheless, classified and closed, and marked primarily by the aptitude for motionless peregrination through the centuries (it is of the painting, the statue, and not the written text, that one can say "Changed into himself at last by eternity."[2] An exalted and *arrested* memorization, against which Time itself will not prevail—this is the immediate feeling that every great painting communicates to us, with the haughty and spellbinding air it has, like Baudelaire's Don Juan, of entering indefinitely into the future while moving backward: all painting, in its essence, is retrospective.[3] Hence its relative insignificance as an element of active civilization: all the ferment that the art of an era conveys is conveyed by literature; a painting may enchant moments in a life, in the pure magical sense, but it has never changed a life (except those of future painters): yet this is what many books have done, and do, from year to year, even books that are not masterpieces. Because literature, and within literature fiction in particular, is in essence an offer of possibility, possibility that asks only to be turned eventually into desire or will, and painting proposes nothing: with an immobile, icebound majesty, to which literature cannot gain access, it invariably represents a last stop.

*

Nowadays, people instinctively see themselves as free agents, circulating in an inert material world and treating it as a simple tool for their convenience. It is difficult to rid them of the idea that things are different in fiction, because they have the reassuring sense of finding themselves on familiar ground. Indeed, characters in a novel, as in life, come and go, speak, act, while the world maintains its apparent and passive role as support and backdrop. Yet something that has no place in real life forcefully brings them together: people and things, their substantial distinctions abolished, have all in equal measure become *material for a novel*—at once acted upon and acting, active and passive, and shot through by an endless chain of the drives, tractions, and twists of the singular mechanism that brings novels to life, that in its combinations effortlessly amalgamates living, thinking matter and inert matter, and that indiscriminately transforms both subjects and objects—to the understandable scandal of every philosophical mind—into the simple material conductors of a fluid.

Do you think people in novels, as in life, possess all the privileges of autonomy and confront a material world they have arranged to their liking? Then come see the novelist at work in his *capharnaum* (as Homais called it)[4] and proceed to his airy alchemical transmuta-

6

tions: kicking his hero's exacting moral conscience into a corner like a pedestal table, because center stage now requires all the space for a still life, or incorporating his character, easily amalgamating him—plumped up, reduced, now Lilliputian, now enormous—into a row of vegetables, an opera foyer, a sunset. For him, ten lines of moral debate or Louis XV furniture, in a certain profound, essential way, *forms a whole*.

In this sense alone, real fiction has a relationship with painting: *ut pictura poesis*.[5] The animation a novel is filled with, in which activity imitated from life is mirrored by the activity of the reading process, an animation that at first glance violently distances it from the fixed images of the painted canvas, is a trompe l'oeil that cannot fundamentally deceive. Just as a painting is made of a certain number of square decimeters of canvas marked by colors, none possessing a value different from the others, a novel is made of a certain number of thousands of marked signs whose equivalence, as the material-of-the-novel, is absolute, whatever the meanings to which they refer, because *the novel as a whole* is the only value, all representations that these signs cause to spring forth being equal for the duration of the reading. The "life" of a novel—since it seems that often there is life—is only attributed after the fact to the apparent an-

imation of these characters by an instinctive and misleading comparison to the real world, where in fact only
the living move and are moved: this is not different, in
and of itself, from the "life" of a painting, in which the
only things that intervene are the relationships of tone
and surface among inert elements. That perception in
one case, intellect and the free play of the imagination
in another, remain preponderant in the face of the work
does not introduce a fundamental difference between
painting and fiction, as far as the deceitful homogeniza-
tion that occurs there between the living and the inert. A
novel by Balzac—for example—which one might enjoy
trimming of its description in the helpful intention of
cutting the fat (this undertaking was called for in the last
century by serious critics), would in no way evoke a
house tidied up and made spacious, but rather a gothic
nave whose flying buttresses have been demolished for
the sake of economy.

*

I am struck by the insightful simplicity, the solid and direct precision, the bursting vitality of painters, sculptors, musicians, and most artists who use the hand, eye,
and ear, when they are capable of speaking of their art;
next to them, in the writer who speaks of writing, every-

thing is too often outrage or retraction, dust in the eyes, alibis. The causes are in literature's profound ambiguity, where a thousand enzymes work and ferment the material as it is being elaborated. Commentary on the art of writing is inextricably mixed up with writing at the outset. The creative artist who steps back and tries to understand what he is doing stands before his canvas as before a green and intact prairie: for the writer, the literary material he would like to recapture in its freshness is already similar to what passes from the second to the third stomach of a ruminant.

*

The blues and golds of *Fra Angelico*: the radiance, the effulgence of an altar's vestments. The blues and yellows of Vermeer: the saturated matteness, the thorough permeation of color by an earthy material, as if the secularization of art had also implied a despiritualization of its matter. The Dutchman's colors are the sap of the earth, no longer the phosphorescence of the Visitation. Ever since Byzantium and Angelico, painting no longer dared cloak itself—though it could have—in the *suit of lights*[6] any more than those in power today allow themselves rows of banners and the fanfare of trumpets.

It seems, moreover, as though all art in ripening has a

tendency to confine itself to the median register of its means of expression: as the demands of its material grow, as the initiative in the artist moves gradually from thought or vision to words and color, one might say an unwritten law compels words and color to be discreet and reserved, enjoins them to veil an overly provocative splendor that would trumpet all their power from the rooftops. In classical art, it is already evident: in Racine most of all.

*

Only painting or sculpture of the first order can capture, on canvas or in marble, images of female beauty that elude time. Neither photography nor film can do this: after thirty years or less, all women's faces begin to appear old-fashioned, because there is a fashion of living faces, and not simply of makeup and hairstyles, that constantly changes, like the cut of clothing (though more slowly). And one suspects that even the loftiest literature—if, as a result of some fateful spell, it truly managed to *show you something*—would not escape this sort of aging, and that, for example, Odette de Crécy in Proust, her "eyes welling with affection, ready to detach themselves like tears,"[7] in fact only represented the better-dressed twin sister of the pin-up girl on postcards popular in 1914, at the low end of the spectrum or—lower lids curved like the shell of a mussel—the still-adolescent stars of the silent screen, in the mid-range, like Mary Pickford. This is because a woman's seduction is exerted—on the artist as on the fabric clerk—according to the canons of current beauty, but the painter, when he paints his mistress, is only in love with his canvas and its demands, while the hand with the pen, because it evokes and can never show, easily turns lead into gold without really having to *transmute* anything. Or, instead of gold, a strange paper currency of entirely fiduciary value that circulates with all the virtues of a precious metal, without anyone being allowed to examine the cash balance.

*

What can explain the repeated calamities of the *rainbow* in figurative painting? It could be that an excess of ostentatious *prettiness* and its provocative, ready-made quality turns the true painter away from it. But more likely there is another cause: what prevents the integration of a rainbow into a painting is not an insurmountable technical difficulty; it constitutes the admission of a painter's failure to submit *all* natural elements, without exception, to the organized arbitrariness of his personal vision. The rainbow is an insertion into the middle of a vivid symphony written entirely in a subjective key, in a dioptric formula resistant to any substitution. And such prohibitions indicated in painting also apply to literature.

*

Duplication in art. Giorgio De Chirico exhibits in a Belgian gallery. On the first page of the catalog, a full-length portrait of the artist: in the grand uniform of the Academician, heavy, ungainly, his face devoid of thought, muttonlike and obtuse, beneath white, woolly hair, hands crossed over a jutting paunch, he brings to mind both an unskilled laborer disguised in the Academy's green costume and Ingres's Bertin. The same heavy build of bourgeois prosperity, the same grin of satisfaction, sly and sated. He is eighty-eight years old. After being submerged in academicism for fifty years, he is now remaking the paintings he painted at thirty without modification—simply recombining their elements, like an Erector set: streets with arcades, pink towers, empty squares, equestrian statues casting shadows, factory smokestacks, locomotives in remote landscapes—"unsettling muses" with heads of light bulbs, mannequins, bobbins, T-squares, artichokes. And these paintings that are so many impostures, these paintings that are tricked-out and soulless—which one might imagine being resigned to responding solely to market demand, gracelessly and after a long sulk—are not easily distinguished from those he painted half a century ago. The same edge of yellow sky at the horizon, below a heavy green firmament, the same magnet of the arcades, the same low walls masking a procession of railroad cars against the light. All of which, in advance and from the start, almost erased for me what surrealist painting at its best might have subsequently offered.

Ostensibly and conscientiously—through a rare combination of precocious indifference, cynicism, and longevity—he was one of the first artists allowed to become his own forger. The big, white, wily tomcat that caught so many mice, the bulky manipulator of painting, peering slyly from the threshold of his catalog at the visitors of the galleries, presents an enigma, a slightly irksome one.

Nothing like this is conceivable in literature: it is significant, too, that the titles of De Chirico's recent paintings, more than the canvases, are what suggest a noticeable flagging. *The Metaphysician in Summer*, *The Joy of Toys*, *Chance Encounter*, do not equal the titles of yesteryear that instantly hit the bull's-eye: *The Oracle's Enigma*, *Pink Tower*, *Melancholy and Mystery of a*

Street. In everything having to do with the production of poetic writing, there is the requirement of an almost sexual generosity, which has no chance of being imitated by itself fifty years down the road. But in painting—when one thinks of the nearly hundred-year-old Titian, the orthopedic paintbrush of the paralyzed Renoir, this De Chirico *redivivus*—it would seem the artist is not offering the artworks equal amounts of emotional substance. When a door has been painstakingly forced, when access has been found to a treasure, the painter has the privilege of minting his discovery, a kingly right to reduplication without real loss of authenticity. Picasso's "pink" paintings, Degas's dancers and laundresses, Redon's flowers, La Tour's "lights," maintain relationships with each other that are both closer and more mechanical than the poems in *Illuminations* (for example) or those in *The Legend of the Ages*: without objecting to this, we sense that they involve both the imperious signature of the unique and the thrifty exploitation of the mass produced. From one work in this pictorial series to another, our demand for modulation is simpler and more succinct than that which we would instinctively emphasize vis-à-vis two poems in the same collection (the only one, to my knowledge, that almost presents this mass-produced homogeneity of the matter and manner

proper to painting is Verlaine's collection, *Fêtes Ga-
lantes*, which, by the way, not insignificantly, seems to
animate a series of paintings by Watteau.)

What we should probably see in this, for one thing, is
the persistence of some historical residue that has not
been completely absorbed: the fact that the painter has
long maintained the status of artisan, the serf of his
clientele (a status literature has escaped much more
quickly because of the written text's ability to be reproduced at will, once beyond its author's hand and voice).
Almost until our century, the painter has been a pro-
ducer of images on demand, for whom commissions
abounded and multiplied for what he knew how to do
best or what he alone knew how to do: lights for La Tour,
composite heads for Arcimboldo, military ironmongery
for Meissonier (the existence of secrets and *tricks of the
trade*, hidden and stolen as enamellers, ceramicists, or
even cooks might have done, is characteristic today only
of painters). The painter, when he copies himself, still
benefits today from the effects of an expired tolerance
that outlives him: we remember that he was bound by
the servitude of the supplier. But this tolerance on the
way to extinction does not—fundamentally—explain
why the literary pastiche remains an amusement without scope while the *faux* in painting is an industry, an

industry rooted partially in the current practice of authentic artists.

It might be interesting to reflect on what separates the "motif" a painter works on from the "subject" a novelist or a poet has set out to tackle. It would be impossible to exhaust the virtual possibilities of a motif without having several perspectives of it, without, more or less, walking around it: Claude Monet's landscape series as well as Picasso's multi-profile faces are two opposed and convergent means of admitting and surmounting the contradiction of a visual art walled up in two-dimensional space. The series, quite naturally, is there in its infancy. On the contrary, what comes closest to a painting in literature—description—does not at all resemble a series of perspectives constantly brought into focus. In literature, all description is a *path* (that may lead nowhere), a path we travel down but never retrace; all true description is a digression that only refers to its starting point as a stream refers to its source: by turning its back on it and—eyes half shut—trusting only in its intimate truth, which is the awakening of a naturally eccentric dynamic. The complete impossibility of instantaneousness—because the reading process is spread out over time, eliminating as it adds at every moment—is the basis for the antinomy of descriptive literature. Literature tries to resolve this by turning vision into movement. But this path, which is its personal solution, a path of great speed and imaginative flow, understandably excludes any temptation for replication.

To describe is to replace the instant comprehension of the retina with an associative sequence of images that unfolds over time. Always hand in hand with the preliminaries of dramatic art, description tends not toward a quietist unveiling of the object but toward the beating heart at the rising of the curtain. Nowhere is this aspect of theatrical prelude more clearly apparent than in the famous description of Meschacebé at the beginning of *Atala* that establishes a tone, is broken up into contrasting movements, comes alive, and ultimately explodes in the final *tutti* of an opera overture.

For me, painting remains the world that calls attention to its closed heart, at times in the form of ecstasies that may be repeated but may not resemble each other. Description is the world that opens its paths and becomes a path where someone is already walking or about to walk.

*

I am reading Matisse's writings on painting: fragments of letters, interviews, technical notes, sometimes a few more extensive and affably categorical pages that one could call professions of faith. There is a quiet honesty, a sedative freshness, a scrupulous and workmanlike proximity to the material of his art that infinitely pleases me. If he is corresponding with Bonnard, they sound like two elegant monks informing each other of the progress on their twin projects, helping each other, without selfishness or pettiness, come closer to the truth.

Only two scientists searching for the solution to some difficult immunological or genetic problem could correspond this way, one imagines, without hiding anything from each other about their experiments or conjectures, vanity counting for little in the face of the objective all-importance of the acquisition of knowledge. Not two literary sorts, alas! Except perhaps in the unlikely case of two contemporary Mallarmés.

Correspondence exists between writers who have no doubt enriched each other; leaving aside the letters exchanged between Flaubert and Maxime du Camp, or between Mallarmé and some Symbolist poet, where the imbalance in the mutual contribution is too flagrant, we could at least cite, in a recent era, what we know of the correspondence between Gide and Martin du Gard. It does not go beyond reciprocal and stimulating critique. None of the almost mystical mutual aid put into practice on the path to perfection, in the quest of this paradise of painting that seems to exist concretely for certain painters, and to which a chosen few, whom Matisse cites here, have surely gained entrance: Giotto, Cézanne, Piero della Francesca, Chardin.

An intimate difference in the nature of the writer's relationship with his art separates him from almost all other artists. There may be saints of music (everyone would cite Bach), saints of sculpture (the sculptors of cathedrals), there are certainly saints of painting (just as it has its Lucifers: Picasso) with a Franciscan approach of Truth rather than Beauty. There are no saints of literature: nothing, even with the distance of glory and death, nothing but heretics locked up in their singular heresy, who do not want communion with the saints. There is a choir of dead painters in some empyrean who celebrate for us the ineffable joys of Peace in real Painting, from Vermeer to Chardin to Cézanne; neither Rimbaud, nor Baudelaire, nor Claudel, nor Racine, nor Stendhal, nor Rousseau, nor Flaubert will join anyone at all in the afterlife (in spite of the efforts of literary handbooks) to celebrate some unifying life together in Poetry—and their garden of Eden will forever remain one of forking paths.

*

The past fifteen years, which apparently will not count for much in the history of our literature, have brought more change in the publishing industry and bookstore business than these have known since Gutenberg. The history of literature, at least momentarily, has slowed down; the history of the book has taken its place. Yet what seems to us today to be a new development in literature in fact fills the history of painting, rich with periods when importance was placed not on *names* and schools but on changes in technique, materials, media, and markets: the invention of oil painting, the passage from fresco to easel painting and its clientele, etc.

STENDHAL — BALZAC —

FLAUBERT — ZOLA

For every period of art, there is an intimate rhythm, as natural and instinctive for it as the rhythm of breathing can be, and that, much more profoundly than its picturesque exterior, more profoundly even than the key images that obsess it, connects it to being and really causes it to exist: only in this rhythm does the world begin to dance in time for it, only at this pace can it pick up and translate life, the way the needle of a gramophone can only read a record at a certain established and regulated speed. Mozart's *tempo* is fundamentally foreign to Wagner's but maintains a close, vital relationship with *Dangerous Liaisons* and *Manon Lescaut* or *The Ingenu*: *The Marriage of Figaro* marks the natural conjugation of its specific speed with the literature of its time; similarly, in another era, Wagner's *lento maestoso* was paired with Baudelaire and Poe, and all Symbolist literature. An equally essential change in rhythm, a similar slowing down of *tempo*, probably more important than the modification of material in a novel or the composition of a character—and which perhaps ultimately presides there and commands it—separates, in the history of the novel, *Cousin Bette* or *The Charterhouse of Parma* on the one hand, and *Madame Bovary* on the other. A novelistic superpressure—where pages jostle one another and content swirls like water in a reservoir emptying from the bottom, as if the world were suddenly trying, in literary terms, to evacuate itself entirely through an overly narrow conduit—congests *La Comédie Humaine* from beginning to end, and confers on Balzac's works the suffocating density of an agitated world reaching its maximum internal tension. And the airier *allegro* of *The Charterhouse* is quicker still: it is a traveler without baggage, unencumbered by voluminous Balzacian carriages. Flaubert's *tempo*, in *Madame Bovary* and also in *Education*,[8] is entirely that of a retrospective journey, of a man looking over his shoulder—therefore, already much closer to Proust than to Balzac, it belongs not so much to the season of unhappy bourgeois consciousness, perhaps, as to one in which the novel slides gradually into nostalgic rumination, its kinetic energy depleted from prospecting what it was as a whole. We should try to reread the great nineteenth-century novels as if they were the hero's final glimpse over his life, this illuminating encapsulation attributed to the dying in their final seconds: such a fiction is rejected from the start by *The Red and the Black* and by *Old Goriot*,[9] which rail against it on every page, but constitutes light itself, the only plausible light, in *Madame Bovary*, with its sluggish, stupefied pauses, where all its scenes, one by one, come to sink into the mire: a life recalled in its entirety, with no real departure, no problematics, without the faintest palpitation of the future. A dreamy, listless *tempo* with a vaguely dreamlike coloration, that is not solely concerned with a personal constant or a subject's demands, far from it, but that is the muffled and rhythmic bass of every era, and that, one might say, as their creative poles coincide, makes *Sentimental Education* an almost totally unrecognizable replica of *Lost Illusions*.

*

Stendhal sings his own praises in *On Love*, *Memoirs of an Egotist*, *Henry Brulard*, not in *The Charterhouse*: the novel mercilessly ferrets out the secret and well-protected images from the heart of hearts, because it will draw pitilessly on the author's last reserves. Even poetry is better at disguise than this. The exceptionally high vital expenditure demanded by the novel is partially responsible (a caricaturist of the end of the last century who left elegant parties at the break of day said it was not until four in the morning that fashionable women's faces finally relaxed—or gave in). And, above all, no color lasts —on the literary genre most battered by all kinds of bad weather—but the colorfast colors, colors carved from the block. Everything iridescent—even if it is charming, even if it is delightful—pitiless years will scour from the novel, with the friction of a scrubbing brush. A superficial emotion may bring color and life to "fleeting" poetry for a long time (Verlaine's collections are full of these poems that seem to shimmer like a butterfly wing, and that nevertheless are protected by an invisible fixative). But it cannot animate a novel. The period between the two world wars, and particularly Anglo-Saxon literature (Rosamond Lehmann, Margaret Kennedy, etc.), was rich in novels vibrating, like aeolian harps, with a lively feminine sensibility, but that did not innervate a single central, internal organizing image: in spite of their qualities, their immediate charm, they went the way of yesterday's snow (and yet *Weather in the Streets* and *The Constant Nymph*, which no one seems to remember today, were not minor novels).[10] It is not sufficient for a novel to be carried by the heat of a sincere emotion; this emotion has to be able to reanimate the chosen images, stored and dormant, the whole secret, private iconography—and not the documents or "true little facts" collected externally—that alone represent the real archives with which a novelist fills his books. The bad novelist—by which I mean the skilled and indifferent novelist—is the one who tries to bring to life, to animate from the outside and on the whole faithfully, the local color that strikes him as specific to a subject he has judged ingenious or picturesque—the true novelist is the one who cheats, who asks the subject, above all, through oblique and unexpected paths, to give him access once again to his personal palette, knowing full well that in terms of local color, the only kind that can make an impression is his own.

Thus, Flaubert, half the time, is mistaken about the choice of subjects he deals with, because he believes their autonomy must be respected. What self-denial in the act of writing *Salammbô*! But, in truth, in the eyes of the authentic novelist, it is the subject that must make room for him and not he who should lend life and heat to the development of a foreign body according to its own law.

*

It certainly seems that of the *four greats* of the French novel—Stendhal, Balzac, Flaubert, and Proust—Balzac seems left behind by criticism today: the quantity of studies on him is no doubt far behind those devoted to each of the three others. The "competition of his works with the registry office," and the disparity in relation to the traditional novel—a fatally minimal disparity for him, since everyone tacitly sought this sort of novel chiefly in his books—everything that built his glory solidly, undoes him in 1978 among the subtlest literary scholars: the model of the French novel, just as Hugo is the model of poetry, we tend to accord him the same essential function as reference and the same sort of disinterest *per se* that we accord a yardstick.

And I admit when I have the desire to reopen him, it is primarily for those of his works that could be considered more or less deviant in relation to the type: not *Lost Illusions*, *Cousin Bette*, or *Eugénie Grandet*, but *Les Chouans*, *Lily of the Valley*, *Béatrix*. Rereading the standard Balzac no longer gives me but a moderate pleasure. I am surprised moreover—having just reread *An Old Maid*—at the differences in quality of this supplier's product (differences to which Alain, out of piety, once directed us to close our eyes).[11] The missteps and chatter of *An Old Maid*, its buffet-table pleasantries, the outrage and at times parodic inconsistency of the characters (Athanase Granson!) surprised me, on this rereading, so much so that I couldn't believe my eyes at times, and, furious with myself, almost agreed with Sainte-Beuve's judgment.

If, as soon as he was published, Balzac had been abundantly and faithfully illustrated, as, for example, Jules Verne was by his publisher Hetzel, if our reading habits did not separate his text from such images any more than *Five Weeks in a Balloon* or *North Against South*, it seems at times we would be better able to sense, or more clearly see, the essential Balzacian singularity, which is a hemming in and almost a burying of each character in the hyperbolic network of the material relationships in which he is not simply engaged, as with other realist novelists, but truly swaddled, to the point of being almost inseparable in the end from these encasings, as concentric and tight as an onion skin, encasings that outline, mold, and almost definitively make him exist for us. Encasings that, most intimately, are called clothes, furniture, and home, and, most externally, kinship, relations, trades, business, fortune. People go into ecstasies, and justly so, over the human swarm of Balzacian characters making up the various repertories, but do they imagine (for example) what dreamlike Galeries Barbès, what hyperbolic *Manufrance* catalog, what accumulation of issues of *Intermédiaire des chercheurs et des curieux*, what *quantity* of universal secondhand furniture could rival the gigantic thrift shop, the colossal flea market, catalogued and described in the thirty or forty volumes of *La Comédie Humaine*? There is more than one novel by Balzac—and, above all, we should recognize, more than one second-rate effort—where the essence of the book seems to be not man's relationship with the world, or man's relationship with his fellow-man or society, but rather man's relationship with the moneyed and material intermediary of these great, intimidating entities: Furniture and Real Estate.

*

The light and playful tone with which Stendhal speaks of the conflict of the social classes (l'abbé Pirard at the Marquis de la Mole's) belongs entirely to the eighteenth century, a century that for Balzac remains as if it never existed. Between them there is not only a mutual exclusion of the space of the novel, but a time lag in the historic *moment* of the gaze, and, because of this lag, there is a sort of distantness in Stendhal in relation to his narrative that marks his books more intimately perhaps than any other feature. *The Red and the Black* is certainly Stendhal at his most brilliant, but, at times, it is also as if Laclos or Diderot had been asked, against the grain of chronology, to recount the Restoration. This does not have to do only with tone, the omnipresence of a will for demystification, or generalized skepticism. The opacity and inevitability of the social structure, whose physical weight we feel on each page of Balzac, have in Stendhal no other reality but a semi-fanciful one. We can leave aside *The Charterhouse*, where money plays no role and where social relations between rich and poor are treated somewhat like those of kings and shepherds in the pastoral novel. But if we take *The Red and the Black*, for example, we must observe that in spite of the apparent realism of the whole, the two true Balzacian realities, money and social promotion, are treated purely as fairy tales there. In spite of all the calculations of his ambition, money comes to Julien Sorel only in the anonymous form of a mysterious bill of exchange—promotion, by the magical stroke of a no less mysterious summons to see the Marquis de la Mole. Moreover, at no moment in the "arriviste" Sorel's career is there the slightest relationship between will and results. This is because Balzac, when he is optimistic, is the novelist of planned success, and Stendhal, the novelist of happiness, always more or less the product of a miracle (here, prison). The only social moral to be extracted from his books is that *goals* serve no purpose, except to communicate the motions through which happiness might present itself obliquely to a life; it is the moral of a class that has "arrived," that of the witty, cynical, pleasure-seeking court nobles of eighteenth-century salons, with the Marquis de la Mole and Count Mosca their old-fashioned brothers, the two true mentors on the life paths of Julien and Fabrice, respectively.

*

Politics in *The Red and the Black*. I like the fact that no made-up name is clearly translatable for the historian here (though, more than once, on the topic of conspiracy, one name comes to the tip of the tongue). My principle has been confirmed: in fiction, everything should be fictional: Stendhal even managed to avoid the name of the reigning monarch. A character in a novel, however lifelike he may be, instantly loses his suppleness and freedom if we encounter him in a scene with an actual historical figure, because suddenly he has been linked to an isolated fixed point: for a moment, he is nothing more than a coat hung on a peg. Thus—in *Men of Good Will*, a novel quite unworthy of *The Red*—this happens to Gurau or Mionnet, as soon as they make contact with Poincaré or Jaurès.[12]

An objection, by the way, that has nothing against the historical novel, where authentic characters, by the mere fact of becoming members of the majority party, find themselves automatically fictionalized, in *The Three Musketeers* as in *War and Peace*. This spontaneous mutation of substance is made obvious by a novel like Dumas's *Queen Margot*, where there are almost no invented characters: the few remaining fictional figures, in the midst of their fully conquered novelistic freedom, suddenly make things awkward for Catherine de Médicis or the Duke d'Alençon.

*

The loges of La Scala, San Carlo in Naples, the Argentina Theater in Rome—rented for the year or granted for life, carpeted, draped, furnished, and canopied in the taste of their tenants—were Stendhal's true second homes in Italy; but, contrary to our customs, people left the glacial and unfurnished grand palaces of that era at a fixed hour to find the promiscuity of shared transports and the warmth of proximity to others.

*

In his processes of magnification, Balzac never dismisses the preoccupations of the caricaturist: faithfulness to the real, swiftness, divination, isolation of the decisive feature, but also, distortion and systematic accentuation for effect. His (scarcely inferior) counterpart in the category of the plastic arts is indeed Daumier, a great painter, but halfway between Rembrandt the engraver and the *Charivari*.[13] In reality, just as a writer like Colette in our time had privileged and at times distorted relationships with a certain right-bank *café society* all her life (guided by Willy),[14] whose sense of elegance, art, innovation, and success had very little in common with the preoccupations of the circles that, say, Gide or Claudel moved in, in order to grasp the nature of Balzac's ambitions, we would have to surround him with a whole milieu deeply marked by the very emphatic, broad strokes of journalism (which fascinated him), and by the distorting pencil of Daumier, Guys, or Gavarni.[15] A world for whom the sign of success is not the work of art painstakingly and slowly elaborated in private, but the punch that instantly makes the Parisian echo chamber resonate—not the exquisite and shadowy marginality of Stendhal, but the flashy career of George Sand, or the dazzling ascent of Thiers carried by the rocket of the *National*.[16]

*

In the end, it doesn't matter whether you prefer Stendhal to Balzac or to Flaubert, or to anyone else, or whether you find his novel production meager, and, moreover, colonized, garlanded everywhere like a forest by its creeping vines, by arabesques without beginning or end, the inexhaustible flourish of his ego; his singularity is that he delivers to his readers an *era and country* completely in the margins of both chronology and geography, an Icaria whose consonances alone are Italian, floating somewhere in the displaced time between Garibaldi and Césare Borgia, flourishing not by trade, industry and commerce, but solely by virtue of leisure and the free exercise of the passions (among them, conversation), having as monuments the residences of Palladio and the prisons of Piranesi, as government and police a congregation of black men straight out of the novels of Donatien-Alphonse de Sade—a country whose forum would be the theater, and vernacular language the opera, and all this lodged in an historically impossible-to-situate *no man's land*, a timeless country made up only of witty people, where—the Revolution placed in parentheses, though spoken of constantly—Byron and Mazzini could meet on familiar ground and converse with Casanova and Cardinal de Bernis. If I read Balzac or Dostoyevsky, the distortion that a sovereign temperament imprints on my vision of the world is imposed on me as on everyone else, and yet, when I reopen my eyes, I am in this world, I am still here. But if I push open the door of a novel by Beyle,[17] I enter Stend-halia, as if returning to a vacation home: worries fall from my shoulders, obligation takes a holiday, the weight of the world is alleviated; everything is different: the smell of the air, the lines of the landscape, one's appetite, the lightness of living, greetings themselves, the way people approach each other. Everyone knows that every great novelist creates a "world" (and perhaps we repeat this a bit complacently, because it is saying a lot)—Stendhal does both more and less at once: he establishes a second, inhabitable native land for his true readers, off to the side, a retreat suspended outside time, not really situated, not really dated, a refuge made for life's Sundays, where the air is drier, more bracing, where life flows, relaxed and fresh—an Eden of free passions flooded by the joy of living, where nothing very bad can happen definitively, where love is reborn from its ashes, and where even true sorrow is transformed into benign regret.

*

What image would remain of Stendhal had he not written either *The Red and the Black* or *The Charterhouse?* A naïve question that cannot be stopped from prowling around in one's head at times, since—cut off from the two powerful fictional breakwaters that reinforce it—the rest of the work seems scattered, circumstantial, incomplete. That of an amateur polygraph, an original mind, full of fire and wit, but paralyzed at the approach of completion? Of a literary Caliban, masking his secret impotence behind borrowings and copyings? The materially considerable mass of what must be called a brilliant writer's scrap heap does not in any way evoke Proust's extraneous matter, material abandoned in bulk at the foot of the enormous edifice of *Remembrance of Things Past*: these are at times the obsessive "fragments" of a beautiful mind in a small town, at times the potboilers of a very talented scribbler, at times the misfires characteristic of a writer who has not managed to place his voice, who is bogged down in subjects without perspective. There is no trace of genius—that's what worries me—in the ten or fifteen beginnings of narratives that Stendhal left in the lurch. Once again he raises the problem, which intrigues me so, of the unexpected passage to excellence—a problem that Nerval personifies exemplarily, but that Stendhal/Beyle, under his multiple names, has raised as well. It is true that three lines of *The Life of Henry Brulard* today seem irrefutably typical. Probably, in 1840, they were no less so for his correspondents—his sister Pauline, Mérimée, Jacquemont—only they were signed Beyle and had the sort of effect on them that entries in the *Journal* of Jules Renard produce in us, though in 1978 for us they are signed Stendhal, and their trace extends incommensurably from every shadow of *The Red* and *Charterhouse*. A unique effect of backlighting enhances the appealing chatter of the everyday Beyle: glory (which for him was really the sun of the dead) does not cause the remarks of a man of wit, long since recognized as such, to sparkle after the fact (which would only be banal) but closely incorporates them, agglutinates them to his masterpieces. The effect of integration that is not exercised to any degree on *Things Seen* by Hugo or the travel writing of Flaubert, which remain heterogeneous to the bulk of their work, is exercised fully on the slightest fragment by Stendhal, which itself hastens to form a whole, indissociably, with the mass of his nevertheless singularly reduced master works. Never has such a reduced radioactive core transmuted and bombarded so thick an inert shell.

*

The increase in the separative power of the internal eye, from Madame de La Fayette to Stendhal, and from Stendhal to Proust, is probably the clearest indication of the progress of "the psychological novel." But, if there is any progress, it is not in the sense of a "truth" held more and more tightly: rather it is in the sense of the liberation of a subtler, richer personal enchantment, which the author views on the interior stage and of which his art extends enjoyment to his reader without enriching his knowledge. Psychology in fiction is pure creation, doubled by an active power of suggestion.

*

The comparison of Stendhal and Balzac is the comparison of two different images of the world, powerfully overdetermined and underlined by literary techniques separated by a century, whereas the gap between the birth dates of both writers, which is only sixteen years, makes them almost contemporaries. Each of them perched in uneasy balance on the extreme edge of two literary periods, one beginning and the other ending, they seem almost to hold hands, like the bottom floors of corbelled houses separated by a street with car traffic. When I go from *The Charterhouse*—where the landscapes of Lombardy and the Alps have the misty, voluptuous blur of those of Watteau—to the beginning of *Béatrix*, the formidable disembarking of the external world in the novel, with its freight train rumbling, suddenly brings me back to the awareness of this gaping fissure: *Quid* of the palace that the Sanseverina inhabits?[18] The odor of the streets of Parma? And yet already all the pathos that the nineteenth century will link to History is present there, with the prelude of Waterloo to usher us in.[19] How many untold pleasures do we owe solely to Stendhal's technical and tangible "lateness," while Balzac's jumble of furniture, barely extracted from its cases, still waits to be sifted through by the exacting parsimony of a Flaubert!

*

Why do Stendhal's intimate obsessions and peculiarities, the maxims he jots down on his suspenders, why does an idle Breton walking the grand boulevards toward the *Longines* clock, or following a charming young lady in the street as she looks for *cornichons*,[20] captivate us, when nothing like this would retain our interest (I am choosing almost at random) neither from the pen of Hugo nor that of Flaubert—and I will add, whether Valéry likes it or not, nor from that of Restif, whose self-indulgence I find tedious?[21]

The cause here is neither a more marked egocentrism (Hugo takes the cake) nor a penchant for confession (which Breton barely has, in spite of appearances). What counts, and all that counts, is the rare coincidence of a single wavelength conveying the rhythms of the *habitus* and those of speech, pell-mell: thus vital tone itself becomes an imperious style of writing, and style becomes gesture, bearing, tone of voice.

*

Napoleon's fall was Stendhal's lucky break. All the same, after the first "dime-store success" in Marseilles was cut short, he nevertheless shot up nicely in the *rice, bread, and salt* division of the Grand Army.[22] Beyle scholars hardly ever speak of this long period from 1806 to 1814, from which literature is absent, not only because professional obligations take over, but because Stendhal (after 1810 especially), being busy, established, official, well received, and receptive, no doubt had less need to write once he could satisfy the desire that we imagine to be vital in him: to speak as he wished, in public, wherever and with whomever he pleased. In the long existence of forced leisure that would be the rest of his life, we do not sufficiently imagine the moments of solitude that, even in Italy, must have prevailed over the others by a fair amount; solitude due to financial constraint, to celibacy, to his constantly offside situation as a man about town without means, a saunterer on both riverbanks in Paris, a foreigner (in spite of everything) in Italy, where he only ever had a tourist's visa. Literature filled the intervals of these overly short hours of *brio* in public, that were, along with the after-dinner La Scala and La Comédie Française, the only lively points in his days as an eternal marginal: it was the military half-pay, after 1815, that allowed literature to play a part—a part so lovely for us and for Stendhal, perhaps, merely large—in a life that included other parameters.

Because in Stendhal's life we scarcely consider its other aspect—for him, perhaps, its main aspect—a bureaucratic career prematurely shattered, and only partially salvaged later in life; we see him only as the "eternal writer" and never as the very young retiree who fortunately had better things to do than to translate Horace (or Carpani). But who in the end realized this rather late.

*

In fact, who read *The Red and the Black* when it first appeared? The book used one of the recipes that will allow a masterpiece to go unnoticed for a long time: an archaic packaging entirely undermined from within by a corrosive temperament and an original sensibility. *The Red and the Black*, which appeared in the midst of complete romantic overheatedness almost the day after the publication of *Hernani*, made Stendhal, at first glance, in both writing and spirit, a faded epigone of the cynical, ironic, blasé fops of the eighteenth century, much closer to Crébillon *fils* than to Balzac, and this outdated veneer camouflaged all the rest. Today we see the book only as the top-to-bottom, in-depth renewal of the elegant, dry novel of the eighteenth century; contemporaries saw only the fake varnish of skepticism and Voltairean mockery, which must have seemed antiquated. It is likely that this dual-faceted Stendhal, who no longer exists for us, did not exist for his contemporaries either. Only it was the other side they saw, exclusively: the rare but not entirely exceptional occurrence at the turn of a century of a book fashioned like Duchamp's ingenious doors, which close one room only to open another, and vice versa.

*

In the writing, one of Stendhal's traits that connects him most closely to the eighteenth century is the breeziness with which he always evokes violent death, in war, duels, murder, suicide, or execution; his tone is always that of Abbé Prévost ("It *is* Lescaut! he shall sup tonight with the angels!"), that of war in laced costume and aristocrats threatened by the guillotine. If we leave aside the apologetics and eloquence of the pulpit which, in the seventeenth century, provides their foundation, the fundamentally common *tremolo* that underscores the evo-

4 1

cation of death dates back only to the nineteenth century. Hugo's *The Last Day of a Condemned Man*, the caricature of this, underscores the pageantry of its entry into the literary sensibility of the time through excess itself.

We try—we try to imagine the alarm of the reader of seventeenth-century novels and even eighteenth-century ones (in spite of Rousseau) faced with the pathos of Madame Bovary's death (and yet Flaubert was a model of restraint for his time) . . .

*

Where does this directness come from, the direct connection Stendhal's prose suddenly affords, even in his potboilers, his musical and touristic rhapsodies, and his recopied notes, which no other author affords to this extent? Why is this prose so intensely alive and so intimately "personalized" through and through, though it presents no very apparent formal qualities? At times I think I can half-detect one of the reasons. This prose is never a spoken prose; it has none of the vocabulary or turns of phrase of casual conversation or aimless discussion. But it almost always has the nimbleness, breeziness, and freedom of a total lack of sequencing. There is no prose in which the sentence being completed leaves one less able to predict the style, rhythm, or even tone of the one to follow. The person who captivates us in conversation is not Goethe debating with Eckermann so pedagogically but the person whose remarks always bestride the foreseeable, in a graceful, unexpected, and sometimes brilliant *leap*. So it seems to me that the secret of Stendhal's prose that makes us "fall under his spell" in a few moments when we take him up again, is to be sought not in the united flow of the writing and its cumulative richness, as in the oratory prose of Bossuet or Chateaubriand, but rather in exquisitely negative values; in the various ways it thwarts expectation at every moment, in the largely open register of its breakdowns.

*

The first truth we should remember when we speak of Balzac, and that we half-forget in spite of ourselves each time we compare him to the other "greats," is that he is at once the first full professional and the first regular "supplier" that the career of the novelist has known in France. His category (this is how we sportily refer to the only writers it is completely licit to compare him to) is not Stendhal, Flaubert, and Proust; it is Dumas, Eugène Sue, Zola, Ponson du Terrail, Zévaco[23] (I am not considering quality, but *status*). Between an independently wealthy artist like Flaubert, who gives his best, from time to time, in work that engages all his reserves, and a Balzac who every evening counts the number of pages knocked out in the day, with one eye on his account book, there is the same difference of state of mind as between a pre-war tennis professional who gave lessons five hours a day, and the crack amateurs he trained who applied themselves with all their might two or three times a year at Wimbledon or the Davis Cup. Balzac's speed (in the sense of an engine's speed) is that of a writer who needs to *endure*, which is to say, a speed that is almost always a bit below his maximum capacity, and that skillfully makes use of all the slopes and landings that allow him to rest (a mechanism of development and amplification of an almost purely verbal province being in Balzac the most common way to spare himself, to arrange resting periods within his creation in order to breathe). It is obviously a mistake to compare Flaubert's careful weighing of an adjective with the stylistic concerns (there are some, but they are on another scale) of a novelist who writes this in *A Woman of Thirty*.

"At last she opened the door. Evidently the creaking of the hinges had reached the murderer's ear to no purpose. Although his hearing was very keen, he stood almost as if nailed to the wall, motionless and lost in his thoughts. The circle of light cast by the lantern shone faintly on him, and in that segment of chiaro-oscuro [*sic*] he resembled the cheerless statues of chevaliers that are always standing at the corners of dark tombs in gothic chapels. Great drops of sweat stood upon his broad, sallow forehead. Incredible audacity spoke in every feature of that violently distorted face. His fiery eyes, tearless and staring, seemed to be looking on at a battle in the darkness before him. Tumultuous thoughts passed swiftly over that face, whose resolute and unwavering expression denoted a powerful character. His body, his proportions, his attitude, were all in harmony with his savage temperament. The fellow was all force, all strength, and he scrutinized the darkness as a visible image of his own future.

"Accustomed to look upon the vigorous faces of the giants who surrounded Napoléon, and engrossed by a sort of moral curiosity, the general had paid no heed to the physical peculiarities of that extraordinary man; but Hélène, being, like all women, extremely sensitive to outward impressions, was struck by the mingling of light and shadow, of grandeur and passion, in a poetic chaos which gave to the stranger something of the aspect of Lucifer rising after his fall.

"Suddenly the storm pictured upon that face subsided as by magic, and the undefinable despotic influence of which the unknown was, unconsciously perhaps, both the cause and the result, diffused itself about him with the increasing rapidity of an inundation. A torrent of thoughts issued from his brow at the very moment when his features assumed their natural shapes. Fascinated, whether by the strangeness of the interview or by the mystery into which she was forcing her way, the girl thereupon saw before her a mild and most interesting countenance. She stood for some minutes in a bewitched silence, disturbed by emotion hitherto unknown to her youthful heart. But soon, whether because Hélène had uttered an exclamation or made some movement, or because the assassin, returning from the imaginary to the real world, heard for the first time other breathing than his own, he turned his face toward his host's daughter, and saw indistinctly in the shadow the sublimely beautiful features and the majestic outline of a creature whom he might well have taken for an angel, seeing her stand there motionless, and as ill-defined as a ghost."[24]

Perhaps no isolated novel by Balzac can *endure* absolutely if compared point by point with those of his famous rivals, but his stakes are not placed there; his bets are on the transformative power of the "masses" in literature, a century before their ascent to the summit of politics, and on the sort of passage that sometimes occurs—and that in fact occurs all the time in *La Comédie Humaine*—from quantity to quality. Starting with a certain literary volume never obtained before him, Balzac must have had the sense that all the stylistic givens changed weight, like a pebble dropped in a river (he proves this later by placing each of his isolated works into the whole of *La Comédie Humaine*), and changed nature, like a detonation that a cave's echo both spreads and amplifies. Because the overall literary interconnection that the stroke of genius of *La Comédie Humaine* achieved for the first time allows not only an echoing effect, the play of a keyboard multiplied by correspondences: it also allows, like the interconnection of an electrical network, the potential of a far-off literary supply station to be mobilized in the service of a narrative that is languishing or *giving out*, and, in fact, the miracle of this body of work that is formally so uneven is that any sense of a bad patch most often disappears on reading: the literary reserves flow on their own as in the interplay of communicating vessels; the whole not only controls the parts, it fills in their deficiencies, instantly.

Balzac ended up being perfectly aware of the virtues of establishing overall relationships, and played with them at times with a premonitory subtleness. When he writes in *An Old Maid* that Suzanne, the sewing-maid, recognized her vocation as a romantic adventuress while hearing the story, told in her youth, of Marie de Verneuil, a duke's daughter, the first episode of which takes place in *Les Chouans* at More's town house, specifically in Alençon where she lives, he injects this down-to-earth narrative with the same sort of emotive enrichment Wagner did by introducing King Mark's leitmotif in *Tristan* into the score of Sachs, the shoemaker, tempted by love, through a clever analogical reminder. What at first was simply a literary link in the conception of the *Comédie Humaine* has with time become osmosis and even blood flow. The ivy ends up sending living roots into the wall to which at first it was only attached.

*

Stendhal: a writer of the eighteenth century publishing in the time of Louis-Philippe—Claudel, projected directly from the century of Innocent III into the Third Republic of Emile Combes—Barbey d'Aurevilly, a *chouan* of the Second Empire—these time lags almost always signal a promising situation of originality, because they allow both participation and remove. Participating in the same privilege are writers (Chateaubriand) forced to straddle a historical hinge by the hazards of chronology, the extreme compression of the ruptured duration they have traversed replacing the effects of a personal historical lateness. The writer's transplanting of a setting from an old civilization into a more developed setting, or the reverse (Claudel again, or Gobineau) produces analogous effects: this would be a good topic of inquiry—no one to my knowledge has done it up to now—regarding Lautréamont.

*

Jean Prévost speaks of "technical progress" and "compositional weaknesses" in regard to *Rome, Naples, and Florence,* which seems written off the cuff in an evening at the tavern, with no memory of the fragments written the day before that seem to wander about on butterfly wings. Stendhal's charm is to want to do everything properly and to do everything carelessly—for the reader it is to feel carelessness prevail precisely where the author is pulling the reins most tightly. "Compositional weaknesses": indeed what is more contraindicated than the strange binary composition of *The Red and the Black* with its two long stretches of Verrières and Paris, each flanked by the brief appendix of the seminary and prison? Two trochees: a particularly disgraceful rhythmic imbalance: who cares? Movement—Stendhal is all movement—is the imbalance and dissymmetry and awakening at each instant of centrifugal force. Perhaps all that counts in a novelist is to know at all times how to grasp the current of life carrying him, *the life of the current*, which, as soon as the riverbed winds, will collide, as we know, with one riverbank and then the other, always blown off course, always de-centered, and never concerned with decoratively steering a middle course.

Quite often, criticism—scarcely preoccupied with the imperious pursuit that motivates the pen hand and scarcely concerned with the current of reading—sees the book as an open field and seeks symmetry in it, the harmony of the land surveyor, whereas all the secrets have to do exclusively with fluid mechanics.

*

If after all these years I am curious to reopen *The Red and the Black* and reread a few chapters here and there, I get a better sense of how it is done; I see with an invariably knowing amusement how Beyle prepares and places his *words* (which do not all surge up in an instant from his pen, far from it). I am surprised by the eclipse of the external world, which suddenly begins barely to exist—muffled, rarefied, stripped of its resonance, like noises to the ear when one steps onto the summit of the Puy de Dôme—and which emerges from the void in isolated sections, emblematic symbols serving to herald the place and time: the lime-blossom tea of Verrières, the seminary gate, the crimson twill tent at the hôtel de Retz, the chiming bells of the clock of the hôtel d'Aligre. It is by treating the outside world only as a hollow imprint of man, buffed and polished at his leisure and as a result almost invisible (parks, promenades, salons, theaters) that Stendhal sticks most closely to the eighteenth century: the salon "magnificents" of the hôtel de La Mole have no other function, we sense, but to ensure the flow of conversation as discreetly as possible. But, as soon as they emerge from the functional gloom, concrete touches capture your attention as intensely as interludes of color in a black-and-white sketch; they easily become a kind of foreshadowing: one could without difficulty find other examples besides the famous—and somewhat simple—reflection of blood in the stained-glass windows of Verrières at the beginning of the book: the *scale*, for example, of Verrières, the hôtel de La Mole (and the scaffold), the *letters*, or notes, all, without exception, heavy with consequence in the novel (there is, in Stendhal's novels, as in his life, an instinctive suspicion vis-à-vis the handwritten text, always considered a possible piece of evidence; the written here is invariably something one hides, camouflages, or encodes).

One singularity appears upon rereading. I have always had a prejudice—I have written of it—against the *ana* of an author, scattered throughout a novel, which are not closely linked to the life of the book and that come detached as soon as one gives it a shake. *The Red and the Black* is filled with these, and no attempt is ever made, quite the contrary, to blend them into the body of the work or incorporate them; the narrative is cut off at every moment by invisible dashes between which the author speaks without concealing himself in the least. Now the particular life of this novel—impossible to doubt upon rereading it—is inseparable from these stage whispers that everything underscores. And I am suddenly brought back to the sort of reflections I once had regarding *Les Diaboliques* on the author's position in relation to the book's action and audience.[25] When Balzac throws himself, for pages and yet more pages, into a development or commentary infinitely more complacent than those of Stendhal, he gives the impression, through an effect of ventriloquism, of speaking *from the other side of the frame*, not as a character in the novel, of course, but rather as an extra character devoted to the commentary, and a bit like a coryphée in a bourgeois tragedy, a spectator of the action, certainly, but in the wings, not in the audience. The literary projection is so violent here, in fact, that the author himself is sucked in, and swings from the other side; even when he speaks, he does not speak among us, but—divided in two—in the Vauquer pension, the Grandet house, or the Cabinet of Antiquities, where he has been transferred in our minds once and for all. His interventions are sometimes on the long side for the very reasons that make it difficult for us to endure the parentheses of Greek choruses (if they seem at times to paralyze the play, it's because they are *in* it). As for Stendhal, he is never *in The Red*. When he stops narrating for a moment and speaks for himself, he occupies an intermediary position between the characters in the novel and the reader—at times facing the reader and drawing him aside by the sleeve in order to share his reflections on how the world goes, at times turning his back on the reader and interrupting his characters, in order to point out his way of thinking to them *ex abrupto*.[26] Between the novel and us, as soon as the lively moments of action wind down, there is the perpetual presence of the intermediary, or better yet a *go-between*, a coming and going that is interjected less as a coefficient of the distortion proper to all creative temperament than as an interpreter combined with an animator. This is why there is no world of Stendhal in the sense that we speak of the world of Dostoyevsky or the world of Kafka: there is just *the world*. But a mysteriously sunny one—as though you were taking a walk with someone who could recharge your life—seen through the omnipresent screen not of a creative and distorting imagination so much as a furor to live, a tirelessly animated and avid humor with inexhaustible mobility, seduction, and luster. A world not transfigured but simply reimpassioned.

I return to Céline's reflection, which once struck me so, and which I have already quoted: "Not much music left inside us for life to dance to."[27] When we no longer have much of this music left inside us, for one reason or another, it is here and only here that Stendhal is irreplaceable, because for a few hours he restores it; he does not have great invention and he knows it (he needs the crutch of the news item) or great technique (though he prides himself on it) or great imagination (and he doesn't care) or, as it is often said, this "psychological depth" that in him, above all, is the vivacity of the phrase and the ingenuity of the stroke—nothing but this intimate *allegro*, this high-pitched and somewhat clipped *staccato* that is all his, but to whose rhythm life does in fact begin to dance again irresistibly.

*

"Even at my age, and even though I claim to know something about it, I would be interested in a professor—the
kind they had forty years ago—who could explain to me
in meticulous detail the beauties of *The Red and the
Black*, a recent reading of which made me see its flaws
above all. I am told that Balzac wrote a great article on
The Red upon its publication . . . why don't *all* editions
include Balzac's article?" (Montherlant: *Carnets*).[28]

Never mind Balzac's "great article" on *The Charterhouse*. Montherlant does not like *The Red*; there is nothing to say about that: literature, like democracy, can only
breathe freely in non-unanimity in the voting. But this
"meticulous detail" interests me, because it is precisely
the touchstone for all allergies to Stendhal: Stendhal
does not have the beauties of detail, whereas Huysmans
has nothing but that. In one page of Stendhal, there is ten
times less to be gleaned for a student's French "explica-
tion" than a page of Balzac or Flaubert; as a novelist, he
is the sum of its parts, because he resides almost entirely
in its *movement* (always this *allegro* I spoke of earlier,
which is truly *vivacious*, in the full sense of the word: to
be sensitive to this or not is almost a question of mental
rhythm, a private wavelength: as far as I'm concerned,

Mozart's allegro exceeds me as much as Stendhal's delights me). As for the beauties of the detail of an "eminent psychologist," it's time to get over it: these are, beyond any experimental verification, pure creations of the mind (the best), reckless collisions of ideas suddenly releasing I don't know what kind of oxygen that gives the style its effervescence and sparkle: Stendhal's psychology has always seemed fairylike to me: one would like it to be true, to make the world more exciting. From the first time I read *The Red*—and I was certainly unfamiliar with it—I scarcely accorded any credit to the psychological truth of its dry and leaping notations, this elegant, sentimental algebra: I felt everything was an invention, and calculated poetry, and that the details of the book itself were subordinate to its intoxicating speed.

Perhaps deep down what prevents Montherlant from "seeing" Stendhal is what brings them together, and only brings them together, in the midst of so many contrasts: the too-eminent incapacity of both, in the novel, for transparency—the transparency of life that is Chekov's, Tolstoy's. An ambiguous incapacity that is at once a deficiency, if you like, but also an irreplaceable quality—which is that of certain very great actors in whom the composition of a role always pales in favor of the stubborn resurgence of their identity. For those people, in truth, the role doesn't really matter: *they* are all we see, or rather see again: their accents, their tics, their gait, their greetings, the tilt of their nose. Now everyone freely congratulates an actor for his *presence*, but there is the (much less clear) problem of the presence of the novelist in his novel, a presence that is a contribution but that also— starting with a certain threshold that Stendhal does not cross and that Montherlant goes beyond—may be a screen. When it comes to fiction, there are cases when this presence becomes oppressive, as they say, and that can be unfortunate. In a book like *Desert Love* (which I appreciate), the writer's *ego* is displayed without rebellion on my part for four hundred pages (a performance!), but everything that has to do with "the story" is more or less passed through the vegetable mill.[29]

*

Balzac as a planner of social harmony in *The Country Doctor*, *The Country Parson*, and even *The Wrong Side of Paris*.[30] The key of progress for him lies in the notables' and proprietors' enlightened despotism (which is not dealt by a lifeless hand! See *The Country Doctor* and Benassis's nocturnal deportation of the *cretins* of the Grande Chartreuse), never in State intervention—the obstacle (*The Peasantry*) is the emerging and exploitative rural class of semi-wealthy peasants (Rigou in *The Peasantry*).[31] Here we have the reflection of an entire current of *ultra* ideas, extended at times by the practice that adopted Catherine II's plan for Russia in France (Villèle managed his lands in Toulouse this way): using large properties, equipped with police rights and extensive statutory powers, as these sorts of colonial administrators, supervising and overseeing, but also helping, educating, and illuminating the indigenous rural masses (Balzac sees French peasants almost as muzhiks). The great social aristocratic dream, which persisted in France until the notables of the Assembly of 1871 and until the Duke of Broglie, this dream of a rural France becoming a sort of antibourgeois, economic Vendée, grazing herds and laboring in unity with the landed gentry and priests, is positively displayed throughout the idyllic *Country Doctor*, just as it appeared negatively in the darker counterweight of *The Peasantry*.

"The moment that the peasant changes from his purely toilsome life to the easy life, or to the landowning classes, he becomes intolerable. [...] You will see an example of it in Taboureau. He looks simple, and even doltish; but when his interests are in question, he is certainly profoundly clever" (Benassis, in *The Country*

Doctor).[32] Isn't this holding up the *kulak* and his negative rapaciousness to public obloquy, just as in *The Peasantry*? And here the monarchist and reactionary Balzac
unexpectedly joins the social politics of the Little Father
of the People.

*

I don't think for a second that Balzac, in spite of his
claims, sought to compete with the registry office. That
is not the writer's ambition; it would be both too much
and too little. Too much because every artist is perfectly
aware of the deep and essential negativity of literature
(negativity on which M. Blanchot has written very good
pages). Too little, because the novelist, for example, is
too aware of the decisive superiority of his characters
over the flesh-and-blood citizens who appear in munic-
ipal registers to want to compete with them. Proust
defined this superiority perfectly: entirely internalized
by the reader, while real personages, perceived by the
senses, remain mostly opaque, everything that happens
to the characters in the novel is born in him; they are in
him, for a moment, as much himself as he is or more—
similar in that to the demon *Ginifer*, Cocteau's ingenious creation in *The Knights of the Round Table*, who

only exists in the real beings he successively inhabits, one after the other, thanks to Merlin's magic, expelling them for a moment from their normal and apparent identity.

*

The overdressed aspect of the Balzacian narrative, always clad, furnished, draped, garlanded top to bottom like a Belle Epoque salon, and all the more so since the epoch in which he is situated is a period of transition, where fashions and styles exist side by side and jostle each other without eliminating each other, trousers and knee-breeches, boots and dancing shoes, Empire style and Restoration style (with echoes of Louis XVI). The profusion of singular objects prevails over the overall look, *interiors* over landscapes, flounces, yokes, embellishments, and fabric over the line of the garment. Certain episodic silhouettes of the Balzacian novel make one think of Wells's Invisible Man, who only really exists by virtue of the leather and fabric covering placed over his central cavity.

No other novelist seems to have possessed this instantaneous remove that makes him see and describe the costumes, furnishings, and carriages before his eyes as "period" costumes, antique furniture, the *highlights* of a carriage museum. This is what simultaneously gives his novels the direct, irreplaceable heat of lived experience, and the seduction that the Dutch or Venetian intimists still have for us: born historical, so to speak, the extraordinary bric-a-brac that fills his books does not become shop-worn; the spirit of the times, emerging fashion, word play in the taste of the day, seem pulled out from the continuance as he records them, and fixed on the spot, somewhat ponderously, as in an eternal frost.

*

"The police chief was able to silence the struggle of his passions" (*Les Chouans*). Sentences of this sort in Balzac (there are many) pierce through the ridiculous like a bullet, and let you see beyond, like a livelier day of pure theater in which characters—all characters—replay the comedy of their life, in splendor and majesty, each, naturally, at their own level.

*

A book's lighting (and even its private equilibrium) can change so much based on weather and mood! I no longer feel quite the same pleasure reading *The Charterhouse* as I did twenty years ago, a pleasure never comparable, far from it, to that afforded me by *The Red and the Black* at fifteen years. All the adventure and intrigue

—for example, the passport complications and quarrels with the police following Giletti's death—slip upon re-reading into the picaresque, and seem a bit fraught. As for Fabrice, who surrenders to immediacy like a leaf in the wind, the charming simpleton who sometimes inhabits this likable exterior annoys me a bit: the only reliable thing about him is his seduction, and, as always on this topic in a novel, Stendhal needs us to extend him credit. The seduction of intoxicating youth can be brought out directly in film or maybe opera; the novel, much less well equipped, possesses almost nothing but dialogue. And Stendhalian dialogue, contrary to Balzac's, is poor in diversity of vocabulary and tone, and does not particularize, unless dealing episodically with walk-on parts for the lower classes. We are always in the midst of witty people—the constant sparkle, the competitive stimulation of the salon conversation, can always be heard; Fabrice, when he speaks, does not speak very differently from Mosca or Ernest IV. As a result, the seduction, of which he must be exclusive and privileged possessor in order to justify the narrative's unfolding, crumbles, scatters, and in somewhat equal fashion for the reader comes to sprinkle glitter on the count, the duchess, and even the prince at times, in addition to Fabrice—a small, prestigious coterie, an enchanted circle of the "king's son" that scintillates above all through its *existence as a whole*. The charm of the novel lies in the intimate grace of these inseparable figures in this intoxicating quadrille, against a background of beautiful trees, lakes, and misty mountains in the distance, and—a strange thing to say—if I sought an equivalent for my impression upon rereading it, I would have to look to *The Embarkation for Cythera*.[33]

The novel only reaches its full height (no pun intended) in the second volume with the episodes of the Farnese Tower. In the first volume, I resent Stendhal a little for not making it absolutely improbable, on this rereading, for the actor who plays the budding archbishop in the film version of *The Charterhouse* to have played the character *Fanfan la Tulipe* in another production. The seduction of this novel *concertante* grows as we go along by virtue of a microclimate so blossoming and tonic it makes all the figures that populate it tenderly akin, just as all plants, in springtime, are less different from one another than the rest of the year. A *blending* that probably results from everything in the book emerging, or rather reemerging, in one spurt: it is unbridled nostalgia captured live by writing. All of Italy, half-lived, half-dreamed, suddenly goes to Stendhal's head again like a whiff of perfume; for an instant, he is able, indivisibly, to be this perfume, this privileged moment. And to express this privileged moment breathlessly, in so volatile a manner: it's clear that time was of the essence! How can we compare this book, offered as a gift, the book of a medium, to the fierce and determined construction of the *Red*, full to bursting with working-class energy?

In the last pages, the mad scramble of events and the speed of the narrative become dizzying. The unhappy and charming Count Mosca, whom we feel a bit sorry for, ultimately dissipates in the wake of his explosive duchess, like a pile of straw behind a tornado. All the court scenes and maneuverings that follow the poisoning of Ernest IV are outrageously implausible. The Stendhalian *allegro* that I love so much is transformed a bit too early for my taste into an *allegro furioso*.

*

What a strange itinerary, a *retro* itinerary, Fabrice's is, if for a moment we put aside the fictional glamour of an Italy detached from the course of History, which mixes Guichardin with Metternich and the Rome of the Borgias with the Parma of Marie-Louise! Still adolescent, he was seized by the great wind of History, he ran to Waterloo; barely back from Italy—he was not yet twenty—

everything was forgotten forever; as though he were extracted inexplicably from one of the dimensions of his life: nothing more—aside from love—but the little trickeries, niceties, intrigues, and coteries of a dwarfish capital in a tiny principality, nothing more than a life, delightfully yet listlessly epicurean, nothing more than "an extra man," as the Russians say, a seductive supernumerary of the court. I know that this was the evolution of Stendhal himself, who in 1815 turned his back once and for all on the pomp of History that let him down, and dreamed only of a garret in Milan and a loge at La Scala. But, in 1815, this very young renunciant had all his books ahead of him: Fabrice has nothing. And if we read it in a certain way, the novel is like an enchanted crown placed atop an empty space. Through a *naïveté* congenital to all creators, Stendhal gave this ideal son (whom he indulged) every gift but one, the only one that could justify him but the only one not delegable. By projecting himself onto him and lending him his brief missed appointment with Napoleon, by making him a "successful" Stendhal—younger, better looking, richer, more seductive, more spontaneous—but not a creator (and for good reason), he made him a strange retired adolescent of grandeur.

*

Behind the agitation and even frenzy that can occasionally inhabit them, these books are fortunate, the ones we
sense have been written from start to finish as though in
gold dust, in the smiling and regret-tinged calm of the
end of a summer day. The perceptive ability of their
reader also seems split in two: while it follows an uncontrollable, turbulent movement and "man's small
steps," it constantly registers the benevolence of celestial
mechanics, the slow movement of the setting sun, and
the increasingly saturated light being poured down
upon the earth. *The Charterhouse of Parma* is written
entirely, and stands out for me cover to cover, against this
halo of ripening sun. And I would place Balzac's *Lily of
the Valley* and Tolstoy's *The Cossacks* in this same favored lot, if only for myself. When you emerge from this
backdrop of starry transparency, the admirable Dostoyevsky shrinks a bit all the same: we sense the human
enclosure and reenter what I want to call the hell of
"souls." And it's true, too, on another level, of Bernanos,
whose work, without forcing the issue too much, falls
in with Nietzsche's view: "The world, a word that has
become a Christian affront." I will not speak of Pascal,
whom I have forsaken, dismayed by his mania for hair
shirts and his relentless determination to hate the world

and himself. There is, in this, a literature of the wretched of the earth and "exiles of jubilation" by decree (as Alain has said) that I can no longer bear.

*

From the comedy of the Italians—somewhat more marked, more spontaneous, and more naïve than that of the French—Stendhal drew a whole fairyland of manners, causing it to blossom like a Japanese flower, which enchanted him until his final days: the love at first sight of 1800—his first descent into Italy—is the best example of crystallization that his life offers, a crystallization that nothing could dissolve, because the seduction of a country and a people is not depleted by living with them: it is deepened and extended by a deliciously passive and available presence, like a beloved woman who is only there when you call her. Italy is always partially, and maybe more than partially, blended with the theater and opera for him, which is to say, with the non-habit-forming drug of a richer, more intense life. Thus, beyond the accidents of real loves, he had the distinct luck almost all his life of keeping the affective charge and heart-opening power of the love potion close at hand, with all of its potency but none of its enslavements.

*

Movement in novelists. In Proust, Zeno's arrow remains truly suspended in the air as long as he wants, like a film stuck for a moment on a static image—scenes in *Remembrance of Things Past* seem to dream of these intimately. In Flaubert, it is like the brief effort of a sinking person to wrest himself from glue, but who is quickly paralyzed in the fascination of the inert: every paragraph, or almost every one, ends with the return of a continuous horizontal line. In Stendhal, the arrow arrives first, but in this drunkenness of pure movement with no reference points, evaluation of progress is lost; without any warning, a page indiscriminately covers the space of two weeks or two years (hence, *The Charterhouse*'s constant shifts in speed, which take the reader by surprise and curiously desensitize him to a sense of uniform temporal continuity). When Flaubert inserts a long temporal break in the narrative, such as at the end of *Sentimental Education*, with a somewhat ponderous integrity, he manipulates the traffic signals, starts a new paragraph, changes tenses, and switches to the *parfait défini*.[34]

> *Il voyagea . . .*
> [He traveled . . .]

I love Stendhal with enough distance, I hope, to understand that his gift for communicating the sense of elation
and freedom born of unbridled movement has a counterpart: he is victim, too, in his own way, of the agile passion for *moving* that he satisfies in us without restraint.
He has no means to express the weight of time, its cumulative effect, the saturnine tragedy it emits (which also
means he doesn't think about it). The eclipse of the
"canker" throughout his books is total. He does use old
people, especially for walk-on parts, frozen forever in
their emblematic age, like Chélan or Blanès: but we
never really see the aging progress in any of his characters. More than once, Count Mosca prepares himself for
retirement—or rather talks about it—only to spring to
life again, better than before, rejuvenated through money
and favor, making a fortune à la Talleyrand on the last
page of the book. At twenty or twenty-five, Julien Sorel
is guillotined, Fabrice walled up in his Charterhouse.
Lucien Leuwen seems more suited to reaching maturity,
but the fate of the book did not want that: the material
destiny of the written thing has its perspicacities.

*

Through Stendhal, Goethe, and Chateaubriand, I have
come to think of romantic Rome, and especially the Ro-

man countryside, as a refashioned and wild paradise. And perhaps even more through the two thick volumes of drawings by German Romantic painters that I leaf through slowly each summer at Sion, all filled with landscapes of Mount Sabins and the Abruzzi, traced with the meticulous clarity of a darkroom, and whose perched village of *Olevano*, reproduced a hundred times from every angle, somewhat represents Mount Sainte-Victoire. Berlioz's *Memoirs*[35] (so suspect on so many levels) convey the disparaging humor of the exile in these places where Chateaubriand dreamed of finishing his life: the author is bored to death there, and in the overflowing of the fountains of the Navone piazza, he only sees the splashing of a swamp. Everything I find appealing about Rome in 1830 as I imagine it—grass in the streets, the shiver of malaria, the silence, the delicate flock-bells of herds of goats, the floating of slender life in clothes too big for it—is precisely what repels him; he dreams only of the Colosseum repopulated with roaring crowds, *colossal* music under the vaults of St. Peter's. In this complex and thundering crank who plays the songs of the *Aeneid* and verses of Shakespeare on his guitar in the forests of the Sabine, there is a perspicacious Barnum of the fine arts considered as exhibition, and the presentiment of an Americanism in music that never really took shape.

His chapters on Italy are an icy shower for the reader who emerges overcome by the pages of *Rome, Naples, Florence*.[36] Is he right or is he wrong? Of Italians, he knew only carters, police officers, and a few *lazzaroni*.[37] But did Stendhal have anything but a landscape painter's view of their filth, misery, and unsociability? While Chateaubriand only traveled there as a magnificent ambassador, Stendhal and Berlioz's points of view are separated by an even greater divide: one that separates the tourist in his *sediola* from the beatnik on the road.[38] Three reactions of sensibility and culture, as well as three levels of observation, and three separate and watertight worlds: for a comparison, you would have to think of modern India as seen by a dignitary from UNESCO, a tourist on a charter, and a hippie heading on foot to Kathmandu.

*

Not everything has been said, though much has been said, about Balzac's *city*, Zola's Paris, and even the city in *Sentimental Education*. Much less, it seems to me, has been said about the city so characteristic of Stendhal: a fragmented assortment of enclosed precincts—salons, gardens, theaters—devoted to the raptures of art, the pleasures of love, conversation and intrigue, and linked to one another through perfectly abstract pathways. The *street* (omnipresent and almost solely present in a novel like *Les Misérables*) does not exist in Stendhal, and the *café*, the intermediary between the street and the salon, barely does either, its social mixture overwhelming to him: it's less a place to meet, consequently, than a place to collide (the Besançon café in *The Red*), a place you can scarcely enter without getting snubbed or challenged to a duel. The secret, elective, and perfect symbol, the quintessence of the City for Stendhal, is *La Scala*—all its boxes side by side and buzzing—lit up on opening night. The airtight quality of social compartments is the rule; osmosis takes place only between contiguous cells ruled by the same conditions of temperature and pressure; all exchanges there are circular.

*

I have always been surprised by the misunderstanding that makes the novel an instrument of knowledge, reve-lation, or elucidation for so many writers (even Proust thought that his glory would depend on the discovery of a few great psychological laws). The novel is an *adden-*

dum to creation, an *addendum* that neither illuminates it nor reveals it in any way: a child of seven knows this perfectly well as soon as he places his nose in his first real book (he will have time in school to try painstakingly to forget this). That the novel is a parasitical creation, that it is born of and nourished by the living exclusively does not change anything in terms of the autonomy of its specific chemistry or its effectiveness: orchids are epiphytes.

I don't know what fictional truth is. There is a fictional presence that everyone can observe in Stendhal, Dostoyevsky, or Dickens: it does not require the corroboration of the reader's lived experiences. Reading a novel (if it's worth the trouble) is not a resurrection or sublimation of an experience that the reader has already more or less lived: it *is* an experience, direct and new, like an encounter, a trip, a malady, or a love affair—but, unlike them, a unusable experience. Last year I reread *The Charterhouse of Parma*, and because I reread it with a purely critical eye, I reread it with an admiring and amused astonishment: there was not one ounce of "truth" in it, any more than there is historical, social, political, or psychological truth in *The Three Musketeers*: there was a well-loved and slightly crazy vision, in addition to a captive and captivating creative passion that asserted itself from start to finish. And—dare I say—there is not one ounce of "truth" in Dostoyevsky: he has other fish to fry.

*

I read Stendhal's treatise, *On Love*, when I was about twenty. Then I pretty much forgot it. It's curious (I realized this recently while reopening the book) that the famous theory of *crystallization*—of all the pages in the book, the one referred to ad infinitum—has with time undergone an unconscious transmutation in my mind: the image of the branch in Salzburg gradually being covered in pine resin had yielded space in my memory to another—that of the tiny impact that makes a supersaturated solution crystallize instantly—no longer a symbol of the embellishing sedimentation of love but of a heightened predisposition toward love, for which any woman could serve as catalyst. An inauthentic image, but just as true in and of itself—or in no way more false—than Stendhal's: a piquant example of the smooth functioning of a possible exchange policy after purchase from the classic suppliers of *profound truths of the heart*.

*

Stendhal, who was perfectly aware of courting the happy few, remains and will no doubt always remain the most anti-popular of all our novelists. When you read Balzac or Zola, or even Flaubert, you see the bricklayer standing at the foot of the wall corresponding to his work, honestly and unequivocally: there is no key to reading linked to a precocious and privileged cultural practice, that must be added secretly to the text. But a fondness for Stendhal, even more fundamentally than for Proust, tyrannically assumes passage through a secondary education, because a certain parodic use of language—constantly implied, always floating around his prose in a virtual state, and that is half the charm of his writing—is only learned in school, along with the precocious reflex to keep one's distance vis-à-vis scholarly Beauty and its established priests. Two or three times, I have seen autodidacts with remarkable literary discernment, whom I tried to make read Beyle, reject him with a slight note of irritation: they sensed marked cards there, a person of dry humor waiting to ambush them whom they could not locate, and ultimately found themselves as ill at ease in this encoded prose for connoisseurs as a self-made man in the Guermantes' salon: Stendhal writes in keys that are never indicated (*intelligenti pauca*) and his chromatic tone is constant.[39] This sort of experience made me understand that there is not a page of Stendhal, in fact, that does not aggressively signify, by implicit reference to a whole implied code of reading, that we are there "amongst ourselves." At once politically leftist in reflex (in the manner of a dyed-in-the-wool radical somewhat partial to Boulangism[40]) and irremediably well-heeled in literature, he creates discord in his admirers through the clash between the born aristocratism of his irony and mockery, and the virulence of his opinions on the res publica—and there is no political person who has not kept his taste for Stendhal somewhat under wraps.

*

A few beginnings from Stendhal's scrap heap:

"On a beautiful morning in the month of May 182–, Don Blas Bustos y Mosquera, followed by twelve cavaliers, entered the village of Alcolete, one league from Grenada" ("Le coffre et le revenant" ["The Coffer and the Ghost"]).

"On a dark and rainy night in the summer of 182–, a young lieutenant of the 96th regiment stationed at Bordeaux emerged from the café where he had just lost all his money" ("Le philtre" ["The Love Potion"]).

"Midnight chimed on the chateau's clock; the ball would end" ("Le roman de Métilde" ["The Romance of Métilde"]).

Finally, someone who would not be intimidated by Valéry's terrorism! As soon as these stories are set in Spain, the resemblance with Mérimée makes itself felt almost brutally, not because we are transported to Spain, but because Italy is no longer there. If not for the soul's secret opening to love that Italy bestowed on him, Stendhal would be a second Mérimée. The wondrous treasure that childhood bequeaths to most writers, and which is lacking in Beyle, is adolescence, and the first trip to Italy linked to adolescence takes its place. The advantage is that any idiotic tenderness is shut out by this transformative light: he himself chose the era of his *green paradise*.[41]

*

Female devotion as prime erotic value in Stendhal (Mme de Rênal, Mme Bissaux, Clélia Conti). But not, as in Laclos, as a chief obstacle, the *jumping* of seduction. Rather as an elective sign of the soul's extra dimension, an aptitude toward this total quietism of love that is Beyle's secret aspiration, that shatters at the end of *The Red* and *The Charterhouse*, and that gives his novels, which deal with such dry topics, the velvety smoothness that is their true power.

*

Perhaps truest in Stendhalian psychology—so famous and often so artificial in its will to be brilliant and *well played*—are the brutally tense, sometimes instantaneous ups and downs that affect his characters' feelings, whose voltage is constantly changing. There is nothing like this anywhere in Balzac. There is a small seed of the fragmentation of the self that heralds and joins the twentieth century of Proust, striding over Flaubert and Zola all at once.

*

In their reasoning, conversation, behavior, decisions, in the jauntiness of their spirit and manners, the real characters in *The Charterhouse* (minor characters as well as major ones, l'abbé Blanès as well as Count Mosca, Ludovic as well as Clélia, Ferrante Palla as well as the duchess) not only reveal themselves to be made of the same stuff—ideal Italianness according to Stendhal—but are members of a freemasonry in which a thousand things go without saying, where a secret language is spontaneously spoken without anything needing to be spelled out, all social distinctions left by the wayside. Nothing is more typical of this point of view than the duchess's conversations with *Ludovic* after Fabrice's escape, conversations in which rank creates no distance; they are immediately related through *virtue*. The others, the Rassi, Fabio Conti, Ascagne, Barbone, Raversi, boldly outlined and with no inner life, play traitors as summarily and as artlessly as in a novel by Alexandre Dumas. *The Charterhouse* is the very singular and somewhat magical novel of a *king's sons'* aristocracy—princes or valets, millionaires or vagabonds, beggars or ministers—who recognize each other, gather, and band together as they meet on roads by chance and by accident, solely through the exercise of mutual tact. And, contrary to what happens in *The Red and the Black*, the merit of each character lies less in his depth and his personal originality than in his intimate inclusion in this privileged *egregore*,[42] successive examples of which charm us more by their organic kinship than their singularity. Reading *The Charterhouse*, I sometimes feel I am listening to an enchanting but unique musical theme, a "little phrase" like Vinteuil's that is repeated inexhaustibly but in a different timbre each time by successive groups of instruments; and that's enough to give me pleasure.

Because the moments of pure inner life, the lively Stendhalian moments of *tempests in a skull* (so frequent in *The Red*) where characters concentrate and gather, are almost nonexistent in *The Charterhouse*, where, most often, reaction follows excitation without any interval, and only passages of pure contemplation interrupt this *alle-*

gro furioso with their long pauses. Abandoned by the enraged tempo that the book communicates to them,
destabilized by the slowing down of the narrative (the
cohesive force that welds the characters of *The Charterhouse* to the fictional body is tied less to its mass than to
its velocity), what would it mean for us to see Fabrice
married, Mosca and the duchess disgraced and in retreat
in Naples? Whereas we can very easily imagine Mme de
Rênal abandoned at Verrières. Let's admit it: in order to
read this wonderful book, a certain state of grace is required that cannot be retrieved at will; reopening it at
certain pages, and until the supple swiftness of the writing woke me up, I thought I was reading Dumas, a softer,
sunnier Dumas, a Dumas who had fallen in love with his
subject. Because it is the climate of love that supports the
book, but it is not really Sanseverina's love for Fabrice,
or Fabrice's love for Clélia Conti; it's the manifest love
of the novelist for his novel, as for an Eden revisited in
dreams.

*

From the (secondary) point of view of fictional mechanics, *The Charterhouse* is set in motion at three successive speeds: the speed of the Waterloo visitor, whose
myopic eye is bogged down in detail; the speed of the
body of the narrative, much swifter; the speed of the last

part, a simple summary, certainly a signature summary, but one that is impatient and rushes posthaste, "skipping" as much as it can. The supple handling of this acceleration gives the book a fairly convincing *legato*, but a reader who went, with no transition, from the Belgium retreat to the Anetta Marini episode, *bowled* at top speed, would have trouble believing he was perusing the same work. The detailed precision of the Waterloo episode makes a long and slow prologue that is not perfectly welded to the rest of the narrative: it is an *hors d'oeuvre*, which must be taken in the best sense of the word: appetizing and gastronomical.

*

The adverb *quite* (used systematically in place of *very*) and the adjective *sublime*, applied to the body as well as the mind, to landscapes as well as character traits, are two of the key words in Stendhal's writing. Lavished throughout his novels, they are there for a reason—one because it is a maliciously clipped superlative and the other because it underscores an all-purpose cliché with a knowing wink—in the imperceptibly parodical smile, the slightly acid tenderness which seems to be the writer's most common expression. The "quite great" fistfights or swordfights that occur at times between characters in the *Italian Chronicles* lose a little of their penetrating and blunt reality, and, while truly admiring the "sublime Mathilde," Julien Sorel does not fail to establish a bit of distance with the Spanish character.

*

The vital relationship in Balzac between man and his shell: in the work of other novelists, characters change domicile; in Balzac, they move out.

*

In Balzac, there are novels constructed around the support of a grand passion: Grandet, Claës, or Goriot (there are no novels constructed around a "character," whose regular features would soon be bursting with the uncontrollable Balzacian dynamic). But Balzac, a novelist of insane vital energy, seems incapable of placing a controlled and managed life at the center of his novels: his Julien Sorel is Lucien de Rubempré. Fouqué in one, David Séchard in the other—two equals—make up the range.

*

For almost a century (it begins with the reign of Louis-Philippe—"Are you going to the Tuileries, madame la duchesse?" "Yes, to the garden"—and it culminates with the world of Proust and the Guermantes salon, where a person going to dine at the Elysée Palace is regarded as a curious animal), images of social ascension in France have been almost radically cut from images of access to political power: a wonderful opportunity to develop a complex and subtle social fiction, whose possibilities Balzac was the first to make use of (and which the fiction of *The Red and the Black*, still marked by the atmosphere of the Restoration, does not possess). The strong and simple pyramid-shaped structure under Louis XIV that confused fortune, prestige, and power at every level would not have allowed anything of the sort, and the Fifth Republic, for different reasons, did not lend itself to this very much more. I do not want to give this remarkable circumstance of our history more importance than it may deserve, but we must note that it is in this sociological "slot" that the great period of the French novel is lodged.

This intimate rift in the dominant classes, rich in nuanced and iridescent conflict, changes of camp, occasional divorces and profitable alliances, provided novelists of the time with a world where "class position" lost its meaning and direct rootedness in reality. A limited world perhaps (the "bourgeois" world) but sinuously fissured, detached from brutal social causality through the intervention of numerous and subtle mediations. Where A Thousand and One Nights of ambition, greed, snobbery, bonds of friendship, family, and love could be deployed in a sort of empyrean (as in Proust) without sinning openly against reality.

*

What we mistakenly call composition, and what it would suffice to call the internal balance of a novel, a novelist like Flaubert seems to seek out and arrange within a previously enclosed and nonextensible space, where any readjustment is a matter of subtraction, where any added contribution is paid for by an unballasting in some other section. But in Balzac, on the contrary, there is always the reserve of a virgin continent on the horizon of his pen, an inexhaustible, fictional Far West where the disharmonies and upsets of balance that occur in a text that seems destined to languish are only stimulants for a masterful forging ahead, for an annexationist bulimia, mortgages taken out on a fortune yet to come. All his problems prompt an expansion of his subject matter; all his difficulties are exhortations to massive scale. Balance is always regained, not through some parsimonious re-trenchment of substance but through the generosity of added creation.

This also goes for Stendhal's *The Charterhouse*, where he frolics on nourishing terrain and it seems he will never lack for resources (the novel comes to a sudden end only because of concern over its excessive costs and the publisher's complaints). But not *The Red*, where balance has to do with a thriftier, more economical sense of proportion. It is very clear that another admirable example—the most perfect of all, no doubt—of this motivating imbalance, this balance always entrusted to the future, always to be found in the vague expansion of creative conquest, is provided by *Remembrance of Things Past*.

*

The charm (the only real charm) in every object that operates through seduction is epidermic: who would imagine praising his Dulcinea's skeleton?[43] She must be able to walk, of course: though some of the limping women are not deprived of love, far from it.

In depth? . . . In depth, all works of art tend to level out, just as the sea stops moving thirty meters below the surface. Even if I read Balzac, whose external charms are hardly ever praised, once his table manners are removed from his books, the very particular, almost glutinous consistency of his words, as nourishing and sticky as jam (so different from the airy dryness of Stendhal, who cracks like sheets in the wind), his elephantine graces, all the more touching, and everything in his prose that makes one think of the abrupt and unexpected agility of the obese, like the incredible Gaudissart—bursting on all sides with absurdities of his own invention—from whom one cannot detach one's eyes or ears, once the timbre of this sensual and fleshy voice, so complacent, is made commonplace, carrying its vision along like the grandiose overflowing of a melting river, what is left to truly hold my interest? A few *infallible-sounding lines* in the social mysteries of the *Temperate Monarchy*, which I do not care much about, material for political sociology, received and signed for, but that, we must admit, cannot really be vouched for.

The criticism of novels often seems to us to deal with an opera reduced to its libretto. Still, a libretto has a certain poise in destitution, an autonomy in poverty, to which a fictional subject, stripped from its writing, could not in any way pretend.

*

There are few tics born of the nervousness of the artist's style—in Flaubert as in Zola—that bother me as much as the repeated use of abstract terms in the plural preceded by an indefinite article: "Des langueurs flottaient ..."

(Languors floated) "Des tendresses le prennaient . . ." (Tendernesses took hold of him), etc. A provocative dual indeterminacy that is an unconditional capitulation of the rigorous mind.

Zola gets away with it, but Flaubert! Still, the exigency and negligence of the most scrupulous artists often call to mind the mote and the beam of the Gospel. Flaubert literally does not see the substantial laxness of these oversights, whereas he categorically hunts down word repetition, relative pronouns, and cascading genitives with the reflex gesture of someone flicking crumbs from his jacket. These genitives which Hugo, to cite only him, handles so superbly in his most finely wrought pieces:

> *Des empreintes de pied de géants qu'il voyait*
> ["The footprints of the giants that he saw"]
> ("Booz endormi" ["Boaz Asleep"])

In reality, every writer is differently sensitized to the swerves of language; absolute correction testifies to nothing but a commonplace, anonymous sense of language. Why would I proscribe word repetition, when it is the contortion of the periphrasis destined to avoid it that is disagreeable to me? Do you want to say, "It's raining?" Then say, "It's raining." Even if it's the second cloudburst.

*

Certainly, *Salammbô* is a literary "folly," a Chinese pavilion, more horned than natural, lost in the romantic gardens, and continuous reading of it can be likened to an arduous session of weight lifting. But if you pursue it to the end, an overall sinister and even oppressive sense of ancient paganism emerges. It does not have to do so much with the barbarian bric-a-brac, a delirious Orientalism, the applied savagery of the images: it has to do with the fact that none of the impulses traversing this human hodgepodge is ever overcome, none—even if it is religious—is spiritualized; at no moment does the possibility of common human entreaty appear. Everything is false in this parodic sword-and-sandal epic, except perhaps the essential thing: the sense, obtained by the most dubious methods but ultimately alive, of distance in relation to the Christian era and even the Biblical world: it is a chronicle prior to "Conscience," prior to the punishment of Cain.

*

Setting aside the wealth of their contents, I admire books that proliferate and radiate freely around a central theme less than the great fictional narratives ruled strictly by chronology (as *realizations* in Cézanne's sense)—and this for a laborer's reasons. Less *Ulysses* or *Remembrance of Things Past* than *The Red and the Black* or *Madame Bovary*. Just as I admire the tightrope walker with bare hands more than one moving forward with the aid of a balancing pole. Or, to use another image, in exchange for all the supple conveniences that works composed *in the shape of stars* give themselves, they deprive themselves of one weapon, one of the most prestigious in the fictional arsenal: the cumulative pressure on the last scenes of a novel (the death of Mme Bovary, for example) exerted by the stored up and uninterrupted series of episodes preceding them. A projectile propelled forward by the gradual reduction in pressure of gasses gains its maximum speed at the mouth of the cannon.

The secret processes of constant accumulation (the image is far too mercantile, but I can't think of a better one), which operate throughout the progression of a work of fiction and no doubt contribute decisively to its enrichment, are one of the least studied aspects of fictional technique (with the understanding that technique cannot be learned and only takes effect in a book *a posteriori*). In any case, there is reason to believe that they are connected more than we think compared with duration in its vectorial form, and can be disturbed by a narrative too frequently "returning upstream."[44]

*

Flaubert's cadences—how doleful and monotonous! Sometimes, it's true, the sentence will start with a lively movement, but it is like a happy stream rushing to throw itself inevitably into a pond. The rhythm of the anapest, short—short—long, stretched to the members of the sentence, seems almost a respiratory necessity for him. All of his writing is the often ill-fated struggle to enliven and chase the page or paragraph beyond this inevitable falling away.

*

The difficulties of reconstructing the past, as Flaubert confronts it in *Salammbô*. The disabled soldiers of Antiquity: a low percentage of the one-armed and one-legged, and, in sum, a remarkably elevated rate of recovery among the injured forces. On the other hand, the reunions of liberally scarred former soldiers must have resembled the corporate banquets at German universities in the time of Bismarck.

*

There are times when all I want are a few modest stories, without plot, apparent magic, or even sparkling poetry, that leave you with the reassuring certainty of having been on familiar ground. As well as with the sense of being filled with a sort of tender internal sunlight that murmurs from the depths of its mysteriously consoling quietude, "Yes, life is like that."

Both Nerval in *Sylvie* and Tolstoy (*The Cossacks*)—so different—give me this feeling equally. Rarely does the work of Balzac, overpopulated by a human seething that at times goes to your head like vertigo. Never Flaubert, where the interjection of the cold gaze and the entomologist's magnifying glass cannot be forgotten for a second. Nor Proust: the uninterrupted crackling of the too rendered, too vivid detail continuously staves off the vague lulling of the mind, similar to dawn in a new climate, that serves as a prelude to this sort of enchantment. And neither does Stendhal: there is a refusal here to mire himself in the world, and a sort of excessively guarded mental autonomy which, out of insolence, offhandedness, or irony, keeps itself—and the reader—*in check* at all times.

They all have other advantages in their favor, of course. Perhaps there is some trace of aging in this more pronounced tendency of mine to let—or to give myself the illusion of letting—*life as it is* emerge through the text. For writers who restore this to me, a certain mental inactivity, slowly allowed to permeate, is necessary, combined with a greater opening of the inner diaphragm in the sensory realm—what Degas, I imagine, felicitously and memorably referred to as, "to train oneself on a trellis."[45] At twenty, even at thirty, life seemed wide open and almost out of grasp; intoxication, with an aftertaste of anxiety, arose from the multiplicity of offered and gradually slaughtered possibilities. The narrowed field that age brings with it sets and weighs down this dazzling, elusive Proteus. The world is closer to us, more solid and more certain, and the writer who senses the imagination's diminished ability to take flight, and for whom Pegasus is restive, also partially rediscovers the resources of Antaeus.

*

I've taken up *Sentimental Education* again, and again the immense respect surrounding the work strikes me as hard to understand. The willful distaste with which Flaubert treats almost all his characters mechanizes them and makes them grimace: nothing but puppets in this chronicle! Their substance seems eaten away by the grayish mold trembling like a mist over the France of the Citizen King, the whole tyrannically controlling the parts (that's why the justly famous reflections on the 1848 revolution have much more depth than all the scenes of Parisian life). What moves me, at times, is Flaubert's inability to really give life to his heroine; radiating with obsessive memory, she is like a *blank* in the middle of the novel from which any depth is erased—bleached out, one might say, like an overexposed snapshot, by the too intense light of love.

In the descriptions, Flaubert here gives up suggesting and evoking, which, despite the "realism," he almost always does magnificently in *Madame Bovary*. He has to say everything, because he never casts his imagination beyond what he is saying. In the nevertheless famous Fontainebleau episode, the forest is described in the style of *Baedeker* or *Blue Guide* itineraries: every stop the visitor makes monotonously sets in motion an all-purpose descriptive rundown:

"Finally they went down into the flower garden.

"It is in the shape of a vast rectangle, giving an overall view of its broad yellow paths, its lawns, its border of box, its pyramid-shaped yews . . ." etc.

"Half an hour later they left the carriage again to walk up the Heights of Aspremont.

"The track zigzags among stocky pine trees and beneath jagged rocks . . ." etc. (Jagged, the rocks of Fontainebleau?)

The book is stocked with abundant furniture, more carefully sifted through than in Balzac: Chinese porcelain vases, shawls, ankle boots, cashmere, bonnets, console tables, tapestries, plates and dishes, *side tables, fish kettles*—how poorly Flaubert is served here by the obsessive provincial scent of *Madame Bovary*'s interiors! For the historian of furniture and costume, everything is rigorously controlled, it seems, down to the slightest detail; *everything is of the period*. What do I care if this listless and dismal odyssey gradually depletes every row of inventory from the Department Stores of the Temperate Monarchy! Flaubert's collapsing syntax, which makes his sentences leaden and prevents them from ever taking wing, discourages me from following him throughout his laborious quartermaster wanderings: there is a hundred times more life for me in *Les Misérables*, and ten times more in *The Mysteries of Paris*.

*

I've finished rereading *Sentimental Education*, undertaken out of bad conscience, with the sole intention of reducing the abyss that separates me from the quasi-universal view of my contemporaries. It has not changed my opinion at all. The most convincing figure in the novel may be, in his inconsistency, "Mr. Arnoux," but he's a figure who tends toward farce, halfway between Labiche and Balzac (it's odd that while reading, the memory of *Perrichon*'s author returned to me more than once; *Regimbart*, as much by name as by his conditioned reflexes, is a pure Labiche character). What an unexpected, melodramatic image, clashing with the slow monotony of the work: Dussardier felled by Sénécal before Frédéric's eyes! The Dambreuse household, what ectoplasm! Without a single somewhat incisive feature to extract it from its grand bourgeois indistinguishableness! As for the final reflection on the bordello—so unconvincing, so artificial, so *induced*—that encompasses the novel's meaning so narrowly, it's like a transgression, in Flaubert's universe, which is nevertheless of another complexity and another extent, of the limited and reductive cynicism of *Maupassant*.

*

What does compete with the balance and efficiency of *Madame Bovary*, unlike *Sentimental Education* where the mocking spirit definitively submerges the whole monotonously, is that all who affect the heroine closely— not only Léon and Rodolphe, but Justin, Father Rouault, and even Charles—are pulled sooner or later from the ordinary by the glint of a central fire, and surround Emma (for everyone is present throughout, or returns, until the end) with an orbiting ring of weak light that is enough to isolate the unalloyed grotesques that are Homais, Binet, or Bournisien, so that, from one end of the book to the other, she hardly seems to notice them. In rereading the novel, what struck me was not the miserable failure of Emma's loves and fantasies, on which Flaubert dwells at length, but the intensity of the flame that brings his heroine to life and plants her, like a lit torch, in a sleepy town in the boondocks of Normandy. I am more sensitive, on this rereading, to Emma's beautiful struggle than to her defeat, which is in no way pathetic, as we too often say. Because, in short, everything that it is possible for her to attempt in her situation— which is hopeless from the start—she attempts, with a certain boldness, and the nostalgic and fascinated passiveness that has been called "Bovaryism" has to do only very relatively with a decisive spirit that in the book often borders on intrepidness. Finally, in the last scenes (when Flaubert, moreover, clearly takes his heroine's side), the bovine placidity of Yonville is disturbed: this flying spark of errant passion is mere inches from setting fire to a village that is nevertheless so exemplarily fireproof.

It is this fury of a frantic will to live—slow to awaken, smoldering and finally exploding in the torpor of a small town like a time bomb—that for many definitively assures the book's greatness. The sinking down natural to Flaubert is not consented to this time, and with counterbalance, retrieves all its poetic potential. Once again, the lighting of a masterpiece changes with time: *M.L.F.*,[46] like May 68 ("Think of your desires as realities"), close to a century later, find a deeply reflective surface in Emma Bovary, and make the book, for us today, a novel of awakening as much as a novel of failure: the awakening of the proselyte still in a savage state.

*

When I read *Nana*, the ravages of the artistic writing dear to the Goncourts suddenly strike me as more extensive than in other novels in the *Rougon* series. It's not bad taste—after all, who cares!—that ruins Zola's style for me, it's the precarious balance of his sentence structure that makes the reader ill at ease, as one might be before a person balancing on one leg or leaning against a piece of furniture in order to stand.

The best part of the book is the captivating account of the stage and the backstage atmosphere during rehearsal. Zola has remarkably sensed the *cozy* and comfortably serene side of these theatrical behind-the-scenes, with their concierges and sleeping cats, muffled sounds around the conspiratorial half-light that reigns on stage—and into which seeps an unexpected, antiseptic, placid daylight (this was particularly true of Théâtre Montparnasse, where the windows of the loges, stairways, and hallways all looked out over the spacious, sun-filled glade of the cemetery).

Zola's novel maintains its precarious balance for a rather long time between the emphasis on the true (Nana's bad patch, her love for an actor in a furnished room, shopping in worn-out slippers between moments of prosperity) and the fake purple passages (the ridiculous meal, the house transformed into a waiting room, clients shoved into the kitchen). Until he swings into involuntary buffoonery in the grand-guignolesque[47] scenes of the final culmination, worthy of the paintbrush of Clovis Trouille. This confirms my notion, which has been mine for a long time, namely, that the "epic" Zola, visionary of the misshapen, so celebrated by critics, far from merits the preference. His best register is actually situated in the *middle range*, and when he climbs into the high notes he almost always derails. He also has a way of *puffing out his chest* and letting us know when he is attacking high C, something Balzac would never allow himself to do.

*

It seems to me it was Zola who first realized how economical it could be for an author to integrate not mere index cards of information into a work of fiction but material already constructed in a literary way—memoirs, souvenirs, testimonies. This seemed clear when I read *The Debacle*, which at times very incompletely digests the travel diaries of Mac-Mahon's aide-de-camp. And this is what gives his novels their equivocal historical marginality; they make one think of trees that have been returned to the wild but that recall being grafted.

Because nothing can dispel the idea I have that the "epic" Zola's reputation is built entirely on purple passages whose audacity *Les Misérables* both secured and supplied the unsurpassed model for: the source of *Germinal*, the Paradou or La Lison[48] owe almost everything, and a bit more, to the sewers of Jean Valjean, the garden on rue Plumet, the elephant of the Bastille. What the *Rougon-Macquart* brings to literature that is really new is the herald of the novel-as-reportage.

*

All the houses, gardens, furniture, and costumes in Zola's novels, unlike Balzac's, have a whiff of the index card and the catalog (from this point of view, the botanic inventory of the winter garden in the hôtel Saccard in *The Kill*[49] is almost a parody: it is a collection of labels from the palm-tree conservatory of some Botanical Garden). In Balzac, the bric-a-brac of the interiors, as excessive, as invasive as it is in places, always seems to have undergone a long, cozy period of cohabitation that organizes it and makes it plausible to us: a strong sense of the human lair emerges from this catch-all room; rather than the storage room of a secondhand furniture dealer, it calls to mind tangles of interwoven bits of thread, shawl fringe, cigarette butts, wisps of straw, horsehair, and the ends of matchsticks. Everything is a garment— fitted, stretched, and worn thin on the person—in the Balzacian environment; everything in Zola, as soon as he abandons the working classes, seems a freshly delivered order from *Worth* or *Ladies' Delight*.[50]

*

Zola: *The Debacle*. The memoirs, accounts, and oral testimonies he no doubt consulted lead the author, with a
plausibility all the more deserved since it is entirely reconstructed, up to the battlefield of Sedan exclusively,
that is, to the limits of the zone of fire, where no docu-
mentation can suffice any longer, even for the most imaginative novelist, because in the limitless play of transfers
and substitutions that is his resource, there is no longer
any equivalence that can animate from within the depiction of a troop under fire, and the strange world into
which it is thrown. A world where the basic components
of mental chemistry lose their stability and become
volatile, where the sense of time and space—to take only
this example—are subjected to such singular distor-
tions.

No matter: at the account of the lugubrious movement of Mac-Mahon's army between Reims and Sedan,
a thousand memories reared their head. The zigzagging
marches in the polders of Dutch Flanders, through the
thick zone of calm, muted and green, bordering the dull
rumble of explosions very far to the north, east, and
southwest. Sas-de-Gand at two o'clock in the morning,

all lights out, its footbridges and chimneys, its cranes and sluice-gates catching moonbeams in the dark night, like a fleet of tall ships in a black lake. The white night of Gravelines, face to the false dawn that turned the rooftops red on the Calais side. The deluge that battered the roadway from Dunkirk to Teteghem, bordered as evenly by trees as by its two rows of English trucks tossed into the ditch.

But in 1940 there was still a lot of room for phantasmagoria. Since Napoléon III, information in times of war has made lightning progress. Leaving for Sedan, the last of Mac-Mahon's troops knew the situation of the war and the list of defeats, which the newspapers did nothing to conceal. In 1940, the mental *blackout* was complete; the incredible airiness of the dream was the sole point of juncture for the incoherent news that could be gathered.

LANDSCAPE AND THE NOVEL

What *speaks* to us in a landscape?

If you have a penchant for vast panoramas, it seems to me it is primarily the spreading-out in space—embellished, appealing—of a virtual and variable "life path," which, stretched out in time, can usually only be represented in the abstract. A life path that could also very easily be a pleasure stroll. Every great landscape invites you to possess it by walking; the enthusiasm it communicates is the intoxication of the road. This shady area, *then* this patch of light, *then* this slope to descend, this fordable river, this house, already forsaken on the hill, crossing through the black forest behind it, with, in the distance, far off in the distance, this glorious sun-filled mist, at once and indissolubly the vanishing point of the landscape, a proposed stage in our day, and a sort of obscurely prophetic perspective on our life. "The broad country, long-silent, extends . . ."[51] and yet they speak; they speak vaguely yet forcefully of what is to come, and of what suddenly seems to come to meet us from so far away.

That is also why, in the distribution of color, shadow, and light in a landscape, everything that makes one material part more prominent by the signs of the hour and the season, makes the physiognomy more expressive, because it more narrowly interweaves the freedom linked to space to the destiny that can be felt in temporality. This is what makes a rocky landscape at noon inert under the gaze, while a morning landscape, and even more an evening landscape, often achieve an augural transparency where, if everything is a path, everything is also a presentiment. This engulfing of the future in the delineation of the features of the Earth, nevertheless so firm and stable, spurs thought that is already partly divinatory, a lucidity that the Earth purifies and seems to turn entirely toward the future: one of the singularities of the figure of Moses in the Bible is that his gift of clairvoyance always seems indissolubly linked to the visual embrace of some vast revelatory panorama.

*

Was Gide right to associate the poetic valorization of the mountain to Swiss Calvinist ethics? (A penchant for purity, or rather nonpollution, underscored by the Protestant phobia of the microbe—the moral value of ascension, the effort toward the summits.) In fact, the penchant for the mountain was born only with Rousseau, thus in a Calvinist milieu, and was imposed in Latin countries, not without difficulty: three quarters of a century after the *New Heloise*,[52] Chateaubriand who traversed Simplon remained mostly attached to the classic notion of "terrible abysses." But the discovery of the mountain as a source of exaltation—a revolution of capital importance in man's geographic *Weltanschauung*—must have had causes of a quite different scope than the abrupt expansion in Europe of a cantonal quirk of sensibility.

In reality, it is not the mountain, but the indissolubly linked sea-and-mountain pair, and even the sea-mountain-forest triad, that sees assured promotion in the early nineteenth century. Its twofold attraction then becomes so irresistible that Lermontov, pioneer of a literature without a past, a literature just dawning, can make out nothing in the Russian landscape but these two elements, which are completely marginal there and which he will go to seek at the bottom of the Caucasus. And it is in England, the England of Ossian and Byron (to whom Lermontov owes so much), that this revolution of the landscapist sensibility occurred, in which

German Romanticism, the original explorer of the domains of night and dream, took least part. In fact, in the construction of what we call European Romanticism, there was a separation of functions largely determined at the time by the particularities of national and religious sentiment and by the unequally felt impact of the acceleration of history: to the brilliance of the British, the landscapist awakening to *great horizons*, to Germany, the discovery of night and dream, to the France of 1815, the tragic sense of history, the universal obsolescence of its forms. As the first organically European collective creation, which neither the Renaissance nor the Reformation ever were, Romanticism made tangible the interdependence of national forms of Western culture. As soon as it was born, there was no delay in propagating the new ways of feeling: for the first time, from Madrid to Moscow, no zone of opacity could slow it down; Lermontov responded almost immediately to Byron, while the borders of the Holy Alliance period, and political and religious censures of all sorts, were infinitely less permeable than in the time of Michelangelo or Luther: a remarkable phenomenon of a spontaneously unified echo chamber, one that never vibrated as perfectly in all its amplitude again. In spite of appearances, nothing like this was produced in the Europe of the Enlightenment, where above all governments spread, filtered, and carefully controlled an ideology completely marked with the stamp of French intellectuality.

*

I do not lament every aspect of architectural modernity. The vast platforms paved with marble between sky-scrapers, when these are well spaced and allow large, quadrangular patches of sky to descend to the ground, the cold edge of their basins and pools, have seduced me already, each time I encountered them in New York or Chicago, at Rockefeller Center or on the waterfront of Lake Michigan. Since before the war, the high, bare ter-race of the Trocadéro has appealed to me. This after-noon, coming back from the Gare Montparnasse and climbing the staircase along the tower itself that leads to the platform, the same charm stirred in me once again, intensely: these beautiful, vast volumes with sharp an-gles and clean edges made my breath fuller and lighter; in this fully molting Parisian landscape, the forcefully cut-out solids, now of stone, now of air, surrounding me and hanging over me, appeared equal in density and hardness to the senses: I walked around as though part of a sharp-edged, stained-glass picture window—the cold wind that ran along these naked slabs, that lifted neither leaves nor dust, reinvigorated me like nothing else.

Once again, with "Parisian Dream," Baudelaire saw this new age advance from far away, so drawn to a modernity still to come and yet already sensed—unlike Poe, for once, whose "Domain of Arnheim" is merely the final vision of an architecture entirely engulfed by water and vegetation—an architecture in which Le Nôtre colonizes and outdoes Mansart in all respects.[53]

*

The unified image of a landscape, a native landscape, for example, that we keep within us and have seen since childhood, is made up of a combination of periodic cycles with very different rhythms—beyond the seasonal changes that are not really grasped as changes but rather as simple attributes of its substance, successively perceived. In Saint-Florent, for example, in the landscape I have looked at forever through my window, these cycles are about thirty years for the poplars, which are cut down, then replanted, to almost double that or more for the willows, while the rhythm of the expansion or renovation of buildings, once more than centuries old, today tends to accelerate visibly. For a long time during my childhood, across from the house on the bank of the île

Batailleuse, I saw a gorgeous row of already mature poplars before me; nothing disconcerted me more than to see, one fine day, these columns of my Parthenon cut down. Since then, I have seen two complete cycles follow each other in this architectural order—and a more robust Nietzschean ragout seasoning the simple ritornello of the seasonal cycle in a significant fashion.

*

Ardennes: the *Old Forest* in question in *The Lord of the Rings* has its headquarters here: all the rest is a matter of layers, cuttings, and transplantation; there are hardly any real forests besides the Hercynian forest.

I went to Hauts-Buttés again, which has remained intact in its glade since 1955, except that the *Café des Platanes* has become a somewhat more upscale restaurant where on Sundays they serve young wild boar with bilberries. The skeleton of the fortress still stands on the edge of the road from Alle to Sedan, increasingly submerged year to year by the undergrowth. The road from Revin to Hauts-Buttés has been covered in asphalt but is already worn down and returning little by little to the wild; on each side of the narrow, peeling ribbon, high and exuberant populations of fern; in the Manises woods, where a path opens to me at the end of a clearing, a walk in the wet, sun-splashed copse is so agreeable at ten in the morning that I am almost tempted to roll around in the damp foliage with its scent of fall, a scent at once earthy and winged. This entire wild canton has become mine, and the changes I find here have gradually blended with those of a native canton: the simple *markers* that border it here and there have practically become part of an actual story.

*

What strikes me in Custine's *Letters from Russia* is not so much the acuity of the political observer as the eye of the landscapist, through which interstitial urban spaces —air swimming over giant squares, between spires, far apart domes, and the colonnades and quays of the enormous river—are evaluated and situated in all their singularity. The strong, appealing image of St. Petersburg that lingers once the book is closed is that of a still unfurnished capital where monuments float in too much space, at the edge of swollen waters that flow to the brim of granite parapets: a Nordic and deficient Brasilia, shot through with the wastelands of its empty lots, where the lifeless spread of plazas and perspectives absorbs and dissolves crowds and noise, where in one furious gallop the meager, rushing traffic races off on wooden streets, enveloped in silence. A city too distended, too flat on the wide horizon, where the ear is disoriented by the absence of echoes and surprised not to hear its own hum: the strange silence of a capital, as though it were snowing in the middle of summer. And it doesn't matter that the limitlessness of the Russian plain is barely evoked here at all. It is present in perspective and in stippling— and all the more present for not being there except in stippling—at the end of these too vast avenues that are diluted into forest paths, and that fade off confused, already incorporated into a forest, amid fences, wooden shacks, and log piles. The taiga blows its green breath through all the cracks in the city, like an animal's snout under a door.

*

Almost all thinkers, all poets of the West favor ideas and images that evoke a waking state, which is to say, the mind's secession from the world, and no less systematically neglect those that depict—the heaviness and awkwardness of the word show how much what it designates is generally held to be negligible, if not undesirable —*falling asleep*,[54] reunification.

Still, in this waking state, it is almost always a matter of already being awake rather than a passage. In the science and literature of the West, so little attention is ac-

corded to truly nascent or expiring states of consciousness! I am not excluding, quite the contrary, "La jeune
Parque,"[55] whose every resolutely recurring movement
finds its starting point and foundation in the most alert
consciousness.

Western philosophy: man is systematically viewed
in relation to the world in terms of maximum *disparity*.
All the states in which this antagonistic tension is re-
leased—sleep, dream, mystical, contemplative, or vege-
tative states, a sense of participation in or identification
with untamed civilizations, certain mental illnesses—
have been relentlessly devalued by it.

PROUST CONSIDERED

AS AN END POINT

I am not in any way diminishing the admiration I have, as everyone does, for *Remembrance of Things Past*, if I remark that the miraculous precision of memory, flooding in from all over to animate its characters and give them the benefit of real detail unrivalled by any imagination, deprives them at the same time of this trembling of the future, of this elation toward the eventual, that is one of the rarest summits of accomplishment in the novel, and an admirable illustration of which I found recently while rereading a scene in *Bitter Victory* by Louis Guilloux:[56] the lunch at the lawyer's where people cross paths before leaving and never seeing each other again, in an atmosphere of lightness and unreal detachment, with everyone on their way someplace and around whom the future acts as a sort of fluttering fan. This *letting go* of the free balloon, a sense of which is offered us from time to time while reading our favorite novels and which is perhaps fiction's crowning achievement because it is like the materialization of freedom itself, Proust forbids himself: its absence is the price paid for the power of resuscitation communicated to his work by an imagination that, more than in any other novelist, remains close to his living roots, which are memory. All of *Remembrance* is a resurrection, but a temporary resurrection, a scene replayed in the vaults of time, by mummies, who before going back to bed, regain not only the speech and gestures but even the rosy cheeks and flowery complexions they had in their lifetime. Only Eurydice, who is sent walking toward us fully breathing, and who already almost sees earthly daylight again, will not come back from the Underworld: this youth always in development, this upsurge of the future in those whom nothing can ever freeze, and that causes us to confuse in our imaginations the characters of our favorite novels with our own encounters, our own loves, and our own adventures, the people of *Things Past* do not participate in. The umbilical cord that Fabrice del Dongo cut with the Lombardy of the Holy Alliance (while, by some magic spell, continuing to receive its succor) Albertine or the duchesse de Guermantes cannot sever with their Belle Epoque salon; as in the rooms of Egyptian tombs, their double resuscitation only flits among the conspiring jewels, cosmetics, sandals, combs, dresses, and talis-

mans of the funereal furniture, and like the characters in
Locus Solus,[57] miraculously cured by an injection of *résurrectine*,[58] what Odette de Crécy summons, clothed in
her morning dress, are not the pathways of our dreams
and our presentiments, but forever the sun-filled rue Ab-
battucci in the year 1900, with its cool, wet cobblestones,
its smell of fresh horse droppings, the *staccato* of its
sound of clogs.

*

The linking of sequences in *Remembrance of Things
Past*—rather than the usual string of fictional scenes
linked by the flow of time—often resembles cellular
growth through the splitting of nuclei. As soon as a new
or unexpected focus of interest becomes dense enough
on the margins of one of the lively scenes that make up
Remembrance, it centers the narrator's attention and
gaze on it and becomes the nucleus of a new sequence,
which immediately organizes its autonomy. So difficult
to link spatially and chronologically to the preceding
one, so capriciously related to it that it comes to the cells
from tissue proliferating in anarchy. The genetic imper-
ative of multiplication and enrichment predominates in
the book at all times over that of organization. The life-
line, so svelte and sylphlike, that presides over the de-

velopment of a novel by Stendhal, yields here to a star-shape through the somewhat stifling yet no less dynamic expansion of live substance. A world with no destination and no hierarchy, animated solely by its infinite capacity for secret proliferation: this is the feeling the world of *Remembrance* sometimes gives us, and at times a page of Proust can recall those fragments of living matter in science fiction novels that have fallen to earth from another planet, and whose inextinguishable propensity to proliferate, like an oil stain, nothing can stop.

*

Guermantes Way remains both the most shimmering and most superficial part of *Remembrance*: it really has to do with the society novelist, monocle secured to his eye, circulating through the salons under the aegis of the parodic phylactery, *I am observing*. And indeed he observes marvelously. But the solidity that supports this worldly iridescence: the composition, the mergers and evolutions of the Guermantes fortune, the duke's relations with his stockbroker, his banker, his lawyer, his stewards, the whole deeply Balzacian cut that would give these glassy reflections a third dimension, play explicitly hard to get here—no doubt for the only time in *Remembrance*. The reigning class's apparently fixed economic status allowed gossipy chronicles in the closed milieu of the Grand Siècle, from Tallemant to Saint-Simon: the period of rapid real estate and financial transformations with which the narrator is faced no longer supports the tics and niceties of the salon of the Guermantes circle, already deeply threatened by the Verdurin upsurge, which clearly has to do with entirely other causes than the fluctuations of snobbism. But no doubt Proust knew this and wanted it this way: all the broken cables, all the cut moorings are a heaven, an inferior heaven, no doubt, but a heaven nonetheless: a heaven of high society in which the duc de Guermantes is God the Father, celebrated and enthroned, and if the actions of Suez and the great estates are the launching pad for these brilliant asteroids, they now revolve, cluster, regenerate, and attract each other based on other laws: they have, at least in a literary sense, gone beyond escape velocity.

*

One of the reasons Proust has not had an apparent literary descendant is because this descendant would be very difficult to identify—because his work represents less the creation of what we call a writer's "world" (that is, the filtering of the objective world through an original sensibility) than the application of a decisive technical conquest, immediately usable by all: a qualitative leap in literature's optical equipment. The resolving power of the eye—the inner eye—has doubled: this is the new capital; like any adjustment of a more sophisticated microscope, it implies both superior precision in the observation of domains already explored *and* access to new domains, which until now have remained indiscernible (a typical example of this for me is the inclusion in *Swann's Way* of a chapter like "Place-Names": *terra incognita* up until then for literature, which a Huysmans, for example, had the capacity to recognize, but did not, lacking the necessary magnification, have the means to explore).

When I speak of progress, it goes without saying that this resolving power of the eye existed, virtually, but it was not sanctioned; no one used it: all the conquests, all the successes of power in art were not inventions but permissions, the rights of transgression that an artist suddenly accorded himself at the expense of the *not-dared* until then. In every period, there is an infinitely small thing that literature considers reject material, as though unworthy of being accounted for, but the threshold of this infinitely small, residual, and negligible thing shifts with time, and this threshold will lower from the seventeenth century to the nineteenth and from the nineteenth to the twentieth: the meticulous sartorial detail of Balzac's characters is situated beyond this threshold for a contemporary of Boileau (and even for Stendhal, a quasi-contemporary of Balzac's, which proves the abruptness of the transformation), but the Lilliputian details by which Legrandin's snobbism is betrayed are likewise beyond the resolving power at Flaubert's disposal. This does not exclude the notion that this threshold, instead of advancing, regresses in time, without necessarily affecting the quality of the literature; we tend to think it does when we compare seventeenth-century literature to sixteenth-century literature from this point of view. Because it's as if the opening of the compass of literary fiction remained fixed, and as if what was gained in terms of analysis was simultaneously lost in terms of synthesis. The baron de Charlus, for example, while "alive" (oh how alive!), is not alive in the same way as Fabrice or Julien Sorel: forcefully incorporated into each of his scenes by an infallible eye and ear and linked to them by an unusual profusion of stitches, he does not detach from them as a Stendhal hero would, liberated by the indivisible *pluses* he has accumulated after each of his appearances in the novel and allowed to mix freely with our reveries and almost our life: rather he is fused to the detail of each scene of the book and seems absorbed in each of them, like characters in the decors of libraries painted by Vuillard, who seem built into the wall of books against which they appear. Hence, the necessity for the long essay fragments and psychological and theoretical reflections that Proust inserts each time his characters are evoked: functional through and through, they play the indispensable role of literary cement; they are the only means of recapturing and reunifying on a more abstract level the characters who tend to scatter and fragment amidst all their fictional appearances, which are each unforgettable, but, from the viewpoint of the work's equilibrium, perhaps risk being overly so.

Yes, I cannot help it: each time I see Vuillard's "libraries" in the Petit Palais, I think of Proust, struck as I am, as I have always been, by the minimal disparity between the density and relief that separates the characters of his book from the teeming, live mass of which the book is made and from which they just barely emerge. They are like bas-reliefs that protrude slightly, caught in the thickness, and that would barely stand out from a smooth wall, much less an already animated swarming, as in the walls in Hindu temples. At times one could even say these characters are born, almost seamlessly, of the simple excessive density of Proust's fictional matter, just as we are shown the first living cells born in a primitive "biological soup" through a phenomenon closer to crystallization than to creation. On more than one occasion, the way they are inserted into *Remembrance* seems to give material evidence of this. When the duchesse de Guermantes—certainly, of all the characters in *Remembrance*, the one most tightly clasped and attached to its nourishment—appears for the first time, announced from afar, already integrated through her name, her residence, her "côté," and the thousand variations connected to this, and to the mass of the work, she can barely separate herself from her emblematic stained-glass window to walk down the red carpet of the Combray church, before nevertheless—for a long time—entering it. And later the figure of the duchess will continue to be enriched by the succor that the work—even in her absence—continues to nourish her with in her hibernation. If it were possible to speak very audaciously of celestial mechanics in regard to fictional mechanics, I would say that, in terms of artistic effectiveness, a constant quantity results, in Proust, from the product of an enormous central mass of smaller satellites, and, in Stendhal, on the contrary, from the product of masses that are almost equivalent, his key-characters having as much weight for the reader as the entirety of the work that hatched them, drawing it to them as much as they are drawn by it.

*

Proust does not seem too concerned with making the parts of his work harmonize with each other, although certain critics attach great importance to the "composition" of *Remembrance of Things Past*. In each part, a few bricks are arranged so as to mortise into the neighboring part; the density, the intrinsic solidity of the material, treated in powerful blocks, allow juxtaposition to suffice for balance, as in those Achaean walls of crude rubble that hold together simply by being piled on top of each other, without the aid of cement. The chronological sequence remains among the vaguest—at least until the outbreak of the war of 14, when the flow of time brusquely accelerates. In fact, this temporal flow (this, they say, is how Einstein's space is distended, based on its population of matter) seems in Proust to depend directly on the density of the literary substance he is carrying: rapid when the narrative is stripped down, stuck and almost arrested when it is saturated with a magma of reflections, impressions, and memories, until it is engorged and gives the impression—so loaded with an excess of elements in dissolution—that it will *take*, from one moment to the next, like a jelly.

Every time I reopen *Remembrance of Things Past*, I am more sensitive to the primacy of the material over the architecture, of the cellular tissue over the differentiated organ, of the density of the verbal flow over the free air space accorded to the characters, of the concrete duration of reading over the figurative time of the narrative. The central mass of the book imperiously comes down and plasters everything against itself that tends to protrude beyond it, through an all-powerful force of gravity, including the imaginative production of the reader who, deprived of air and movement by the stifling, compact jungle of an overfed prose, never manages to spring beyond it, to play off it freely: how many times has the reader of Proust, when his stimulated mind set off and started to imagine for his own sake, had the feeling that two lines or ten lines down the author was already lying in wait on his path to nip this nascent independence in the bud, that he had rushed ahead to mark every possible path in the literary *rally* with his own colors. In every novel, a balance is established, different each time, between what is said, and the élan that allows the reader to complete things on his own, *freestyle*: in Proust, the compact proliferation of the explicit reduces the implicit left to the reader to the smallest share. Let's admit it—and this limit compensates for another he has forced—Proust rarely compels us to dream, but he compels us to feast: this is food more than aperitif.

*

In *Remembrance*, characters' relationships with money are the kind we see in oriental tales. No "average finances," or very few, and only among minor characters; "wealth" appears everywhere as an absolute—indivisible and equivalent to the possession of secret treasure chests or caverns from which gold flows inexhaustibly like oil from a prophet's jug. As luxuriously as they live, these wealthy people out of fairy tales still live well below their means and at all instants are in a position to permit themselves scarcely believable *extras*: for their anniversary, the Verdurins offer precious stones to members of the "core group" (just as Catherine II passed around a salad bowl full of gems to guests at her dinner parties), or they leave on a cruise on a yacht for a year, simply to allow the faithful *Biche*—who was prescribed this by Cottard—to breathe the sea air; Swann, to entertain Odette, whom he is taking to Bayreuth, thinks it might be fun to rent one of the King of Bavaria's castles for the season, etc. This behavior—more American than

French in the world of the salons, and which makes one think of the steel and railroad kings, of the Carnegies and Vanderbilts rather than the fortunes of the Belle Epoque, still sitting solidly on their assets but short on immediately available funds—gives the insertion of *Remembrance* into real social history an unreal and even fabulous character that ultimately serves it well. Just as our era has rediscovered a taste for mixing sweet and savory flavors, the pleasure we have in reading Proust has to do in part with the strange precision, the paradoxical precision of an ahistorical realism, with the world, analyzed and shot through by such enlightened psychology, existing in a substratum of an economic fairytale world that takes us back millennia beyond Balzac, and that, striding over *César Birotteau* or *Lost Illusions*, joins *Ali Baba, The Magic Lantern*, and *Sinbad the Sailor*.

Petits châteaux de Bohème—Les nuits d'octobre—Chansons et légendes du Valois:[59] even aside from *Sylvie*, there is an omnipresent infusion of memory in Nerval, a song of times past that takes flight and unwinds from even the tiniest recollection, from the recent past or long ago, and that I do not see in any other writer. This is not a quasi-hallucinatory resurrection of the past as occurs in Proust's best moments, so close at times to the illusion of false recognition; rather it is the blind contact, magically evoked in his prose, that one feels on finding one's childhood home and garden. As if this past world were the only place Nerval *finds himself*, instinctively, infallibly, and he immediately convinces us of it. And to do this he has no need of the miraculous visual or aural detail of Proustian memory: what is riveting in *Sylvie* is not the half-dozen charming details by which he is clearly able to compete with *Remembrance*; it is his process alone, it is the inimitable disconnectedness, the freedom of his wanderings, that persuade us at all times that wherever he goes in this lost past, he is always at home.

Perhaps in the haze, in the Nervalian mist that constantly blurs too much precision, there is also the sense that this delicious "fadedness," which is the specific tint of yesteryear, would vanish in the overly mordant vivacity of Proustian resurrection, whose singularity is to transfer to memory the direct aggressiveness usually proper to sensation. The past never *sings* in Proust: it resurges into consciousness and almost surges into violence; in Nerval, it is less material content than tone and lighting, an affective slide toward an autumnal yellowing, a minor key that comes to tinge life the very moment it is being lived (ever so slightly and as though from a distance) with the immediately timeless colors of memory. There is never the search for gold or lost time in Nerval, never the high-strung imperialism of Proust, who will not rest until he has laid a feverish hand on the dissipated treasures: there is rather a docile acceptance of the saturation of the present, already obsessed with the past the moment it is being lived. What perhaps best wears the true colors of memory in Nerval is not the resurrection of Valois in *Sylvie*, but the writer's sleepwalking approach when in the middle of the night, at the beginning of the narrative, he sets off through the streets of Paris in search of a carriage in order to find the *Bouquet* festival; it is this nocturnal wakefulness of a consciousness for which the hands of time, each time they really turn, begin infallibly to turn backwards. Reading the short story, it is this dreamlike night path in *Flandre* that gives one the intense feeling that Nerval only really traveled it in the opposite direction.

*

A continuous *density* of the streets, salons, faces, lighting, memories, landscapes, tone of voice, and conversations impels us to search, in the domain of gastronomical equivalences, for dishes remarkable for both their personal heterogeneity and their entirely solidified consistency, like puddings and *jellies*.

*

There are never real conversations in the paralyzed scenes of *Remembrance*, only descriptive "bubbles" of unequalled expressive force ("I knew what she was getting at"—"Ah! You're sending me to heaven!"). The only thing Proust is unaware of is movement; in this sense, he is the antipode of Stendhal, who *is* movement and who needs almost nothing else. The salvaging of the past, obsessive in him, does not in any way mimic the anticipation of the future: what memory delivers, and particularly what flashes of memory deliver—which Proust seeks above all else—are lightning visions, pictures fixed in the moment by a magic wand, enchanted tableaux. The evocation of fragments of the past is therefore perfectly interwoven into the fictional present, which, when it is the pure present, is static, that is, panoramic and descriptive—projection toward the future is never interwoven here: you have to be entirely devoted to it, like Stendhal. When Proust evokes the narrator's desire to see Venice in *Remembrance*, this desire already has the delicately faded colors of reminiscence: for the reader, there is no moment when these sails are filled with wind.

*

There is a certain legitimacy in dreaming of an audience with Ranuce Ernest IV or a conversation with the Sanseverina, but one cannot imagine an encounter with Mme de Guermantes, Albertine, or Gilberte, any more than with one of the figures that populate the *Mémoires* of Saint-Simon: once extracted, whether by the Sun King's liturgical court rituals or by the exacting and exclusive ecological equilibrium of the Proustian environment, they are no longer anything but fish washed up on shore.

Quite often in a novelist's use of the first or third person an apparent counter-use can be observed. At times the *I* is used with partiality where the narrative is markedly objective, while the *he* is used in narratives whose emphasis is decidedly subjective. There is nothing deliberate about this, nothing but the practice of this instinct which, from a book's first pages, peremptorily resolves the most complex and tangled problems without giving them clear thought (choice of tone, "distancing" or close participation, the *sfumato* or clarity of outlines, etc.). The truth is that the sum of final decisions that every first page implies, whether brutal or subtle, is dizzying. The possibility of intervention left to the author does not tangibly exceed that which an education may subsequently exert *a posteriori* through the years on someone's "nature"—and it is probably good that the initial trigger, the act of engendering, is left in both cases, physical and mental, to blind impulse, to the adventurism of pure desire. The beginning of a work of fiction, in the end, may have no other real objective than to create, from what is irretrievable, a fixed anchoring point, a resistant *given* that the mind can now no longer shake. Because, of all of fiction's problems, there is one problem raised prior to all others, that we leave between parentheses, and that is nothing other than that of Archimedes' screw: what can we use to leave the closed circle of the evasive, the substitutable, and the fluctuating? How can the mind in the labor of fiction escape the fate of Jules Verne's *Nautilus*: *Mobilis in mobile*?[60] What allows literary "creation" to deserve its name is that—in the beginning—the novelist goes beyond it, as in real creation, to the mystery that consists of stirring up and fabricating something, without using his hands, and which can then become opaque to his own mind.

*

I am not very sensitive to the observation of various sorts of "unities" in a work of art, but I am acutely aware of its basic unity. All the disparate elements in the nature of a work's material jostle me—so much so that, in a work of fiction, I cannot let the name of a single real place remain. I allow myself at least a similar preoccupation in *The Charterhouse*, where the very authentic city of Parma finds itself subtly derealized by the implantation of the Farnese Tower. This is not a *little game* aiming to pique or confuse the reader; it has to do with literary honor itself, the intimate nature of the novel, which is to let the reader *be* in proportion to everything that is being said, but in the concomitant annihilation of any real reference.

*

Who would deny that the richness of a work of fiction is constituted by the multiplicity of the (partially clandestine) relationships established between its various elements? Only everything is in the current, passing through the numerous, delicately networked conductors of a text: supposing that one managed to detect them all—an objective accounting that would not, in the end, be unthinkable—one would still have to determine how these "intratextual" contacts were hierarchized and led into one other. A determination of the greatest importance, because the current of reading is not divided, and, in the matter of reading novels, all things raise a question less of existence than of intensity. The current of reading, blindly, among all the branches that a book presents, follows the threads of a larger section, and, in reaction, certain modern exegetes of the text call to mind the electronic maps one finds in metro stations: a thousand paths are interconnected and apparently interchangeable, but if you press a button, the shortest trip between departure and end point will be illuminated. There are certainly as many readings of a text as there are readers, but for each reader—when he is not setting himself up as an artificial promoter of marginal readings—there is one trajectory through the book and, indeed, only one. The line of reading never branches off; if, for a moment, we lose sight of a character with the sense that he will reappear eventually, this sense is not stored off to the side in our memory: it is incorporated immediately into the overall sense that our reading promotes at all times, and that gives it nuances without being distinct from it. This memory of elements already absorbed and consumed that fiction creates as it advances—a memory that is entirely integrated and active at all moments—and that is one of its fundamental prerogatives, contradicts not the existence but the segregation of "levels of meaning" set forth in a text. These levels do not attain real presence, because they are never followed separately by attention, but rather perceived synthetically in the manner of a musical harmony: thus the richness of a book has to do less with the consciously registered multiplicity of these "levels of meaning" than with the undivided fullness of the resonance that they organize around a text as the reading gradually progresses. The refusal of any separation, the imperialism of the overall feeling that makes any real reading of a novel an indistinct tallying, very generally prevails over the intellectual pleasure of comprehension that disjoins, the fundamental, unitary rapture born of listening to a symphony.

*

Valéry's reflections on literature are those of a writer in whom the pleasure of reading is at its minimum, the concern for professional verification at its maximum. His natural frostiness in the matter makes it so that each time he attacks a novel, it is in the manner of a leader of ancient gymnastics criticizing a lack of economy in the motions of coitus: he takes offense at wasted energy, the stakes of which he does not wish to consider. One might wonder, when he condemns the novel, if the cause is indeed the carelessness of the novel's approach, which he expressly invokes, and not the novel's effects on the reader, which—in relation to all other literary genres— are an affective rattling, at once more massive and less defined: of all the forms literature takes, the novel, even a quality novel, is the one that comes closest to the art of appeasement. Valéry speaks admirably of literature, if one is only concerned with its methods and their implementation, and if one wants to place the modest requests of the reader between parentheses: nothing that touches on the ingestion of the written thing is ever dealt with by him, and it would seem he has never found himself in the position of consumer but only that of inspector of produce and controller of weights and measures.

*

On the subject of Hugo's novels, Michel Butor makes an interesting remark on the narrative pauses that often yield to either very lengthy interior monologues or broad descriptive, philosophical, or historical amplifications. He compares them to *arias* where the operatic action is static for a rather long time.

The comparison is seductive; I do not believe it to be completely apt. The *aria* of traditional opera in fact corresponds to a passage from quantity to quality; the excess of intense emotional accumulation abruptly transmutes the dialogue, or eventful recitative, into a motionless, lyrical ejaculation. The narrative pauses of the novel to which Butor alludes seem to me much more often to fulfill another function: that of an organized delay, a braking in the action, whose goal is to let all the reserves capable of orchestrating and amplifying it flow toward the dramatic *apex* already in view. Thus, in Balzac's *Les Chouans*, the long description of the panorama of La Pèlerine, is clearly intended to enhance the simple

guerrilla skirmish to come with all the exemplary historical and geographical resonance it is capable of rousing.

One of the novelist's hidden problems, a problem the
author resolves or tries to resolve based solely on instinct, is, like a general in the army, to ensure the coordinated progression of the heterogeneous masses that his
narrative sets in motion and whose individualized characters only constitute the advanced point, the most alert,
most mobile homing rocket. Every novel then lugs
around its own logistics ("lugs" is not pejorative here),
more or less voluminous, camouflaged, or constricting,
never totally absent, from the flying column of psychological monotypes in the manner of *La Princesse de
Clèves* or *Adolphe* that advance without support or baggage to the massive phalanxes, regulated in their march
by the cartage of their *impedimenta*, of the social novels
of Zola.

One of the singularities of *The Charterhouse*, very
different from *The Red and the Black* in this regard, is
the complete and felicitous insouciance Stendhal maintains throughout vis-à-vis the foundations of his work,
which do what they can to remind the reader of their existence, and—great rarity—manage to succeed: the narrative moves quickly without slowing down an instant
for them; it is a superbly successful novel of almost ethe-

real suggestion. The Italy of the Holy Alliance is present there entirely, in its landscape and society as well as its stagnant political climate, but it is only there in a fragmented way in the individual parcels that characters transport with them everywhere without appearing hampered or weighed down: their literary fatherland remains stuck to the soles of their shoes.

*

And why not, definitively, "The marquise went out at five o'clock"? In fact, two distinct lines of operation converge in the offensive against the novel and assure its effectiveness: one against the style of "information pure and simple," thought to have currency; the other against the arbitrariness of fiction.

The entirely traditional maneuver of intimidation here involves taking the part for the whole, the inward part for the whole. Because, with the second sentence, the arbitrariness of *la marquise* already yields to a concern for the novel's coordination and coherence—a life of relationships, within the narrative, begins to awaken and to replace the peremptory assertion which the first sentence has knocked down, like a fist on the table. In fact, if dealing with a real novelist, the arbitrariness in the novel imagined by the author of *La jeune Parque* never really goes beyond the first sentence he quotes from it: there is no more exemplary case of wanton quotation and suppression of context than that of the famous *marquise*.

What seems clear in Valéry's broadly instinctive position here is the fundamental retraction of the mind before the native vice of any absolute beginning, of any Genesis. No artist, of course, can remain entirely insensitive (even if he disregards it) to this vice of the *incipit* that marks all the arts that organize duration: literature, music, as opposed to visual art, the execution of which is also certainly inserted in the unfolding of time, but that, in completion, erases any temporal reference and is more purely present as a circuit closed upon itself, with no beginning or end.

It may be that there is humor in Valéry's sentence, for the novel's servitude only exemplarily amplifies the servitude also inherent in the writer of verse. The novel, less pure, serves as a scapegoat for what poetry itself cannot totally purge itself of: the initial gratuitousness. What writer has not dreamt of breaking his attachment with the contingency of the world—of erasing his beginning?

*

Cruel novel. There is one subject for a novel that to my (mediocre) knowledge has never been dealt with, or at least never in all its scope. Its hero is a lover in the grand style, not a Don Juan, but a seducer, one of those true lovers by vocation, with a succession of flames, of which the musical field—composers, singers, and conductors—seems to provide more specimens of than others. From year to year, he switches idols, always enflamed, always exclusive, always transported. But his ex-lovers do not die (they only die in books). And since he is naturally sociable and cordial, and also deeply professional, a man of work and habits with little taste for the pleasures of breaking up, all his mistresses leave the flamboyant scene of passion one by one, without, however, disappearing from his life: they reenter the familiar and politely indifferent circuit of daily female colleagues and cohorts. Toward the end of his life, he moves among the old *Dilettas* and *Unicas*,[61] like a sacristan at dusk in the sweetish, smoky scent of candles he has blown out one after another. A world much worse than a world of inert objects: a world of uncharged batteries.

*

Chemical analysis: an authentic process, because the synthesis of decomposed elements reconstitutes the analyzed body in its integrity and weight. The "science" of literature or the text: the sum of the means detected and processes decrypted is not only always incomparably inferior to the total that the work represents, but is also still absolutely heterogeneous to it. The work of art is not—is never—a combinative of elements that go, for example, from the simple to the complex; for the writer, it is much more like a volume sensed from the beginning in all its scope and that allows itself to be colonized freely, unequally, and thereby to be progressively distorted by the writing. The mechanical distribution of the writer's work along the temporal vector being traveled is a source of false images, all of them related, closely or distantly, to that of a river gradually swelled by its confluences: as much as a page of work apparently moves toward the whole in order to construct it gradually, the sensed totality always comes from the opposite direction to secretly meet the page in the midst of being written in order to orient and inform it. Modified by each page, as pages are gradually written, but always present in all its mass; elastic, distortable, but indivisible. And more and more crushingly present as the work (I am only speaking of the novel here) fills out and comes closer to its realization, its end; it seems to me critics scarcely pay atten-

tion to or even suspect this constantly growing and ultimately all-powerful force of attraction of the whole over
the part, that makes the composition of a novel something less like a free voyage of discovery than the delicately guided comportment of a spaceship preparing to
land on the moon. The climate of the novelist's work
changes progressively all along the route: nothing could
be more different from the almost breezy freedom of the
first chapters than the anxious navigation, nervously
surveyed, of the terminal phase, where a sense of maximum risk is mixed with the intoxicating impression of
being pulled in, sucked in, as if the mass to which the
book has gradually given shape in turn began to capture
you in its field (perhaps it is this impression novelists try
to convey—so poorly—in their own way when they in-
sist that their characters "escape them"). The fact,
which has often intrigued me, that about two thirds into
each draft of my novels I have taken a long break—a
break of several months, accompanied by disarray and
malaise—before going back to it and finishing it, is perhaps not extraneous to the feeling I have had more than
once when completing a novel—of "landing," danger-
ously, rather than concluding.

*

Everything we introduce into a novel becomes a sign: it is impossible to insert an element that does not change it to some degree, any more than you can insert a number, algebraic sign, or superfluous exponent into an equation. Sometimes—rarely, because one of the novelist's cardinal virtues is a beautiful and intrepid unconscious—on a day of critical inclination, a sentence I have written will *conjure up horrors before me*, as Rimbaud wrote:[62] as soon as it is integrated into the narrative, assimilated by it, caught irrevocably in a pitiless continuity, I sense the radical impossibility of discerning the ultimate effect of what I have shoved into a delicate, growing organism: food or poison? Happily, a great attenuation of responsibility is among a novel's features; you have to move forward without thinking too much, have the optimism to at least believe you can make the most of your blunders. Among the millions of possibilities presented each day in the course of a life, some will barely hatch, or escape massacre, like insect or fish eggs, which is to say, have consequence: if I walk through the streets of my town, the hundred familiar buildings I pass each day—unperceived, and gradually obliterated—seem as though they never were. In a novel, on the contrary, no possibility is obliterated, none is without consequence, since it has received the stubborn and disconcerting life force of

writing: if I write in a narrative: "he passed a house of
modest appearance, whose green shutters were closed,"
nothing can erase this tiny scratch on the reader's mind,
a scratch that immediately enters the composition with
everything else; an alarm goes off: something has hap-
pened in this house, or will happen, someone lives there,
or has lived there, and it will be dealt with later on. Everything that is said sets off expectation or recall, everything
is taken into account, positive or negative, even though
the novel's totality will occur through agglutination
rather than addition. Here the weakness of Valéry's attack against the novel appears: the truth is that the novelist *cannot* say, "The marquise left at five o'clock": such
a sentence, at this stage in the reading, is not even perceived: it only deposits, in the dark of an unenlightened
night, a theatrical prop meant to become significant later
on, when the curtain is actually raised. The whole to
come is waiting to incorporate the part into its workings,
to reintegrate this building block initially suspended
in the air, and no judgment of gratuitousness can be
brought to bear on such a sentence, since there is no
judgment on the novel but the final judgment. The
mechanism of a novel is just as precise and subtle as the
mechanism of a poem, only, because of the dimensions
of the work, it can discourage the exhaustive critical

work that the analysis of a sonnet does not always deter. The critic of novels, because the complexity of a real analysis exceeds the mind's capacities, works only on intermediary and arbitrary sets, simplified groupings spread out and taken in blocks: "scenes" or chapters, for example, where a poetry critic would weigh each word. But if the novel is worth the trouble, it is line by line that its adventure has taken place and line by line that it should be discussed, if it is discussed. There is no more "detail" in the novel than in any work of art, although its mass suggests there is (because we are rightly persuaded that the artist was not able to control everything), and any criticism reduced to summarizing, gathering and simplifying, loses its right and credit, here as elsewhere.

Said before, and to be said again, this way, or another way.

*

Why would the shift of proportions and precedents that Wagner introduced between the playing, the remarks of characters onstage, and the all-powerful choral commentary of the orchestra, like a rustling in the forest, be forbidden from operating in the novel? Downplaying the protagonists' loves and quarrels, *reasons* and skirmishes, in favor of the mother-pulse of the great orchestra of the world? As soon as I started to frequent the lyric theater, I was fascinated by these breaches, so gaping and so eloquent, in the continuity of the singing, breaches in which the tenors, basses, and sopranos on-stage—and not merely the audience in the depths of darkness—seemed to silence themselves to let the flow of a whole sonorous tide come pulsate around them, as if they created silence, and taboos, around the confused revelation unfurling, of everything developing for them, yet outside them. Why would the novel be forbidden from wrangling from opera this asset that Mallarmé wanted poetry to take from music? These unique moments of really and truly inspired, profound and surging listening that have always seemed and still seem to burst the wall at the back of the theater and open it wide to let in the guiding hum of the world becoming Sibyl and becoming Pythia—music does not have the sole privilege of making space for them, of providing an outlet for the prophetic trances of their vapors.

*

The novel has certainly declined as a creator of characters in the twentieth century: here Mme Nathalie Sarraute has been proven right. But I doubt the real cause is the one she advances, namely, the growing distrust of both the reader and writer vis-à-vis fictional figures that take on life. I see this rather as the effect of the writer's inordinately heightened trust in his capacity to animate literary works from start to finish, solely through the scarcely disguised production of his inner self. In the novels of Malraux, Colette, or Montherlant (of which I am far from thinking any evil) there is nothing *but* Malraux, but Colette, but Montherlant, it's fairly clear. The one and only living type they brought into the world— the fictional world—was their *ego* cast as various natures, a constant in countless hypostases; that the perpetual dialogue with one's self can be substituted shamelessly for the more humble attempt which, until now, was the novel's—to imitate the accidents, encounters, and variety of creation—is not the effect of the reader's growing incredulousness vis-à-vis literary personification, but rather the author's almost insolent faith in the capacity immanent to fiction to make *everything* acceptable, including a new edition of the mystery of transubstantiation as well as the miracle of the wedding at Cana.

*

The failed books of writers who in their old age try without success to reflect a new era that is no longer made for them often mark the brutality of the click that separates one moment of civilization and society from the following, marking it better than others, because what might be called a psychological adjustment movingly fails to be made. Thus, in one of the last books by Jules Verne, *Master of the World*, an unsuccessful book published on the eve of his death, the old magician foresees—as Moses sees the Promised Land—the literary advent of the great detective tracking State secrets that will flourish with Lupin and Rouletabille (*Great Eyrie*, the Master of the World's lair, opens the way for *The Hollow Needle*), and the Prairie-du-Chien–Milwaukee race and its flying machine in clouds of dust is his attempt to adjust to the *hundred per hour* fever of the first Paris-Madrid. Likewise, a very poor novel by Paul Bourget that I read in my youth called *Le danseur mondain*[63]—a pale and tentative reconnaissance into the *terra incognita* of the postwar period.

*

"I am too swift—too precise, to tell stories. I operate in exactly the opposite fashion, sweeping the narrative aside. The glittering outcome weighs down on me. I am not good at lingering" (Valéry).[64]

How, indeed, with such innate demands, can one be attached to the novel, whose secret resource is dispensing slowness pills?

Leaving aside this allergy (which, after all, is legitimate), Valéry's objections to the novel are reduced to two.

1) arbitrariness ("The marquise went out at five o'clock")

2) the multiplicity of possible variation, "so malleable" (*sic*) and all fairly devoid of consequence ("the countess went out at six o'clock").[65]

Let's examine this.

"*The marquise*" is in fact infinitely less variable than it would seem. "The duchess" would set off the roar of the heavy artillery of Balzacian nobility and introduce another social register from the start: the high intrigue of the salon, mixed with Church and politics. "The countess" is already too colorless a title to be employed isolated from the name, except with a particular intention—caricature, for instance. "Marquise," moreover, remains rigorously connoted by the adjective *exquisite*,[66] always musically present just below the surface: delicacy, grace, the suggestion of courtly intrigue without the threat of drama, rush up at its call. Far too many things—in fact, a whole tonal switching in the narrative—are already set in motion by this choice (and in a book's first sentence!) for the novelist to rely on chance.

Aside from a certain quality of light and air, which has

its importance, "at five o'clock" suggests leisure, and thereby announces the probability of or plans for an important encounter before dinner. "Six o'clock" would inconveniently cut the afternoon too close to its end, would only announce the mechanical constraint of a dentist's schedule or a train station's timetable. Five o'clock—a working hour—is the luxurious hour of leisure in the novel, just as the third floor[67] is the beautiful floor of a building: another connotation that is immediately inscribed in the reader's expectations. Etc., etc. . . .

Part of the novelist's equipment is a sufficiently sharpened sense of the meaning and precision of the conjectures that each of his sentences will cause to arise in the mind: this is what allows him to "remain in contact," a demand as imperious in writing as it is in the waging of war. Half his talent is projection: with the first page—and even the first sentence—scarcely completed, he closely watches a whole intersection of trajectories already under way, some short, others long or very long-term. The persistence of overlapping images, the sudden emergence of complementary colors, halo-like images, and a whole singular retinal chemistry is activated in the reader as well, to whom the author cannot be insensitive: in fact, at every moment, reading projects a partially illuminating phosphorescence into the reader's future that depends less on the immediate images the text causes to appear than on certain values proper to the novel with which they are or are not filled, and that are an integral part of temporality. One might say that all the attention a poet places on the capacity of his words for immediate deflagration, the novelist transfers, probably with less precision, having to do with a difference in scale, to the possibility of his sentences' delayed effect. In Dostoyevsky, for example, the literary power of the dialogue—reticent, allusive, indirect, never explicit—consists almost entirely of the enormous kinetic energy with which it recharges the reader's mind, whereas the panoramic and ambling novel of Tolstoy, whose merits lie elsewhere, and almost all in the immediate order of nature, arrange and accumulate almost no energy at all (the pleasure afforded by reading *War and Peace*, exceptional in the novel, is perhaps what comes closest to a fulfilling and nourishing meal, which is sufficient in and of itself from moment to moment, and almost free of anticipation).

In fact, if the reader's mind anticipates the text in all reading, if the focal point of his attention is always cast a bit and often well beyond the words the eye registers, there is no doubt that this shift toward the future

reaches its minimum in reading a poem—and a poem by
Mallarmé more than a poem by Hugo or Musset—and
its maximum in reading a novel, not only a cloak-and-
dagger novel, but one by Kafka or Dostoyevsky. The
naïveté of the belief in a possible assimilation of fictional
life with actual life can be measured by this simple observation: if, in a section of lived life, the great majority
of the signals the outside world emits in the direction of
consciousness concern what endures and persists, the
less numerous but filtered signals that the text of a novel
dispenses deliberately concern that which changes or
will change. And the most significant, perhaps, concern
what will change in the long run, the verbal tense of
choice in the novel being not the future but the ulterior
future (while the tense does not exist in conjugation,
fiction is nevertheless animated by this mode of projecting toward what lies ahead).

What is truly irritating about the novel to minds obsessed with precision—Valéry's, for example—is not
what they say it is (and what it is not), it is the imposing
delay in elucidating its methods, in comparison to poetry, which is more finely dissected. It is not naïveté
or the vulgarity of its procedures and pretensions, it is
the unequalled complexity of interferences and interac-
tions, premeditated *delays* and modulated anticipations

that work toward its final effectiveness—a complexity and entanglement such that they seem to add a dimension to the literary space, and, in the current state of "the science of letters," allow only instinctive piloting and the hazards of navigation with no visibility. Everything counts in a novel, just as in a poem: Flaubert knows this (though Valéry thinks him stupid), and he does not cross out any less, or any less meticulously, than Mallarmé. But the field of combined forces that the novel represents is still too vast and too complex today for any sort of precise intellectual seizure, and the calculus it would require has yet to be invented.

*

Spontaneous and immediate vitality, as a feature of the novel. Meaning, when in doubt, novelists would do well to favor the soft pedal. If a novel could somehow reproduce a fragment of lived life in the *tempo* of reality itself, a fragment populated by all of its objects, all of its movements, all of its characters, the reader would see the *accelerated quality* of newsreels from the 1910s revived, shaken from an inexplicable dissipation of energy. It is the slowness alone of the mechanical act of reading that reestablishes a relative equilibrium. Without that, even a description by Chateaubriand, the Meschacebé, for example, would resemble the final fireworks in a July 14 display.

*

The difficulty of making characters believable in a novel, when their external charms are rendered as universally accepted and matched by a basic villainy: the seducer, the charmer, the handsome rogue. A narrative of black deeds that is immediately credible to the reader has no convincing counterpart in the physical attractiveness with which the novelist gratifies their perpetrator. Proof—if proof is required—that in the reader of novels, the characters' physicality is almost entirely reconstructed on the basis of an overall sense that is formed of them, and where the material features the author attributes to them are rejected, as needed, in the most cavalier manner, in order to be replaced by others. In the heroes of novels, for the reader, *the body is in the soul*, as in Spinoza (this is why, when we read, we have a hard time accepting the naïve heroine succumbing to the blandishments of her dark seducer). I sometimes wonder if Balzac, when he dwells at such length and so laboriously on the material description of his characters, is not simply yielding to the instinctive need to balance the stage: the clarity of a literary protagonist's physical appearance is infinitely less important for readers than that of a real individual, but his "presence" is very important.

Once again, remarks of this sort emphasize the scarce amount of directly informative value that description has in a novel, and its aptitude, on the contrary, for evocation by a variety of means. What words in the novel call to life is almost never a specific image, but rather always a dynamic system in motion. What characters let us sense, what we think they are marching toward, counts infinitely more than what they are (and which the cinema is so much more apt at showing us than the novel); in fact, they don't really exist until they are under way.

*

Of a poem, there is no form of memory other than its exact memorization, line by line. No reconnection with it is possible aside from its literal resurrection in the mind. But the memory one retains of a long and exacting work of fiction, of a novel, last read or reread years ago—after all the work of simplification, reconstruction, fusion, and readjustment that the elision of memory brings with it—would, if the matter were not so evasive by nature, provide a very interesting topic of study. In fact, if such a study could ever present some reliability, it would provide new information on the structure and secret resources of works of fiction.

We would have to compare the memories that avid readers of good faith distantly retained of the same work, and have them recount *their idea* of the book—or rather what remains of it, omitting any references to the text—from memory, to note the fairly regular recurrence of the shipwreck of entire sections that have sunk to the bottom of memory, and flashpoints, on the contrary, that continue to irradiate it, and by whose light the work is reconstructed in an entirely different way. Another book would appear beneath the first—the way another painting appears beneath an X-rayed painting—that, to the economic map of a country, would be a little like a map of its energy sources.

And after this reduction to only the radioactive materials activated by the sifting of memory, we would obtain surprising gaps. Memory would restore certain masterpieces virtually in keeping with their outlines, with the gradation of their episodes, their overall arc, the balance of their proportions—which, for example, happens for me with *The Red and the Black* (but not *The Charterhouse*) as well as with *Madame Bovary*. In other cases, with the entire carcass consumed, all that would be left would be a sort of incorporeal phosphorescence: of *Dominique*, nothing but a certain shivery and autumnal tone, of *Dangerous Liaisons*, nothing but abstract desperation, dry as tinder. And what remains in my memory of my recent rereading of *The Charterhouse* is something else entirely: the pell-mell wreckage of a treasure-bearing galleon on a shoal. The army's descent on Milan. Waterloo. The divine page on the shores of Lake Como. The Farnese Tower. Clélia's birds. The escape. The prince of Parma (with the help of the film). The orangery of the Crescenzi palace. The whole thing as airily built as a house of cards, but uniformly bathed in the lively, giddy ozone of high altitudes.

And how interesting it would be to apply the filter of memory—to the second degree, so to speak—to a work like *Remembrance of Things Past*, already entirely sifted through by memory!

*

The difficulty a novelist feels in evaluating his investments, as he distributes them in his work. Everything he inserts counts; each indication of the text will bring up memory, expectation, and presentiment in the reader's mind. But he does not know which exactly: how to judge if he is fulfilling them?

Because the poet has every reason to count on the readers of his poem: kept on a leash from beginning to end and word after word, there is scarcely more difference among them, from the best to the most mediocre, than between a good and a mediocre interpreter at a concert. But the reader of a novel is not a performer following notes and *tempo* step by step: he is a director. And this suggests that, from one brain to another, the sets, cast, lighting, and motion of the performance become unrecognizable. Whatever the explicit precision of the text—and even, if need be, *against* it, if he so desires— the reader decides (for example) on the acting of the characters and their physical appearance. And the best proof of this is that the interpretation of a film adapted from a familiar novel almost always jars us, not because of its arbitrary nature, but most often because of its fidelity to the formal indications of the text, with which, while reading it, we have taken the greatest liberties.

*

I like when a novel retains some trace, like a wisp of foam left on the beach by the tide, of the tic of the day, the fashionable "saw," the slang used the year it was written: thus, the words ending in *rama*, the slapstick conversations of the Vauquer pension in *Old Goriot*, as well as

"Outil!" (for "Oui")[68] that dates specifically from the early twenties Nuit du Vél' d'Hiv' in Paul Morand's *Open All Night*. Proust is full of these ephemeral spices of the language-of-the-day, particularly in the vocabulary of Saint-Loup, a veritable flytrap of the jargon of pseudo-symbolist circles circa 1900, and in that of Bloch. Such trinkets of the period, which remain pinned to the pages of an old and famous book, seem to make it say: "I was not born to become a classic. I had my younger days, and I have not forgotten them, when I still felt the *Recently published* and the new paper, when my pages were cut between the morning daily and the after-dinner *dress rehearsal*, and there was no sense of disparateness—I could breathe there, and I was made to breathe there." *Intentional* classicism, the essence of which is to sever any of the work's connections with the annals of its time, makes the great mistake of eliminating the very references by which the reader can measure the extent of the transmutation that signals true classicism: involuntary classicism; thus, a book like *Adolphe* (which I admire as much as anyone) was born with the wrinkles of a very young old man.

It is also significant that this residual foam of time that charms us in a novel, when it survives, chills us in a play. Nothing, for example, has done more to age the fin-de-siècle boulevard theater, that of Porto-Riche and Bataille.[69] The theater is always rather naturally linked to the spirit of the time and to the requisitions of fashion, so we resent it for adding more: when it yields to an era's ways of speaking, it is as if it has brought with it, welded to it, its original audience, with its *turns of phrase*, fans, plumes, flounces, and collapsible top hats.

*

The subject. I am disconcerted, when I read their comments, journals, notebooks, and correspondence, not to find a preoccupation with this problem in almost any writer. It would seem the subjects of their books come to them continuously—one chasing out the other as soon as a project is complete—and cause them no more concern than painters seem to have for the motifs of their paintings. Whereas for me, the sudden engagement of an idea—or rather a sense—of the prospect of a book, each time, has been an event as improbable and unpredictable as the thunderbolt of love.

Everything happens as if there existed, accumulated periodically in the writer, a literary richness not converted into cash, to which nothing gives currency, nothing gives shape and worth, nothing gives an outlet, if not the miracle looming up from chance—when it looms up

—of a sort of *reduced model* that is both simple and eminently expressive, that can be held in the palm of a hand, and yet promises an infinite capacity for expansion, like a fine crystal that, simply through contact with it, makes a whole supersaturated solution crystallize in its image. I do not know if there are recipes for getting one's hands on an "open sesame" such as this—which, of course, only opens the cave of your own treasures once. As for me, I do not have one, and that is one of the reasons I've written so few books.

Modern criticism has good reasons to put aside such a question. I come up against it almost every time I reflect on literature, and find things there that make me dream: all these books that existed in writers potentially and that did not see the light of day, because malignant chance refused the key that would have freed them and that was just within reach. The key, which is to say, the subject, at once revealing and crystallizing, which with a single wave of the wand marks the effervescent and formless literary flood with efficient lines of operation, concentrates it at points where effects of leverage will play in its favor, and sets it in motion with flying colors and rallying signs. The subject seems to give you everything all at once—now, in the moving and blind chaos that you inhabit, great masses of shadow and light suddenly shift, paths converge, forces are gathered and set in motion, movements are coordinated, now that one direction, both unifying and multiplying, animates the diversity at your disposal—now that you have both the place and the formula.

One of the surest signs of a subject's internal vigor and its affinity with your own inclinations is that, in its initial simplicity, as soon as you hold it more closely, more specific pathways are potentially inscribed, pathways that craze it throughout, and over which, to your surprise, almost no ambiguity is allowed to hover. A true subject has a secret slope: if you try to specify it, even on some minor detail, it will not leave you hanging, any more than a drop of rainwater that falls on a vigorous relief is left in doubt about what direction to take. It is back in a few lines, lets itself be taken in at a glance, and has an answer for everything.

A true subject leaves no kingdom and no order, whether human or terrestrial, extraneous to its main theme. In this regard, I have often thought that one of Goethe's most certain advantages resided in the almost infallibly broad sense he had of a subject, as soon as he stopped writing and relaxed. We can suppose that Hugo felt all the importance of the problem perfectly but let himself be taken in at times by vulgar forgeries: it was enough for him to let the subject too advantageously strike the pose.

It could be, after all, that my idea of a real subject is strictly personal to me. It has nothing to do with summaries that *fill in the blanks*; it has more in common with the line of a musical phrase, as charged with energy as it is impossible to break down.

*

It is fairly surprising that the very limited theme of the complementary male pair in a constant state of dialogue (master and servant, master and disciple, master and pupil, master and "damned soul"), a pair launched across a real or fictional world whose layers and density it traverses successively, has had such a large part in the masterpieces of world literature: *The Divine Comedy*— *Don Quixote*—*Faust* (to say nothing of *Don Juan*, *Candide*, or *A Harlot High and Low*). Which is to say, the key works of three of the great European literatures, and several of the major works in French.

*

Almost as soon as I started writing, I was sensitive to the novel's distinctive feature, of all genres practiced, of being an insatiable consumer of energy. In Clausewitz's book, there is a particularly remarkable chapter called "Friction in War." In the novel, lax structure, roughly adjusted cogs, destructive friction, and loss of energy lie in wait at each page. How can you not wonder what force leads such exhausting work to its completion?

Contrary to what happens in a poem, if language guides and inflects the fictional adventure in the midst of being realized, it is never at its origin. There must be a certain state of lack, an urgent and radical dissatisfaction. An impression, or a complex of impressions, that has yet to be given shape and that nevertheless obsesses you like a real memory—something as precious and demanding as a forgotten name that you try to retrieve but that never existed, and that will be the book—is no doubt the fuel that feeds the literary motor. The winds and currents, that is, the fortunes, that make language sail, often decide the itinerary; but no one ever set out on an unknown sea without an imperious phantom waving on the other shore, impossible to dismiss. The difficulty specific to fiction is a haphazard compromise with ever-changing elements to be made on every page between a container without a plan, which is the spontaneous production of writing, and a plan without a container, which is the instant appeal of the *tone* that is sensed and still has no material support, for which an instrument must be found and furnished, which will be the book.

The tightrope that the novel walks over unsteadily must be held solidly at both ends. If everything is controlled by a too-specific, too-articulated plan, the entire work will stiffen and slip into fabrication; if everything is left to the potential of pure "textuality," everything dissolves in speech without resonance or harmonics. The narrative is the refusal of pure chance, poetry the negation of any defined and premeditated will-to-write. You must agree to move through this deceptive chiaroscuro, to go constantly from following paths to clearing paths. This cannot be done without a masterful sense of direction—in every circumstance and encounter—which is one of the novel's major gifts. Across initially unimaginable landscapes, which only getting under way can bring about, the novelist must never lose sight of his own specific organizing North.

Does this guiding magnetism act as imperiously from one novel to another? I do not doubt for a second that, for two novelists as different as Stendhal in *The Charterhouse* and Alain-Fournier in *The Wanderer*, the materialization of an internal music, impossible to capture except in the deployment of a wide-ranging narrative, was their sole concern. For Flaubert, at least in *Madame Bovary*, I am inclined to believe it completely ("to give the impression of the color yellow"). In Balzac, apart from novels like *Les Chouans* or *The Lily of the Valley*, the mechanisms that come into play remain mysterious to me. The two parts of *Béatrix* are obviously not guided by the same star; even when the novelist carries me along without resistance, I do not understand, do not feel, what is steering his narrative so imperiously. In Huysmans, whom I have been rereading lately, this hunt for the interior meteor has a minimal role: centrifugal forces play freely in full exuberance; the limitless sweet tooth for language and the hunt for felicitous expressions invade and take over everything: pure juxtaposition without progression, samplings of distinct flavors that explode one after another in isolation against the palate, this is the substance of *Against the Grain*, and this continuous mosaic of flatness is perhaps even more notable in religious books like *En Route*, which should organize a sense of omnipotence from start to finish, and which crumbles—deliciously—in enumerations, recapitulations, and inventories, shot through with disconnected playlets.

*

A novel that one undertakes to write, whatever extreme freedom of treatment one has promised oneself to bring to it, does not at all behave like the subject of a poem, which exists temporarily while awaiting successive metamorphoses and whose ductility, docility, to the crafting of language and to the verbal adventure remains limitless. In the subject of a novel, there is a minimum of resistant internal structure—hidden blockages, complex internal echoes suddenly awakened by fortuitous collisions, automatisms that will come to light, phenomena rejected, and, on the contrary, affinities suddenly revealed. The contradiction specific to the novelist is that, of his subject, only language used according to its own capacities will awaken possibilities, but at the same time, words do not possess the omnipotence over him that the words of a poem do, because the novelist's passion for his novel did not wake up opposite an ectoplasm, but opposite a figure that cannot be distorted at will, that simultaneously possesses both the blurriness of the dream and the lines, rhythm, and certain *movements* of a perfectly concrete and, to him, enchanting clarity, a figure that, in a certain way, he will not rest from seeking to meet by means of his novel. The novel only lives by the freedom language gives it, used according to its true powers, but it is only pulled from nothingness by the constraint of a demanding image imposed on the novelist throughout, an obsession not entirely literary in nature. "Adorable phantom who has seduced me, lift your veil!" pleads the maker of novels—but the silent apparition places a penholder in his hand.

In fact, no one tries to grasp the relationship between the novelist and his subject *before*: before the moment he starts writing, which is to say, trying his luck. The act of writing erases almost all memory of this incubation period, at times very long, at times very short: the scaffolding is taken down. The subject seems to act vis-à-vis the unexpected propositions of writing a bit like an unknown chemical substance, eager to enter into composition with certain bodies, insensitive to others. That's why the formal organization of a novel means so little, and a better hold on the intuitive sense awakened in love, on the contrary, is so important: "to compose" a novel—instead of constantly watching and tracking the resonances and harmonics that arise as it progresses—is to submit to geometry that which has to do with chemistry. But these harmonics, on the one hand, and these unexpected resistances, on the other, will only be awakened in the *work in progress*, only gradually, as it advances.

*

Salome-Herodias: a subject so vigorous in and of itself that it has engendered only successes, from Flaubert to Strauss, by way of Wilde and Mallarmé (and I still remember the dazzling Salome by Koralnik, shown on television a few years ago, in the pictorial style of Gustave Moreau). I was thinking of that while listening to Richard Strauss's *Salome*, above and beyond anything I expected. In a subject like this, everything works toward fascination: the double crepuscular lighting of the end and beginning of a world that, against the riotous color of baroque backgrounds, gives characters the silhouetted clarity of objects illuminated from behind, the double resonance of works spread simultaneously in two mental and historic spaces, as if the Baptist's underground prison had suddenly endowed language with the echoes of a very resonant crypt—the possibility of action developed at will and enriched by related scenes or contracted within a single expressive painting (the dance of Salome as well as Gustave Moreau's *Apparition*). Thus the *Salome* of Wilde and Strauss can produce what no classical tragedy has quite managed: absolute dramatic unity in time as well as space: nothing but a continuous scene, in a single place, of an hour and forty-five minutes, with no contractions, breaks, or cuts of any kind, and no slack periods. The enchantment I experienced while listening to it helped me understand what was truly concealed behind the rule of the three unities, so absurd because awkwardly formulated: the requirement of the absolute closure of the dramatic space, the refusal of any crack or crevice through which outside air might penetrate, and any resting period that leaves room for distance.

*

When Malraux writes that the novelist's genius "is in the part of the novel that cannot be brought back to the narrative," every lover of literature approves without giving it a thought. The difficulty begins when you really try to isolate this part: promising work, not clear intellectual surgery, but rather the bloody and confused mess you see in the butcher's stall, because the passage from bone to flesh, like that from "story" to written text, is made through an inextricably tenacious network of adhesions, vessels, ligaments, and aponeuroses. It is not true that the *story* told by *The Charterhouse* or by *A Harlot High and Low* does not rely intimately on the genius of Stendhal or Balzac, because the integration of these narratives into the combinatory system of the imagination has been total, and their existence is no more distinct than a transplanted organ, also exogenous, that has been infused with life.

Certainly, as far as the choice of a subject, no novelist is infallible: Flaubert is infatuated by a sword-and-sandal epic like *Salammbô* or the *purana* of *The Temptation of Saint Anthony*, Stendhal by this invertebrate *Leuwen*, which we suspect he did not abandon en route without reason. Balzac alone finds a way out almost every time, because his mode of composition, so wide open to possibility, always leaves him time after losing a battle to engage in and win another, as at Marengo, before the appearance of the words *The End* (sometimes, as with *Béatrix*, the opposite occurs). As far as subjects, how do we distinguish in advance between an inert *implant*, to which no living tissue will ever cling or attach itself, from a bone graft that will develop in symbiosis with the writer's metabolism, at once nourished by everything articulated to it, and in turn able to support, organize, and sort it out? A problem whose solution nothing can guarantee but the work itself in its final state, and which only a flair for the wild can help orient, as it gropingly makes its way.

WRITING

Why do we write? The old and perfidious question that the journal *Littérature* revived after World War I has still not received an answer. It is far from certain that there is only one, and also far from certain that a writer's motivations do not vary throughout his career. When I began writing, what I was seeking, it seems, was to materialize the space and depth of a certain unbounded, imaginative effervescence, like shouting into a dark cave to measure its dimensions based on the echo. A time no doubt comes later in life when all one seeks in writing is a verification of one's powers, a toe-to-toe struggle with physiological decline. In the interim, between the excess and scarcity of the flow to sort through, it seems at times there is a vague zone where habit, which can create a state of need, the defensive penchant for giving shape and fixity to a few select images that will inevitably fade, and resentment against the moving, formless wave of the interior film are interlaced inextricably. Sometimes the writer simply wants to "write"; and sometimes, too, he just wants to communicate something: a remark, a sensation, an experience to which he would like to adapt words, because a writer's ambiguous, alternating relationships with language are a bit like those one might have with a maidservant-mistress, and no less hypocritically exploitative from start to finish.

Why refuse to admit that writing is rarely attached to a fully autonomous impulse? You write first because others before you wrote, then, because you have already started writing: the question should really be asked of the first person to dare begin such a practice: which basically amounts to saying that it has no meaning. In this business, spontaneous imitation counts for a lot: no writers without insertion into an uninterrupted *chain* of writers. After school, which places the apprentice-writer in this chain and already makes him glide with authority over the rail of *redaction*, it is the fact of ceasing to write that actually merits contemplation.

The dramatization of the act of writing, which has become spontaneous, like second nature to us, is a legacy of the nineteenth century. Neither the seventeenth nor, much less, the eighteenth have known it; a drama like *Chatterton* would have been incomprehensible then; no one ever woke up one fine morning saying: "I will be a writer," as one might say, "I will be a priest." The gradual and natural need for communication, as

well as the intoxicating apprenticeship of language's resistances, has in everyone preceded and eclipsed the
cult worship of the *sign of election*, the prerequisite of
which specifically marks the advent of romanticism. Before that, no one ever used this strange, intransitive future tense that alone truly, and mistakenly, erects the
writer's work as an enigma: *I will write.*

*

There are two poetic languages juxtaposed in Racine's
tragedies. This high-temperature fusion of precious language, fluid and free of slag—a singularity that makes the
language of love inimitable in his plays—is not found to
any degree in his narratives of dreams and marvels,
whether in *Phèdre* or *Athalie.* Immediately, on the contrary, clichés, redundancies, insipid hyperboles, and
bombastic commonplaces turn the style to ice; everything becomes an ornament, a cold ornament: these are
the daydreams, miracles, and devices of pseudo-*Iliads*,
for which the seventeenth century was so prodigious,
that we have perfectly forgotten, and whose affected
style, "poetic" amphigory, and unfathomable ennui have
been conserved for us only through the lapses of a poet
of genius.

These localized *delays*, where the innovative writer

struggled with the pen against an earlier sclerosis that forms again in patches, are almost always attached to the parts of his writings where he is least at ease, to those treated, through a residual weakness vis-à-vis the hallowed old-fashionedness he has come to abolish, *as a certified copy*. Happily limited in Racine to dreams and solemn "recitations," which is to say, to residues, this paralyzed "delay" is tragedy in its entirety, immortality's laborious chore, to be imposed on the sprightly pen of Voltaire. Just as, later, the expiring glory of the epic will impose it on the pen of Chateaubriand, rich enough, fortunately, to be able to jettison a whole cartload of writings, such as *Les Martyrs* or *Les Natchez*, marked by an almost paralyzing backwardness of style.

There are many reasons to believe that French writers are often more burdened than others by these formal and inherited encumbrances. French literature is the only one to have known not one but two successive crises of the idolatry of the outmoded: the Renaissance, then classicism, the masterpieces of which are largely derived, half-length at most, from the astringent block of "the ancient." For close to three centuries, and to our misfortune, literary old-fashionedness in us has never lost its right for a capital letter.

*

What at first distinguishes the literary criticism of our era from the criticism of previous centuries is a starting position that is never formulated, since in each of these eras it seems to go without saying. For the critic of times past, the position is worded this way: "It is in this manner and for these reasons that an enlightened mind must judge the work of M. X." For the critic of the contemporary era, "The human sciences are my guarantee. Therefore, I do not know, *a priori*, any more about the meaning and structure of the work by M. X. than the author himself." The former doubts the author's capacity to judge his work, the latter his capacity to understand it. The former is content to deny the writer access to the accurate perception of values, the latter relegates him to the rank of a simple piece of nature, produced and not productive, a secretion of language: *natura naturata*.[70]

*

Thesauruses. They are certainly of some use to a verbal memory that becomes more restive with the years. But they are so limited! The word I am looking for (or rather whose sudden appearance I watch for patiently in the vicinity of another used as bait) is certainly related to it somehow. Only most often—alas!—it is from the left hand rather than the right, and proper dictionaries only know legitimate unions.[71] Mysterious family resemblances, which are all the writer has to go by in the chiaroscuro of vocabulary, leap over the barriers of official unions; for the writer, language is most vibrant in its adulterous compromises. Families of legal and overly sanctioned words, the writer despises you!

The main advantage of rhyme in old poems was to oblige the writer, by its technical requirements, to run the blockade of the tight circle of substitutable words, to give back language its beautiful colors through the proven virtues of exogamy.

*

Even in prose, sound has to be able to stand up to meaning. You cannot be a writer without a sense that sound, in words, comes to ballast meaning, and that the weight it is then endowed with can lead it legitimately at times into strange centrifugal excursions. Writing, like reading, is movement, and as a result the word behaves like a moving object whose mass, however reduced, can never be taken for granted, and can noticeably inflect the direction.

*

"All artists know these moments of sudden confusion caused by the proximity, the presence of another's mastery. It has to do with the fact that every practice of art constitutes a new accommodation, itself full of art, by the personal and individual element toward art in general. Even after clear accomplishment and success, the artist is forced to wonder when he compares himself to others: how can I speak of what I have just done here in the same breath as the works of the masters?"[72]

Here in its essence Thomas Mann captures all of the artist's malaise in situating himself. His awareness of the *modus vivendi* established with art, an always singular, always lopsided arrangement that finds no comfort in the *habitus* of artists of the past, comes to overdetermine the vivid sense the writer has in the face of another's success—if they really possess a personal style—of never having the slightest possibility of producing such works, of being capable, at most, of "doing as well." But what does "doing as well" mean in the matter of art? The sense of being powerless to replace the other is so trenchant and so sharp, and the assumption of equality that arises in him so bold, so unsupported! What you have done, and which I admire, I know myself to be clearly incapable of doing, and my confidence in what I am doing is surrounded by strange wonders toward which I sense no path in myself; I can neither execute these wonders nor annihilate them, or even equal them, really, since any comparison here breaks down: the proximity of other works for the artist is an inextinguishable provocation to competition, as well as a negation of any sanctioned rule that would make it possible.

*

At ninety, no writer, if he is still writing, can hope to maintain all the quality of his production. But in painting, Titian and Picasso—others, too, no doubt—manage perfectly well. No writer is brilliant until full adolescence at least. But, in music, Mozart—others, too, no doubt—was. Which tends to corroborate physiologically the hierarchy of the arts as promulgated by Hegel (which is fine by me).

Historical counterproof would provide the same result: of all the arts, literature was last to appear. And one day, no doubt, it will be the first to be eclipsed.

*

There is no "world" of any kind without an internal organizing principle, without a sort of dormant "will to be together," without a vanishing point, even one that is infinitely far away, toward which the lines of perspective converge. We sense it instinctively rather than being able to demonstrate it; hence, the appeal of Teilhard de Chardin's theories for the general public, which are a good example of wishful thinking, and a doctrine of gratification in Malraux's sense.

The "worlds" of art and artists can be recognized in the vanishing point's tyrannical presence, here more than anywhere else—with the exception of religious worlds, which are also the only ones to name the vanishing point. Art worlds: intermediary worlds. Less magnetic than that of the mystic, more so than that of the stroller or dreamer.

*

"POISON PERDU"

Des nuits du blond et de la brune
Rien dans la chambre n'est resté
Pas une dentelle d'été
Pas une cravate commune

Et sur le balcon où le thé
Se prend aux heures de la lune
Il n'est resté de trace aucune
Aucun souvenir n'est resté

Au coin d'un rideau bleu piquée
Luit un épingle à tête d'or
Comme un gros insecte qui dort

Pointe d'un fin poison trempée
Je te prends. Sois-moi préparée
Aux heures des désirs de mort

["LOST POISON"

Nights of the blond and the brunette
nothing in the room remains
not a summer lace,
not a plain cravat.

And on the balcony where tea
is taken at the hours of the moon
there is no trace at all
no memory remains

At the edge of a blue piqué curtain
gleams a pin with a golden head
like a big sleeping insect

Point of a fine steeped poison
I take you. Be prepared for me
At the hours of desire for death]

... the sonnet attributed to Rimbaud, to Nouveau, and even to Verlaine, was so extensively and so bitterly argued over, with a result that is still so uncertain today. Verlaine judged it "inferior to everything we know by Rimbaud," while certifying that it was indeed of his hand. Breton, without making a decisive pronouncement, did not, it appears, have a very high opinion of it. I myself cannot make such a sorry case; in fact, this very uneven sonnet subject, very marked by a literary period, this quasi-anecdotal sketch, has an inexplicable tendency to haunt me: once it is brought up by chance, I have a hard time expelling it from my mind.

At first sight, it is by Nouveau, or—though less likely—by Rimbaud writing a pastiche of Nouveau; in any case, it is scarcely possible that the first, fourth, fifth, and sixth lines were written by someone who did not have close kinship with Nouveau. Yet it is difficult to imagine Rimbaud writing the first and fourth lines, which do not have much to do with his vocabulary —difficult also to imagine Rimbaud choosing a subject like this, much more "Baudelairean" in the mediocre sense of Baudelaire as offered by *L'Assiette au Beurre*.[73]

The eleventh line is so execrable it suggests parody, or—if one accepts the partially oral transmission of the text—a memory lapse that the editor filled in with any-thing at all.

But the fifth and sixth lines, gliding syllable after syl-lable on the labile flow of the *l*'s with a dancing grace— a fluidity, a confidential and vaporous strangeness—are delightful, and call to mind a poet of the first order. A poem by Nouveau in which a distracted memory left gaps that a negligent transcriber patched in places would ultimately be the most likely hypothesis, unless the transcriber, as well as the authenticator, was never-theless Verlaine (which certainly could be argued).

Remarkably, in these two lines that are the *highlight* of the sonnet

> *Et sur le balcon où le thé*
> *Se prend aux heures de la lune*
> [And on the balcony where tea
> is taken at the hours of the moon]

the consonant *r* (in *prend* and *heures*) takes over for the dominant consonant *l* without any loss of fluidity: the oiled glide of the text lubricates and softens the strong consonant (which is rare), giving it a sort of lisp.

Among supremely gifted poets—here, Verlaine, Rim-baud, and Nouveau—who led not only a communal life but almost a united life in poetry, who collaborated on certain poems and most often on pastiches of great virtuosity, most of which are probably lost, there is a smaller commonality of poetry that expands abnormally and that can, in order to stand out, reduce literary meaning to a conundrum. "Lost Poison," which gives everyone pause, shows us the limits of criticism's resolving power. If ever poetry was close to being made by all, and not by one, it is indeed here. Let's stop trying to unravel it.

*

Three-quarters of the most beautiful French poetry was written between 1845 and 1885. How can we doubt it? I wonder if the percentage Valéry is advancing here is even somewhat modest. Beyond these limits—and aside from contemporary poetry, which has a different approach—what is left that really haunts my memory? A few verses by Villon, a few sonnets by Du Bellay, a few poems by Apollinaire, two or three playlets by Musset (*A St Blaise . . . —La Chanson de Barberine*).

And that is what makes all the anthologies of French poetry so derisory and fraudulent, concerned as they are with balance and symmetry, uniformly trying to force the sterile years, to make them blossom in spite of everything, as their title gives them an obligation: how to accept that poetry does not know the regular rhythms of horticulture, that so many decades, even centuries, pass without knowing their springtime?

What remains is the case of Racine, who poses a quasi-insoluble problem, a problem that Shakespeare—where poetry crazes the text at every moment, fills it with stars and perfectly isolatable asteroids, even as the drama subjects them to its powerful gravitation—does not pose at all in England. This is the problem of a poetry that is both "pure" to the highest degree and soluble to the last particle in the dramatic action it has just served, crushed under a *state duty* that lessens none of its integrity. Shakespeare's poetry bursts forth at all times in sublime singing exercises: not a syllable in Racine is allowed to suspend the intelligible line of tragedy even for an instant. Where do we classify (but why classify?) the author of a poetry that is purely unalloyed yet ineffably delinquent?

*

No verse is as *heavy* as Baudelaire's verse, heavy with the specific weight of ripe fruit about to fall off the branch it is bending. As sap changes into inert succulence in the fruit in which it accumulates, it is able—alone in this, no doubt—to transmute the black blood of existence into a stabilized chunk of compact and comestible flavor.

Lines sway ceaselessly beneath the weight of memories, worries, sorrows, pleasures recalled. This is the weight of accumulated experience: at times it seems naturally to add up not only his own disillusioned experience but that of the entire species: what other poet could write, as he did, without sounding ridiculous, "I have more memories than if I'd lived a thousand years."[74]

His lines invite you to repeat them with your eyes closed; as though centered on a gustatory explosion whose incomparable *body* suggests essence, elixir. Heavy, and also seemingly blind: this density (which has nothing to do with Mallarmé's compression, so intentional) has its negative counterpart: nothing in Baudelaire makes one think of flight, of soaring, to which he is not suited (the weakness of a poem like "Elevation" when he ventures into being ethereal!). Compact and saturated, substantial beyond all possibility, in sum, the pulpiest, most engorged matter in all of French poetry.

*

There is a judicious idea in the title of Mauriac's *Mémoires intérieurs*. In a life near its end traveled backwards through memory, the only branches that deserve to subsist without any concern for balance or chronological continuity and that no longer do are those in which the secret sap is still rising. Everything that makes up the "framework of a life" (the biographer's crutch that inevitably hobbles him) would have to be abandoned deliberately: to make this framework the sinew of a biography is to confuse the wire with the branch of the fruit tree that twines upon it, but draws nothing from it and ignores it completely. Anything that was not hours of profound listening and perfect branching—between oneself and the world—would have to be pruned and Cingria's beautiful title, *Bois sec, bois vert*, adopted as a principle of pitiless sifting.[75]

*

The ease of writing, and the absence of particular inclination in the talented author who writes on various topics, are the designated prey of fossilized literary forms, because they are the chosen foils of the *firsts in gymnastics*; thus—alone among the young literary lions of their time—Voltaire writes his *Henriade* and his tragedies, Cocteau his alexandrines, his dramas in verse for the Comédie-Française, and his boulevard theater.

*

In the beginning was the Word . . . Certainly. But as soon as the first words were uttered, they were no longer alone: meaning was born (nothing can stop that once words of any kind align themselves), and meaning, we too often forget, is both irreversible significance and *direction*: meaning is a vector; as soon as it is in motion, the machinery of language immediately creates an induced current in the mind that then breaks free from its inductor. This current is already a projectile: the mind is "launched" (every writer of good faith, I think, would admit this movement, which is the dynamic of writing itself), the lively force thus awakened comes up against language, uses it, changes direction, composes with it, but no longer belongs to it alone; farewell availability, farewell purity!

*

A writer's almost carnal weakness for words (otherwise he wouldn't be a writer), for their corpulence or stature, their weight of round fruits falling one by one from the tree, or on the contrary for their virtue of changing "their absence into delight,"[76] of gradually fading in favor of their broadened wake, can sometimes gradually transform over a lifetime without disavowal. When I started writing, what I wanted first and foremost was the vibratory quivering, the violin bow over the imagination. Later, much later, I often preferred the succulence of compact words, rich in dentals and fricatives, that the ear could snatch one by one, like a dog catching pieces of raw meat: in a way, like going from word-as-mood to word-as-food, the path that leads prose from the precincts of *The Fall of the House of Usher* to those of *Knowing the East*.[77]

*

Sometimes while writing a book, I have reproached myself—a greedy reflex—for *speaking* of an idea I'd just incorporated, annoyed later, in my possessive instinct, at the idea of premature divulgence. In fact, such indiscretions do not involve any risk: if the idea really belongs to the book, it will remain unusable and even invisible detached from it, incapable by nature of immediately entering into another composition. If it's just small change, there's no problem in giving it to the needy.

*

A literary work is very often the placing end to end and close knitting in a continuous and tightly woven fabric—like those blankets made of pieces of multicolored wool—of passages that rely solely on real experience and passages that rely solely on conformity to the whims of language, without the reader finding fault with it or even noticing these constantly changing references in the order of "truth."

*

In sensual writing, as that of an artist usually is, it seems to me it should pass on something of the body's seasons and humors. Never mind a poet like Claudel, who has a traditional view of the world and a liturgical language to intone this view, but it always seemed odd to me that a writer like Montherlant—whose career spanned fifty years, whose language was set and established starting with his first book, and who spoke only of his opinions, pleasures and displeasures, vexations and moods—was able to use exactly the same instrument to translate the grandiloquent outbursts of youth, the equilibrium of adulthood, and the acridness of old age.

*

Writer: a person who feels at times that something is asking through his intervention for the sort of existence that language offers. The sort of existence that the public capriciously, intermittently, and uncertainly inspects and that the author alone guarantees. The public is a network that can always be short-circuited without invalidating anything essential in the literary phenomenon: the visionary witness lit up in the author's brain is necessary and sufficient. The current that moves through the pen does not *go* toward anyone; we must be done once and for all with the misleading image of "dear readers" looming on the horizon of the escritoire and the writer, like the crowd around an orator, into which he pours intoxicating liquor. Literature goes from the confused, aphasic self to the self informed by the intermediary of words, nothing more: the public is not admitted into this act of self-satisfaction except as a voyeur, and generally in exchange for money—and that, I concede, is the unsavory side of the matter.

*

How difficult it is and how interesting it would be, when studying a writer, to discover, not his admitted influences, the *great intercessors* he claimed as his own or who were claimed for him later on, but the ordinary stuff, what he read as a youth that sustained a starved literary adolescence from day to day, pell-mell, and haphazardly: first, the Paris of the daily papers, defunct journals, obscure authors who flourished for an instant, like a rain shower, the flavor-of-the-day, boulevard theater, Parisian firebrands, deliveries from *Magasin des familles*, pamphlets long since gone to seed. The only great writer of the past who tells us about these things is Stendhal, the great exception (above all, it's true, in regard to his musical tastes). The literary bulimia characteristic of the adolescent, or the student who plans to write, like the silkworm before the chrysalis, is such that quantity necessarily prevails over quality: the more imperious his appetite, the smaller the divide, regarding his taste, between truly chosen foods and those that will soon be lucidly disdained. For those destined to write, there is a moment in their formation—a decisive moment—when they read everything or almost everything, and "everything," first of all, is whatever is at hand, what "people are talking about," what smells of fresh ink, and has the same effect on them as gunpowder to a warrior. The voracious eye that is glued to the freshly printed page at eighteen or twenty can in no way make out a literary landscape in perspective with its foreground, middle ground, and its blurred distances, but sees only a riot of colors, a *flatness* juxtaposed with violent, clashing colors that all catch a retina that is still new.

Will this run-of-the-mill stuff in which the writer has paddled about evaporate without leaving any trace? That is not certain, for it is at this moment of springtime flooding, of mixed waters, that he has also tried, and more or less begun, to write: the tics of the period, which he has contracted naïvely and defenselessly, will leave a mark on his way of writing, always refashioned, often ennobled, and sometimes, if he is brilliant, saved: Proust, who, one suspects, of all writers, may have read more that was mediocre than good while very young, is full of these redemptions. Such readings, profoundly incorporated into the writer's beginning automatisms, are perhaps to ways of writing what childhood impressions are to color, to the orientation of sensibility: not chosen, often banal, always repeated, and magnified by the acquired mastery of the resources of language, like the disordered distances of childhood by the learned chemistry of memory. And there is an enigmatic continuity, a strange *melting* of literature from one period into another, beyond all the revolutions and ruptures that are perhaps partially illuminated there: by the fact that the writer in formation is sustained inseparably, inextricably, all at once by pure novelty, which affects him with its extreme point, and by the things written and published around him that reflect the taste of the moment: that is, a continuity maintained with the day before yesterday.

This thought occurred to me, I recall, when André Breton, whose disinclination for the novel we are familiar with, one day lent me the novels of Jean Lombard (whose name, I admit, was unfamiliar to me), recommending them: like *Quo Vadis*, but Byzantine in taste as well as period, they suddenly made me measure the place that a whole bloodless *string* of symbolism might have had in his first readings, something he had long since surpassed but not entirely eliminated. In any case, as far as these novels, he kept them.

*

"If you knew what I threw out, you would admire what I keep" (Valéry).

No. That sort of ostentation about your scrap heap would only lead me to suspect that every pearl makes you think of vinegar first. And that, at times, is indeed what I suspect.

*

"I suppose all men of letters are like myself in this, that they never re-read their works once they have appeared. Nothing in fact is more disenchanting, more painful than to examine one's phrases again after an interval of years. They have been in a bottle, so to speak, and form a deposit at the bottom of the book; and, most times, volumes are not like wines which improve with age; once clarified in the fullness of time, the chapters grow flat and their bouquet evaporates" (Huysmans: Preface to *Against the Grain*—written twenty years after the novel).

This passage certainly does not exhaust all the singularities of a writer looking at his first books after years have passed. Superimposed onto the changing taste of his era, to which he is more or less bound and which is moving away, is the natural allergy in middle age (or advanced age) to the "portrait of the artist as a young dog," the crisis of juvenile originality. The new violence of the thrust, the *impetus* that Claudel spoke of that animated his first books and that the virgin reader sometimes experiences like the weight of a hand on a shoulder, mean nothing to him anymore. All this has evaporated like the rapture of love: the only positive thing left is the impending obsolescence of the form. All the stages of personal immaturity that have been surpassed, and that are distorted and embellished at whim by the memory of others, have precipitated for him into solid crystals with jagged edges; if he rereads himself, it is up to him alone to confront what he really was. Of the constantly renewed substance that constitutes the warp of a life and of which the benevolent law of nature is for all beings, from year to year, obliteration and oblivion, he, in each period, has taken and conserved samples.

*

"Point of a *fine* steeped poison" ("Lost Poison" again).

It is the point, and not the poison, that authorizes this unexpected predicate. The adjective *subtle*, so often associated with the idea of poison and adaptable to the idea of a "point," provides the hidden shift that allows the transfer of the adjective from one noun to another. A good example of how in poetry, and in prose that tends toward poetry, all words made less isolated form a solid, welded chain along which values circulate and permute and exchange their supports based on a very open system of free trade. For exegetes, that is an insolent dismissal of every literal rendering. Each word veers and is transmuted, and makes a hidden facet shine beneath the light of those to follow, refracts them one after another as a gem refracts a gleam that is external to it; the last word of the sentence can return to exert a retroactive effect on the first. And the lines of "Lost Poison" help us understand that the power of a sentence is quite often only explained by restoring its catalysts (here, for example, the adjective *subtle*), absent from the text but lurking in the background and appearing as its linguistic unconscious —its hidden proximity allowing the complex reactions of its chemistry.

*

Prophecy since Nostradamus has disappeared from the literary and even paraliterary scene. It falls to the side of the "ridiculous refrains, naïve rhythms" that Rimbaud spoke of in *Season in Hell*. For an instant, in a few of the sonnets of *Chimères*, the tone shows again on the surface—an admirable resurgence. For golden verse of this sort, Mallarmé possessed an incomparable instrument in the imperious coining, the aloofness of tone, the esoteric ruggedness, and the sense of proliferation: at times one is seized by the regret that he did not feel absolutely Visionary. A line like:

> *Tison de gloire, sang par écume, or, tempête*
> [Torch of glory, blood in foam, gold, tempest]

could be by Nostradamus, if Nostradamus had been inspired at times. What a shame that the Mallarméan poems, instead of the laborious and rather shabbily rational riddles to which they have allowed their "subjects" to be reduced in the depoeticizing replies of academics, did not choose to look out only over the —superbly unverifiable and definitively irreducible— *dark flights scattered in the future!*[78]

There remains Rimbaud, of course, in whom all the

great rejects of poetry of centuries past start to thrill again so powerfully. But *his* problems, his impasses, his furies, his remorse, and his mortifications are what make this apocalyptic upheaval in *Season*, and as far as opening completely onto the world of prophecy, his *I* has not yet fully agreed to be an other.[79]

*

The difficulty of demarcating literature (it's reappeared lately with debates on the legitimacy of including the human sciences). Its domain resembles a spotlight violently illuminated at its center (poetry) and gradually fading at the edges into total darkness. Just as a painter is someone inspired only by the play of line and color (and not by the desire to depict a tree, a genre scene, or a dream), a literary person is only someone more or less inspired by the manipulation of language. But, as the share of inspiration that comes from language may take any proportion in a work, from 1 percent to 99 percent (absolute non-literature remaining as impossible as pure literature), the borders of literature dissolve in an ungraspable melting.

Surrealism, by authoritatively rehabilitating the *subject*, reexamined in the matter of painting similar criteria which around 1920 were on the way to being established absolutely. A good number of Surrealist painters, from the viewpoint of "pure painting," are situated in a clear-obscure zone, very far from the central luminous core: a painter like Magritte may even be situated at the limits of the strictly pictorial domain. Which does not detract at all from the value of his inventions; only, in his paintings, where "the idea" and humor take up almost all the space, the paintbrush takes on the role that in a piece of writing would have fallen to the simple language of information.

*

What often remains foreign to a critic but is almost always so present to the author: the notion of *vital expenditure* implied in a work and in its evaluation.

READING

I've gradually changed my opinion on this: the emotion felt by the reader of a novel, or the listener at a concert, is not a resonant chord that gives off the same note whatever the means of percussion shaking it: it is entirely molded on the complex verbal or sonorous construction that gave birth to it, and as such is not exchangeable, and would not accept being exchanged, for any other. It is not a resuscitation of emotions already experienced, but a new, irreplaceable experience each time. Ultimately, in terms of true aesthetic emotion, there is no distinction possible between cause and effect, and I do not think for a second one goes to listen to *Tristan* in order to remember that one was once in love. If anything, it would be the reverse (La Rochefoucauld knew this already), the feeling of "love" is transposable, as we know, from object to object: the kind one feels listening to the music of Wagner or reading *The Sorrows of Young Werther* is not; it is irrevocably a part of a succession of notes, or words, that cannot be replaced. The notable merit of art is to pull "emotion" from the undifferentiated vagueness to which common psychology relegates it and link it solidly to an individualized figure each time: to this way of giving affective chaos access to a distinct, if not clear, existence, it seems to me Valéry, so hostile to all art compromised by emotion, should not have been so insensitive.

*

The reading of a literary work is not only the decanting from one mind into another of an organized complex of ideas and images, or a subject's active work on a collection of signs that must be resuscitated in a new way throughout, it is also the reader's reception, in the course of a fully regulated visit, where not a comma can be changed in the itinerary, by *someone*: the conceiver and the constructor, now the naked proprietor, who gives you a tour of his domain from start to finish and from whose company you cannot be liberated. As for me, I am extremely sensitive to the nuances of this reception, to the point of feeling awkward throughout, even when visiting a splendid property, if I must do it as an undesirable or as indiscreet company. The reception of a Hugo, for example, at the threshold of one of his books, is superbly disdainful of my lowly self and instead addresses the *dear reader*, a respectable collective of tourists crossing the threshold of a historic mecca.

Malraux, who inevitably makes me ill at ease, always seems annoyed and somehow impatient at having to address someone of such little intelligence as you. The amusing, piquant, inexhaustible companionship of Stendhal is that of someone with whom you are not bored for a second, but who doesn't give you a chance to get a word in edgewise. Rereading him recently, in the forced leisure of my deserted bedroom, I rediscovered one the major charms of Nerval: a kind, simple, and cordial welcome, a sort of drifting and discreetly fraternal alacrity that never insists and always seems ready to let itself be forgotten if you wish.

And there is also the one who abandons you along the way or refuses to take you by the hand (which is not always unpleasant) and the one, on the contrary, who watches the customer at the door and places himself in the window in a proprietary way, like a prostitute in Amsterdam. As impersonal as it may wish to be, a book of fiction is always an empty house that everything betrays from room to room, as though still casually inhabited day after day, from the coat hung on a peg to the dressing gown flung on the bed to the disorder of the worktable—and I'm always happy when I have the impression of surprising the author hot in his tracks and as though about to move out.

*

What do we mean—what does the writer mean when he speaks of *his readers*? It is common to transfer the attachment we actually have for only one work to a name without thinking about it. The admiration devoted to an author, even if it is absolute, is often accompanied by complete indifference to a new book by him whose publication is announced. The writer is finished for us, because we want to keep him as he is; the action of curiosity is extinguished. Certain readings even proscribe in advance, or later prohibit, everything that might subsequently come from the same source: a mechanism of self-sterilization that calls to mind those plants whose first harvest is luxuriant but that secrete a toxin making the soil unfit for their reproduction, and theirs alone, for years. One could understand, perhaps, because of the passage from painting a character to evoking a period, that devotees of *Sentimental Education* are almost never those of *Madame Bovary*—and vice versa—but there are also few readers enamored in equal measure of *The Charterhouse* and *The Red and the Black*. Let's be frank: the love we have for a book, the insubstantial and enigmatic but all-important *plus* with which it is marked for us, implies, like any other love, a *minus* in the interest we may have in everything that resembles it or is related to it. Only, what everyone accepts in love, where exclusivity is appropriate, is far from proper in literature, where the author is considered the common denominator of all his books, and we yield to this pressure of a received idea without even realizing it. If I am asked, I will say, without even thinking, that "I love Balzac." If I ask myself more specifically about my actual taste, I notice that I return to *Béatrix* and *Les Chouans*, sometimes *Lily* or *Séraphita*, and reread them without tiring of them. Other books by Balzac, if I happen to reopen them, most often give rise only to a somewhat distracted ratification of respect: the pleasure they give me—largely commanded by universal glorification—is that which fifteen or twenty other novelists could give me. Likewise, "I love Wagner," in reality, means *Parsifal* and *Lohengrin*, from which I would not cut a single note, and partially *Tristan*; from the rest I would only select a few motifs, scenes, and isolated orchestral passages here and there; the *Ring Cycle*, its mood, its heroes, its plot, remain as foreign to me as a *saga* translated from Finnish or Old Irish. Happy are those, like Proust, who manage to submerge a name and a life, and then resuscitate them, in a single, totalizing, and recapitulative work. Or even Joyce, who can be reduced to *Ulysses*, or Musil. For others, for almost all others, to be "loved" in fact means that, of their substance, which they have tried to make indivisible and incorruptible, the most fanatical reader—betraying them intimately—tosses aside just as much as and maybe more than he keeps.

And what if the literary handbooks taught in high school from now on relied only on books or plays, and not authors? A history of literature, contrary to history plain and simple, should comprise only the names of the victories, since the defeats are a victory for no one.

*

The pedagogical sediment, the fold of education and academic research strongly mark our approach to works of art. Even before we love it, they want to *explain* it to us. What concerns the instructor in a work of art, for professional reasons that, by the way, are valid, is not the free saturation that allows one to take pleasure in it but the external footholds by which it can be grasped: there is no organized discourse for intimate communication with a book, and a teacher seeks the loose end sticking out of the ball of thread that will ostensibly allow him to unwind it. But the secret of a work resides much less in the ingenuity of its organization than in the quality of its material: if I enter a novel by Stendhal or a poem by Nerval without prejudice, I am first and foremost only the *scent of a rose*, like Condillac's statue[80]—without eyes, ears, or localized perceptions—and the artwork thereby offers me its distinctive operative character, which is to occupy my entire inner cavity immediately and without any differentiation, like a gas that is expanding. Revealing its total elasticity and the undivided immanence of its true presence: it cannot be subdivided, because its virtue resides entirely in each particle.

What too often leads explanatory criticism astray is the contrast between the material reality of the work—expanded, articulated, made of encased and complex parts, and if one chooses, able to be disassembled into its detail—and the rigidly global character of the impression of reading that it produces. To not take into account this effect of the work, for which it is entirely built, is to analyze by the laws and means of mechanics a construction whose sole aim is to produce an effect similar to electricity. And there is a similarly misguided aggravating circumstance: the maker of the work of art, each time he has nourished his work and needed to check it, has also been turned completely into the "scent of a rose," eliminating everything from his mind except a certain blind and almost olfactory guiding impression that alone allows him to choose between the paths offered to him. The entire work has been conceived and executed under the control of this sensed essence of the work, which is perhaps not that which is communicated to the reader (this is the profound ambiguity of transmission in a work of art) but whose nature is identical. Only when you "explain," when you analyze books, you say nothing of this passage from the complex to the indivisible, which is also in its own way a leap from quantity to quality. You take apart the interlocking cogs, but what about the *current*—how is it produced? And why doesn't some other no less solidly and intelligently arranged machine produce it? The insufficiency of these methods would be so much more apparent if, instead of analyzing functioning works that have already been sifted through, you approached them at their source, where no seal of approval yet designates and distinguishes them: taken by chance from the pile of manuscripts heaped on a reader's table in a publishing house! For the nature of your methods would then lead you, for all to see, to analyze a false work just as subtly, just as brilliantly as a real work, which is to say, not to take apart a malfunctioning machine the way one would a functioning machine, which is only normal, but—which is less so—to fuss over what in literary terms does not exist as if it enjoyed a plenitude of being.

*

In the matter of literary criticism, all words that lead to categories are traps. They are necessary and must be used provided these simple comprehension tools, precarious tools, random tools, are never taken for the original subdivisions of the creation; so much energy is wasted marking the borders of "romanticism," dividing works of the imagination into card catalogs of the *fantastic*, the *marvelous*, the *strange*! With works of art, it is judicious to keep an eye on their associates but to let their civil status float a bit.

*

This novel, this poem, that I've written, that is a presence for you if you read it, but a presence that dissolves in its consumption, a fruit that you open, that you take and reject based on your appetite and taste, is for me at once a present and a past, a past-present, a past totally retrieved in the present. What Proust sought, he sought with perfect coherence, pen in hand; the acuity of memory, even an all-powerful acuity, could not give it to him, but only the power of art, for the memory never restores a present-past. The "open sesame" that resided neither in the paving stones nor in the madeleines, but solely in the privilege of writing, and what this writing resuscitated for him was not Illiers, the flowers of la Vivonne, or Tante Léonie's garden, but only the irreplaceable past-present of *Remembrance of Things Past*.

*

There is nothing more effective than rereading a polemical piece of writing several years later to detect the accelerated change that endlessly decimates and repopulates the literary scene, for lack of literature; the aging of fictional works is infinitely slower and more gradual. As if the real taste of a period changed with the rhythm of the slow and insensible oscillation of changes in climate, but its conscious enthusiasms or furies, quite to the contrary, with the jerky rhythm of fashion. Just as the famous battles of history preferably take place around an uninhabited ditch or crumbling mill, the most feverish literary tempests carry in the crest of their waves (people or works) extras without consistency: how strange, for the new wave at the time, to choose to fight in 1830 for *Hernani*! The myopia congenital to polemical writing instantly and grotesquely freezes this lack of perspective: it charges against windmills whose names today must be looked for in specialized dictionaries: thus Beaumarchais attacks the counselor *Guzman*, Balzac Gustave *Planche*, and Péguy Mr. Fernand *Laudet*.[81]

*

Just as we hardly ever make new friends after forty, past this age, in the "literary world" we no longer have the familiar kinship, sustained conversation, and real dialogue with the works—even the admired works—of generations that follow. A family is thus gradually extinguished around you, which, like any family, certainly does not preclude private disagreements and lifelong quarrels, but which, like a grandparent who lives with a grandchild, lumps the two preceding generations into yours. Only, in matters of artistic filiation, affective relationships seem to move in one direction: they tend to move backward, from descendants to ancestors. I can understand and even be truly interested in what has come after my generation. But there is an age difference that forbids the older child the transports of intimate fervor in art, just as in life—in the opposite sense, it's true—it closes off the prospect of love.

*

Armand Hoog raises the question of the *time* in which our reading of a novel of the past, Balzac or Stendhal, is situated. He places it in a sort of undated *no man's land*; neither completely part of the period of the creation, nor completely that of the reading: the past is at once past and relived in an original contemporaneousness.

This is subtle, and plausible at first sight. Then, upon reflection, one suspects that the accommodation, the temporal adjustment that occurs spontaneously in the process of reading, could well be more capricious. The terrain of reading *The Red and the Black* is strictly a vintage time for me that is never lost from sight, which is that of dated History; no need here to recall the subtitle: "A Chronicle of 1830." That of *On the Marble Cliffs* (the vagueness of the period of the narrative has nothing to do with it) is from end to end the dreamy and temporally decompartmentalized resuscitation of memory: the affective color of the past, nothing more. That of a detective novel (even one as dated as *Arsène Lupin*) is essentially a time wide open to possibility, a time of pure expectancy—the present already out of balance and entirely swallowed up by the future. The time of history—

the time of memory—the time of expectancy, or rather of imminence. There are no doubt others, even harder to define and more complex. It would not be impossible for the first page of a book to guide this temporal adjustment that reading implies with the same authority of a musical key at the top of a score.

*

Having reopened the notebook of a contemporary writer, I skim it a bit distractedly and peck randomly at a few reflections here and there. Randomly? No, or at least not entirely; when I see the name of a writer, I stop for an instant to read what is said about him: in the literary brotherhood, this is one of the last curiosities to dissipate. Malicious? Of course! What writer, who at times yawns at Saint-Beuve, has ever paused while reading *My Poisons*? And I see nothing wrong with it. In a "colleague's viciousness"—so decried—there is a salubrious scouring agent. Malraux is right—absolutely right—to say that the *retort* in art does not exist. But it is also true that literature—fundamental literature—only *endures* and consolidates when beaten relentlessly by bitter humor, just as piers harden in salty water.

*

What I want from a literary critic—and what is rarely given—is for the critic to tell me, better than I could do myself, why reading a book gives me a pleasure that cannot be replaced. You only speak to me of what is not exclusive to it, and what it has exclusively is all that matters to me. A book that has seduced me is like a woman who places me under her spell: to hell with her ancestors, birthplace, background, relationships, education, and childhood friends! All I expect from your critical discussion is the right vocal inflection that will give me the sense that you are in love, in love in the same way I am: I only need the confirmation and pride that the parallel and lucid love of a complimentary third party gives the lover. As for the book's "contribution" to literature and the enrichment it is supposed to bring me, know that I will marry even *without a dowry*.

In the end, what foolery and what imposture, the critic's trade: an expert in *beloved objects*! For, after all, if literature is not a catalog of femme fatales and iniquitous creatures, it is not worth bothering with.

*

In cartography, the unsolvable problem of *projections* arises from the impossibility of depicting a curved surface on a map without distorting it. On any fairly extensive map, a distortion will appear in relation to reality, either in the proportions between surfaces, or in the drawing of the contours. There is no remedy for this, but there is a palliative; provided the depicted surface is very small, just this side of a certain threshold of largeness, the distortion will be considered negligible.

I tend to think, in a field of objective study that is more accessible to me like literature, that a similar problem is raised, a problem that is also unsolvable. Almost always, in the matter of literary analysis, only the remarks that arise from an almost pinpoint observation are convincing in their immediate rightness (Proust's remarks on the use of the imperfect tense in Flaubert, precise in terms of their objective, limited in their scope, would be a good example). Everything that theorizes, everything that overgeneralizes in the "science of literature," and even in simple criticism, seems subject to caution. A multifaceted impressionism, like these fragments of large-scale maps, impossible to assemble exactly but, taken one by one, almost rigorously faithful, is perhaps the best map that one can draw up of the ways and means, the provinces and paths, of literature.

*

There are two types of voices in French poetry, as different in vocal expression as the soprano from the contralto. Poetry that tends toward the *staccato* of triumphant proliferation, rich in *r*'s, frictatives, and dental consonants; in it, Hugo, Mallarmé, Claudel, and sometimes Rimbaud, are rejoined beyond the abyss.

> *Et, tachés du sang pur des célestes poitrines*
> *De grands linges neigeux tombent sur les soleils*
> [And spotted with the pure blood of heavenly breasts,
> Great snowy linens fall over the suns!][82]

> *Ce vieillard possédait des champs de blé et d'orge*
> *Il était, quoique riche, à la justice enclin*
> *Il n'avait pas de fange en l'eau de son moulin*
> *Il n'avait pas d'enfer dans le feu de sa forge.*
> [Boaz owned fields of barleycorn and wheat—
> A rich old man, but righteous, even so.
> There was no foulness in his millstream's flow,
> There was no hellfire in his forge's heat.][83]

And poetry whose signal power consists primarily in spinning out without snapping and clinching the arabesque of a magical cantilena: Lamartine, Nerval, Verlaine, Apollinaire:

La connais-tu, Daphné, cette ancienne romance

Au pied du sycomore, ou sous les lauriers blancs

Sous l'olivier, le myrte, et les saules tremblants

Cette chanson d'amour, qui toujours recommence

[Do you recall, Daphne, that old refrain

At the sycamore's foot, beneath the white laurel,

The olive, myrtle or quivering willow,

A song of love . . . that always begins again!][84]

Vous y dansiez petite fille

Y danserez-vous mère-grand

C'est la maclotte qui sautille

Toutes les cloches sonneront

Quand donc reviendrez-vous Marie?

[Little girl you danced there

Will you dance there old

The hop and the skip there

All the bells will be ringing

Marie but when do you come home][85]

Who could decide between ambitions that are nothing alike and so radically indentured to their means? The former seems to proceed anew in the august mode toward the naming of creation, the latter to take up where the song of the sirens left off.

Rimbaud? Rimbaud practically wrote at the age his voice was breaking, he had both voices at once, exemplarily and successively. The most intriguing, most unclassifiable case to me remains Baudelaire: the song of a castaway of Eden, so bursting with life force and memory he often gets bogged down; the more mature voice, the *elder* voice of French poetry.

It was a line from *The Graveyard by the Sea* that made me think of this bipartite condition. The lines of poetry that Valéry quotes in his *Notebooks*—almost always by Hugo—reveal what side he tends toward even more clearly than his own: in an artist, what is admired is often revealed to be more extreme than what is produced. Never an allusion to Nerval, Apollinaire. Baudelaire himself is practically disdained—Rimbaud, it is quite clear, annoys him on every level. The published *Notebooks* have changed Valéry's lighting; the first draft underscores his cutting rejections and his impatience with every debate: he draws the figure of the intolerant skeptic.

*

"Baudelaire and Rimbaud, Claudel and Valéry, Breton, Malherbe and Mallarmé cannot all be right, all together. Or, if they are all right, all together, without us knowing how or why, or in what way or by what accord, in any case we are always to cherish what somebody—somebody we value—places above all else ... So yes: either poetry exists, and we should find a way to agree on that, as on the earth's rotation and blood circulation. Or else it is only an error of the mind, a still incomplete formulation of something to be discovered, like the salmagundis of pre-Copernican theologians. And we have the duty to elucidate this problem" (Georges Mounin: *Avez-vous lu René Char?*).

It is always unpleasant for us to see a problem like this raised, since the allergy to Boileau and all the Poetic Arts has long outlived romanticism and may even be its most untouchable legacy. And yet it is raised, and at times with such provocative brutality: as shown by the immediately venomous, sometimes open, sometimes latent war between various poetry anthologies published after the war. Where the full light of poetry blinds you, I see nothing at all—and even when our tastes align most closely, the area I mark off and close off for my own use in the treasure trove of *universal poetry* will never intersect entirely with yours. Never mind that we cannot agree on the necessary and sufficient conditions of poetry, if at least there existed some *reliable* test as to the effects it

produced; unfortunately, aside from the clearly over-
used term "poetic feeling," there is nothing in common between what a reader of Lamartine felt around
1820 reading "The Lake"—not to go too far back—and
what Valéry felt around 1890 reading "A Throw of the
Dice."[86]

It is admirable, in short, that we have been able to say
and write so many ingenious, profound, beautiful, and
even undoubtedly *accurate* things (an added bonus) on
the subject of a phenomenon whose causes we cannot
define—and whose effects we cannot agree on.

*

What a splendid engagement: the *Lohengrin* "pre-
miere" in the Goethean town of Weimar, which Liszt
conducted and which a chance trip to Germany led
Gérard de Nerval to review, at least in his imagination! It
would be nice to see it and hear it all again; the sets, the
costumes, the timbre of the voices, the atmosphere of
the elegant little room, even the comments of the audience during intermission, and the provincial cancan of
the dwarf city. Even if the cursory review that Nerval
wrote of it is not entirely, far from entirely, on par with
the event. But so what! nothing can prevent even the

most innovative poet of his time from being a century or two behind, most often in the areas of painting or music. Nerval's music is that of harpsichordists in the time of Louis XIII, and, despite all the magic of *Les chimères*,[87] an abyss separates him from Baudelaire, whose peerless new modernity has to do with the fact that, in all domains simultaneously, and for the first time, taste was forging ahead.

Music aside (he rejected it), one such simultaneous progression of the awareness in all the aesthetic domains at once—the progression of a rake and not of a single point—was more valuable perhaps and more meaningful for Breton (as for Apollinaire) than a real breakthrough in the poetic field alone. In this, he joined all the standard-bearers of absolute modernity: Baudelaire and Mallarmé in first place, before Apollinaire. An ecumenical demand in the matter of art that is totally absent, on the contrary, in Rimbaud—who does not care about the music, painting, or sculpture of his time—as it is absent in Claudel, and that perhaps translates, when it is brought to excess as in Cocteau, whose insubstantial and evanescent poetry seems at each instant to seek the more robust fixative of Stravinsky, Picasso (or others), a certain lack of plenitude in the singular gift: neither

Baudelaire, nor Mallarmé, nor Breton, so remarkable for the rare quality in the gift, is noted for his overflowing generosity. In all the related fields with which it is fascinated, modernity like this, consciously or not, seeks the comfort of riding a wave that will unfurl evenly at the same time over its entire length.

"From time to time, at rather long intervals, I dream of her, and these dreams place in my life, for several hours after the work has come, an uncommon movement, as when our soldiers pass a large fire in Smolensk or on the Berezina" (Benjamin Constant to Prosper de Barante, a few years after breaking up with Mme de Staël).

As so often when I read Benjamin Constant, lines like these unsettle me, not violently but persistently. I see in no one else this way of suddenly speaking to you about yourself in hushed tones, as you are reading, in a sort of intimist and shivery clairvoyance.

Constant's life ceases to be interesting as soon as it is visited by public success, which places all his concerns and curiosities under a candlesnuffer. Parliamentary glory ages him brutally; it is for him the ironic promotion, *in extremis*, of a retiree of life. No more love affairs after the Chambre Introuvable:[88] the already senile man on crutches acclaimed by the youth of the Ecoles (from which chasms separate him) calls to mind Béranger by his fireside, near an old maidservant-mistress who is preparing to inherit.

Babet, un peu de complaisance
Mon lait de poule et mon bonnet de nuit!
[Babet, a little kindness,
an eggflip and my night-cap!][89]

And how sad, too, and parodic, this last image of his political career: "the wheelbarrow of the gouty deputy" on the steps of the Palais Marchand, blessing the paragon of the Temperate Monarchy. He died shortly after that of a setback at the Academy: the final reprise in a minor key of what had been one of the leitmotifs of his life, a familiarity with the pitfalls in the game of snakes and ladders.

*

There is in Céline a man who started marching behind his own bugle. I get the sense that his exceptional gifts as a vociferator, which he was unable to resist, led him inflexibly toward themes with a high-risk content, the panicky, besieged, frenetic themes, among which anti-Semitism, specifically, made to draw him in. The drama that the demands of an instrument received as a gift can bring out in an artist—demands that are at times half monstrous and above all *fully used*—must have come into play here in all its scope. If someone, to his misfortune, has received the rat catcher's flute as a gift, it will be hard to prevent him from taking children to the river.

*

The register of Dostoyevsky's novels is as different at times from that of "psychological" novelists as a normal card game from one into which a joker has been slipped.

*

I have often asked myself why Alain—whose student I was for two years, to whom I listened for two years with attention and quasi-religious admiration, to the point of imitating his writing style, as two thirds of us did—ultimately left so few traces.

An admirable stimulator of the mind, his mind was not on the future. At the very moment we left his class, in 1930, brutal changes in scale unseated his thought; a world was being established, a frantic, violent world that rejected all of his temperate humanism. The rules of parliamentary democracy, predominantly radical, seemed to him a permanent contribution: there could be *bad elections*, leading notable conservatives and supporters of clericalism toward key portfolios, nothing more serious. His political problems were those of the French constituent of the petite bourgeoisie in a small town, knit together against the encroachments and contempt of the rich, the important, and the official; with infinitely more philosophical culture, and certainly elevating the debate a good deal, the horizon of his battle as a citizen and the measure of his resistance to the arbitrary remained pretty much close to—with a century's distance—that of the winegrower of La Chavonnière.[90] Questions such as colonialism, communism, Hitlerism, the destiny of Europe, the technological explosion, and the new world balance went beyond the horizon of his somewhat departmental wisdom, and I think also upset him: he kept them at a distance. His anti-historicism was instinctive and almost absolute; the experience of Combism,[91] which he supported, and that of the war of 14, which he participated in, were the only lessons of history he took into account: in 1939, he automatically reclaimed Dreyfusard positions and those of *Above the Battle*,[92] and remained there, with no regard for enormous variations in nature and intensity; the tree hid the forest, and Boisdeffre, and Hitler; he roused "republicans" against Gamelin's saber.

We might wonder what he thought of communism; if it entered his frame of thought, I think he thought of it as a sort of overly petulant, overly effervescent radicalism, without any sense of its specificity: something *to bring back to the fold*. The industrial world remained closed to him. Until the end, he wanted to continue seeing the nascent world through the spectacles of 1900. I remember a sarcastic quip he leveled one day at Jean Perrin and nuclear physics, then being born: "They *saw* the atom!" *They* were going to do a little more . . .

He did not like either limited situations or characters. An admirable commentator of Balzac, Stendhal, and Dickens, he acknowledged very little of Claudel except the very Corneillean *Hostage*, of Dostoyevsky only *Crime and Punishment*: neither *The Possessed* nor *The Idiot*. I have no doubt he would have rejected the Malraux of *La Condition Humaine*, or rather ignored him, as he would do with Bernanos. If he knew it, I think he had the same opinion of surrealism as Valéry: a salvaging of scraps.

Once gone, I rid myself of him, in respect and recognition. I sometimes read his *Propos* on literature, on Dickens, which is that of a topnotch reader (he was, he is, in his strictly marked domain, a wonderful literary critic, free and airy, and capable—how so!—of stepping back and taking stock). Perhaps I resented him somewhat for making me mistake a narrowly situated and dated way of thinking for a timeless awakening to the life of the mind, one that reflected the end of a period of the world rather than announcing a new one, through the still-masked decline of a rural, closed democracy. An almost anti-Copernican way of thinking, like that of his sworn enemy, Barrès, where the world still gravitated around the bourgeois couple of France and Germany. The other day, by chance, a little-frequented bookstore reduced me to opening a volume in Anatole France's fictional series: *The Elm Tree on the Mall.* I knew nothing about the book; after sixty pages or so, a strange thought occurred to me: "Say, Alain!" Not, of course, that anything in him recalled the intellectual breadth and very moderate side of the "good master" of La Béchellerie.[93] But I felt keenly that this world of the novels of Anatole France, with its emblematic figures, like those on a deck of cards—the General, the Duke, the Bishop, the Prefect, the Finance Minister, the secular Instructor—was the same narrow world of his youth, the *hand he was dealt* that he did not seek to change, and the limits of which, as the framework of a thought that was nevertheless so free, he had accepted without ever questioning again.

*

Tell me who your friends are . . . I've just leafed through a work devoted to Barrès, illustrated with numerous photographs of the period. What intercessors he chose for himself! What a confederacy! In his study: a portrait of Taine, a photograph of Monsieur Renan. In snapshots taken throughout his life, mustached deputies, collectors from the Bazar de la Charité, military chaplains, Alsatian nuns, generals, missionaries—Rostand, Déroulède, Anna de Noailles, Maginot, Castelnau, Gyp, Paul Bourget, Jacques-Emile Blanche, Marie Bashkirtseff: the upper crust of the Belle Epoque for readers of *Illustration*, which is to say, the second choice everywhere . . . There is not a single truly lofty figure of the period with whom he had a close friendship or engaged in a debate—he for whom all doors opened; he seemed to avoid them all, using the subtle white cane of the blind. Neither Proust, nor Claudel, nor Valéry, nor Gide, nor Apollinaire, nor Breton ever crossed paths with him. Are we to believe that for him the literature and thought of his time remained in the French Academy? And what to think of a mind that chose his interlocutors so well among the dead and so poorly among the living?

*

There are two elements in *The Devil in the Flesh* that do not completely fuse together. On the one hand, the concrete images, filtered with the assurance of an impeccable eye, whose mark in the memory can no longer be erased: the madwoman on the roof, the linden trees of the Marne villas, the picnic lunch in the country, the olive wood fire, the face surrounded by flames. And on the other hand, a psychological algebra that will take up almost all the room in *Count d'Orgel's Ball*, that chills the book at intervals, and where the arrogance of adolescent sagacity works hard to post from day to day the point on the chart of the Tender with the imperturbability of an old Cape Horner.

But the genre of the novel knows the dispensation of favors that poetry does not know, favors that allow a punctual success to have repercussions at times on longer, more barren passages and transfigure them in its light. A few well-placed radioactive cores can suffice to dissolve by extension all the intercalary zones of inertia. As soon as poetry ceases to be present in a poem line after line, it also ceases to inhabit it, as brutally as a current ceases to inhabit an electrical wire, making it impossible for the reader not to stumble immediately on the padding. But the life of the novel, like impressions of light that linger on the retina, relies on an afterlife of strong images beyond the verbal felicity that gave birth to them; in the mind of a novel reader, the speed acquired counts for almost everything; sometimes the need for a break is accompanied by the pure pleasure the cyclist feels when forging ahead turns into coasting. So, when I read a novel by Radiguet, these relays of energy that are truly *found* images make me pass over the psychological inserts where I am given a too clever elucidation without even noticing. In the entire first half of the book, at least, where the force of concrete suggestion remains flawless. In the second, where these energetic recharges are more rare, one gets the sense that Radiguet is writing beyond his age and that child prodigies do not necessarily carry the same conviction in psychology as in music.

What dominates my memory of this rereading is the image of the Paris of the last two years of the First World War, and especially its suburbs, the "voluptuous suburb" Montherlant once spoke of. Without the book trying to depict it in any way, and from the sole fact that the scabrous story the novel recounts fully captures it in its prejudices, a whole layer of the suburban petite bourgeoisie of 1918 is revealed here in lost profile, rooted as couch grass, barbed as a blackberry bush, more present, weightier, than it would be in a work of social criticism. The still somewhat rustic surveillance network of neighbors and domestics, the mayor and the milkman, the baker and the cheese seller, thrown like a net over these dreary residential villas in the heights of Marne. The umbrellas and boater hats of families on Sunday walks. The moral order dictated by retirees with canes and goatees and limited real estate. The pale stubs of candles, suburban night trains' scent of coal. Henri II dining rooms in restrained millstone pavilions. Young ladies married off between the piano and the watercolor, the reign of which has ended while that of the school of Pigier has not.[94] An entire suburban fringe lies enclosed within its suspicious walls, sealed beneath its pruned linden trees, free of cars, movie theaters, culture, or horizons, already as robbed by Russian bonds as by Victory bonds, relieved of its gold, but all the more attached to the cant of its small-minded and jealous morality, pulling rank and holding court, and keeping domestics on a short leash, while sensing its substance gradually slipping away, between visits to the cemetery, visits to the notary public, and the reading of *press releases*. And these are the precincts of the stagnant, fretful slumber of a bourgeois suburb that today gives the book not the whiff of scandal of its publication but the unexpected explosion of a miniature 1968.

*

The outcry of all the Catholic defenders against Gide shows how unable Catholicism was at the beginning of the century to discern its truly irreducible enemies. What whipped up controversy against him was the image of the devil, the age-old expert in "the flesh," as we know; behind this convenient decoy, Valéry got them off the scent of Lucifer himself. There was no solitary intellectual pride in Gide. An inquisitor of the Middle Ages, even a second-rate one, would not have been fooled for a second.

*

In Chartres, a dazzling sun encourages me to visit the city for a few hours between trains: the sudden desire to see the stained-glass windows again, prompted by rereading the first pages of *The Cathedral*.[95] A few German tourists (it is six in the evening, but only four, to judge by the height of the sun) wander in the nave behind a guide; before the dark Virgin, surrounded by candles, an officiant dressed in a sort of cherry-red burnoose (great changes seem to have taken place in the liturgical wardrobe), reads passages aloud from the Bible for the dozen or so elderly people in mourning. The most beautiful, most mysterious stained-glass windows are the most somber (especially one, toward the back of the chancel, of a dark blue brightened only by a few bursts of vermilion). The kinship of these windows, which distance and thick lead settings make almost non-figurative, with Oriental carpets leaps out at the eye immediately. Rather than the sharp fire of cut gems, the colors are at once, for the blues and reds, that of faintly glimmering cabochons that still recall the veinstone, and for the browns and yellows, violet browns and almost golden greens, an appetizing succulence that I did not remember at all: a flow of honey, plum, raisin, the transparency of ripe grapes. It seems to me that if I lived in the city, I would stop by every day to satisfy a hunger for color that can only be awakened and appeased in this place in two separate forms, as different in nature as bread and wine.

As for the rest, it would indeed require the fruity tongue of Huysmans, the essential materiality of his epithets, to speak of this colored glass that is not only mystical but at times so compactly sensual it can almost make you salivate.

The upward thrust of the hillside on the Eure, behind the apse, gave me the impression of an outdoor sacristy scattered in the greenery, an annex loosened from the temple, clarifying the trees of a sacred copse. Rue du Massacre, rue de la Foulerie, a cast shadow, clerical and

benign, made of delicate silence, of cloistered medita-
tion that has scarcely become secular, falls from the slope
topped by its enormous vessel and floats to the edges of
the curved Eure, which the index finger, trailing the
shadow of the spires, visits like a sundial.

In no cathedral town that I know, whether Amiens,
Bourges, or Reims, is the urban tenor as subservient to
the central vessel; mediocre development and the level-
ing effect of the low plateau on which the city is founded
give all the differential scale to the élan of the towers.
One does not get the sense that the church has risen
from the city, as in Claudelian imagery, but rather that a
modest functional grouping—hotels, mills, markets,
lodges, public offices—huddle in the shelter of a primitive and monumental privilege, like a hamlet of colo-
nization under the walls of a fortified castle. Throughout the pages of his book, in sun and winter wind,
Huysmans strolls and wanders the streets by chance:
wherever he goes, he never leaves the magnetic field outlined by the central magnet.

*

Lewis and Irene, by Paul Morand, features an edenic
capitalism, capitalism before original sin. The book
takes place in a sort of paleoliterature, well beyond the

half-century that separates us from its publication, as cut off from the contemporary intelligentsia as pagan works might have been from the Fathers of the Church. And at the same time, it recaptures a sort of piquant innocence: this dilettante of mineral prospecting and this lady from old money, who have not yet discovered that they are doing evil according to Saint Marx, are like an ancient Christian Daphnis and Chloe, unaware that they are indulging in *sins of the flesh*.

As odd as it seems to me today, this book mattered in my life. At sixteen, which must be the age I read it, Lewis presented the very image of the *glamorous life*, circa 1924. The convoluted cocktail out of Morand's shaker: a background of artistic racketeering that called to mind Stendhal as C.E.O. or Vaché after a *dime-store success*, the nonconformist snobbery, the *a little dry* approach, aristocracy replaced by speed, erotic cynicism for sociability, with the zest of up-to-date culture (Lewis reads Freud on the plane from London)—all of it rose to my head. Since it was *business* one tackled in these superior forms of existence, go for business! I thought seriously for a moment about taking the entrance exam for Hautes Etudes Commerciales, for which a preparatory class had recently been created at school, to gain access to this poetry of life.

Reread in 1977, the book, spoiled by a few modernist follies that date it too closely to the age of the *Bugatti* (jasmine releases its perfume "in two strokes"),[96] incorporates a new expedient for the novel, the short circuit, the use of which, unfortunately, was limited due to high risk to the fuses. As good as it seems now, in the literary tradition of the interwar period, like the equivalent of one of these deceptively plausible technical solutions caught at the time in an impasse: the seaplane, the zeppelin, or the hydroplane—one of the most pressing secrets of the novel seeming to be, on the contrary, the ability to create slowness from material duration meagerly counted.

*

Nothing more admirable in Chekhov's *The Steppe* than the precision with which the young child's passive wonder is rendered against a background of vague insecurity, a child separated from his family for the first time and passed from hand to hand throughout the vast world, sleeping in strange beds. The fresh violence, the fragmented singularity of all the irruptions spaced throughout the telling of his odyssey: the faces, conversations, buildings, bad weather, and landscapes are almost dreamlike but maintain a shade of aggressiveness, at once intoxicating and distressing: the world leaps out at us unexpectedly in this second birth, wresting us, naked and exposed, from the familiar cocoon. In a life, aging is nothing other than the continual increase of constants without novelty at the expense of fresh possibility: in *The Steppe*, this possibility that hurls itself in the way at each instant dominates everything and still has the power of instant seizure: at every moment consciousness is engulfed by new images.

*

Rimbaud. I'm looking at his adult portraits, those of Isabelle and Vitalie. The mark of the family, the dents and rough surfaces of peasant stock, are there, all-powerful, accentuated by age, imprinted on the nose, chin, and cheeks in harsh strokes. He belongs to his line so profoundly, to Frédéric and Isabelle, to Vitalie and *mother Rimbe*—blood weaves this nest of vipers so tightly—the thread is so solid that brings him back from the ends of the earth to Charleville, to Roche. His *people*! He was never able to protest this pull his blood ties had on him. How poorly the solitary grave of Charleville suits him!—and after the most dazzling escapades, all these hard, bony replicas of himself seem to have given him a rendezvous in the terrible promiscuity of the family tomb.

*

Of his period, Musset allows only the most fleeting, most ephemeral things to filter through: a popular tune, a street phrase, the year's fashion—*espagnolades*,[97] Byronic Don Juanism, "the German Rhine," Murger's working girls—everything that is sprinkled here and there over Balzac's novels only to situate the narrative in time and establish local tone.

But it is precisely this flawless superficiality that has given him his best chance, not to be forgotten. No writer of his period restores to us, as he sometimes fleetingly does, in a sentence or verse, not the substance and breadth of his time to which he has no access, but its transitory songs, its flavor, and, in his best moments, almost its bedspreads. He has magically found a fixative for the impalpable pigment that makes the iridescence of a period fragile and unique and that stains the historian's fingers, like colored dust from the wing of a butterfly as it alights.

*

We can well imagine Saint-John Perse as a protégé of Mecenus and *amicus curiae* under Augustus, celebrating the triumph of Urbs as well as the lex *Julia de maritandis ordinibus*,[98] or even, in the last century, as a poet laureate, playing a prelude on his lyre at the crowning of the empress of the Indies! He was made for these official dedications and these jubilatory feasts, and there is something in the trembling of the mirage of his consecratory and seminal poetry like the hollow imprint of an imperial accession that the Third Republic could not give him to celebrate: he imagines *Anabase* for lack of being able to see the commission of the *Recessional*. For the world he celebrates is an arrested world, a world stuck forever at the hour of its solstice—a world that passes from the hour of History to that of sidereal stability, of taking stock and census.

This singular poetry is a discourse without orientation or slant, a mixture rather, a fundamentally exclamatory verbal matter of an absolutely *sui generis* consistency and flavor, the most limited sample of which barely matters when an excerpt suffices for immediate identification, to the point that it seems to contain its own pastiche. This vague and hackneyed mixing, once started, can last anywhere from ten to two hundred pages: nothing in this circular motion allows the reader to get his bearings or situate himself near the beginning or end: it is the theatrical unfurling of a wave on a beach, a grandiose sound that only refers to and announces its own repetition. One can open the collection anywhere and bring the page to one's ear like a seashell; it is always the same oceanic cantilena, effortlessly bound to itself, biting its own glittering tail until sated.

I use it, at distant intervals, a bit like chewing gum, which at first gives off flavor with each chew, but whose taste wears out in about ten pages, to my vexation. Still, I take him up again: the number of poets one can return to is not that large.

*

Who would take it upon themselves to come to any conclusions about Rimbaud's thought—he who never came to any conclusions? The eternal insurgent, made up of short furies and unmet responsibilities. *Season* is all violent, clashing movements of the soul, with some of the disheveled, unexpected interference of a heavy swell that knocks and crashes against the piers of a floating dock. It has always drawn me in and fascinated me, and kept me riveted, the same way that an afternoon of rough weather in Sion keeps me on my balcony for hours: an undone fury that immediately is reconcentrated and pure, the inconceivable torrent of energy imploding.

That is over: one of Rimbaud's key-phrases, not accorded all its weight. As if something in him stopped at a given moment, stopped raging, inexplicably. In him, "that" happens, but that is never resolved—the organization is splendidly electric, the psychical configuration tumultuous and rather dynamic for being nothing but collision, salvo, or sleep.

In his very beautiful book, Yves Bonnefoy makes a few appealing hypotheses about Rimbaud after *Season*.[99] Did he drug himself methodically? Did he throw himself (as he always threw himself) into serious, perhaps initiatory studies: rhythmic music, alchemy, mathematics? Did he seek some secret universal harmony? It's clear starting with *Season* that there is a fixed attraction in him for practical knowledge, applied science ("I will make gold and remedies": always this enraged craving for the concrete). It's unverifiable. . . . But we should here accord a bit more attention to Verlaine's indirect testimony (always suspect or systematically neglected) in a half a dozen of the parodic *Vieux Coppées* that he dedicated to Rimbaud around 1875–76. He must have gathered these testimonies as rumors spread; to confront them, he kept a precise and violent image of Rimbaud, the hostility of which exaggerated his features without betraying them. Now, what do we decipher in this ridiculous (but no doubt truthfully ridiculous) Rimbaud that the *Vieux Coppées* evoke? The depths of boredom, first, the chronic existential ennui, the hollow and incurable wandering. Then the taste for applied science, which is practical and even militant ("I am founding a new school"), which Verlaine twice calls Rimbaud's *philomathy*: the study of languages, patents for inventions—the word *Polytechnique* itself, so expressive, is uttered here. One comes away with the sense that in the Parisian bohemia of letters—apt to caricature, but receptive to all hearsay—between the poet of *Season* and the trafficker of Ethiopia, there must have floated the vague (but supported) image of an exasperated wanderer who traded poetry for knowledge and started off in quest of some positive key to the real world, not without some proselytizing along the way.

*

Was Baudelaire a clairvoyant, as Rimbaud believed and said? Morals are his Muse, and almost the entire register of his poetry has the gorgeous iridescence that a sensed and partway open paradise causes to play on the retina of the heretic. Once or twice he has tried to immigrate into a world washed of original sin ("Giantess"); he has never been able to breathe there with any continuity. The world's radiant innocence, the fundamental note that every poet emits most naturally, is practically the only one he lacks. There is a *Flowers of Evil—Season in*

Hell filiation that in its close consanguinity has no parallel in French poetry, only here the same components, the same tangible servitudes ("Parents, you have made me a slave of my baptism")[100] are interpreted by almost opposite temperaments. It suffices to reinsert them both chronologically in the chain of everything before and after them that matters in poetry: Hugo, Vigny, Nerval, Verlaine, Nouveau, Mallarmé, Apollinaire, so that the strange poetic microclimate that brings them together and isolates them from others looms up and comes into focus: the obsessive presence of Christianity as the fatal value of exile—a masochistic Christianity that renounces Pius IX, expels the century, and transfers to poetry everything it takes away from possible insertion into real life.

*

When these days of disgrace return where, for a moment, all books taste like nothing but papier-mâché, where a saturnine *acedia* discolors the soul and deadens all written poetry, all that remains for me are two or three fountains—small, inexhaustible—where water continues to spring forth in the growing desert and inevitably revives me; a few "Chansons" by Rimbaud ("Le pauvre songe," "Bonne pensée du matin," "Comédie de la soif," "Larme," "Eternité," "Jeune ménage"),[101] one or two small poems by Musset ("A Saint Blaise, à la Zuecca...," "La Chanson de Barberine")[102] and—perhaps most directly, most naturally tapped into this deep ground water—Guillaume Apollinaire. More than "Chanson du Mal Aimé" (so beautiful, but whose tone from the start is that of "great poetry"), all I need is "Adieu," "Marizibill," "Colchiques," and "Clotilde," all I need is to repeat the first strophe of "Marie" for the world instantly to take on the colors of morning.[103]

The colors of morning? Yes, but the colors of a morning that is irremediably lost. There is a magic—a black magic—lying in wait at the heart of the chanson that surges up so fresh, so insouciant and light, a magic that the great, elaborate, ripe poems of Baudelaire and Mallarmé do not know (they contain others). There is both the spontaneity and grace of new life moving in its nascent state and the retreat of the *never again* inherent in all poetic fixing.

As for the rest, half the poems in *Alcools* leave me indifferent, if only because their quirky erudition, which seems at times to come from *L'Intermédiaire des chercheurs et des curieux*,[104] traps the imagination at almost every page, and also because Apollinaire is a wonderful inventor, or unearther, of more original proper names and more ethereal flights of fancy than Hugo himself, the only one, in any case, to rival him in this regard. "Zone" is a major poem, whose power, justly hailed by Breton, possesses an infinitely appealing combination of romantic eloquence and the acidic bite of modernity (modernity—which cannot be resuscitated, as we think it can, new and changed with each period, but that only knew one true springtime, between Wilbur Wright and the assassination in Sarajevo—has above all, in the space of a few years, infused Apollinaire's verse and sometimes his prose). Among the other collections, I place the postcard sent to Lou above all else: "To die and finally know irresistible eternity . . . ,[105] a form of high conjuring, an entirely magic phylactery that a lover must have kept all her life between her flesh and her blouse, as Pascal did Saint Epine's manuscript.

I am not inclined toward the works in prose, and *The Rotting Magician*,[106] long unobtainable, which I wanted to read so badly at the time, disappointed me very much.

The grace of Apollinaire's poetry, which is somewhat that of a schooner setting sail, rolling and pitching in the wind, and from time to time embarking on the open sea, makes it, with the verse of Claudel, one of the most spontaneously contagious poetic rhythms there is for the reader who is also an apprentice writer. And there are few influences that are both more auspicious and less burdensome to bear than his. What would Aragon's poetry be without Apollinaire? And yet his visible presence still gives Aragon nothing but free space.

*

It seems to me we barely notice the strangeness of Rimbaud's vision of the world: a totally unified world in which the human species moves and undulates among others en masse, like a population of nettles or asphodels. No encounter is an individual adventure: each Being that emerges or appears—from Beauty, Power, or Damnation—immediately becomes symbolic, refers directly to some Genesis: as though individuality had yet to be born, with no more currency than it might have had in the Garden of Eden. No social differentiation is ever significant. Instinctively, the vision refers not theoretically, as with the philosophers of the Enlightenment, but concretely to an Adamite period preexisting social organization. In this sense, with all his status in the world of the seventh day, he is the last link in a chain where Proust (where everyone is completely caught in a network of social sign systems) might represent the extreme opposite.

*

Impeccable rhetoric, a keen sense of the musicality proper to language, an unparalleled ability to fill vocabulary words with meaning to the point of bursting, the alliance of the classical ode's orderly eloquence and Mallarméan condensation are not *all* poetry: if Valéry's millionaire poetry today gives many of us the impression of a splendid and rather cold declamation, if the mixing of his components seems at times to dislocate it internally, it is because, barely a few years after *La jeune Parque*, which apparently came to crown and kill French poetry all at once, surrealism was to shine the brightest light on poetry of a completely different kind: a low-calorie poetry. The simple, original taste of words (I wanted to say "offerings," as in modern gastronomy) with none of the congestive semantic stuffing proper to Mallarmé. No longer the poetry of "L'Après-midi d'un faune," but that of Rimbaud and Apollinaire (with Baudelaire at the origin of both branches), and, for that, Valéry lacked poverty (I am using Mozart's beautiful expression, quoted to me one day by Robert Bresson), as he lacked the opening natural to all possibility in the image. Suddenly his poetry—poetry beyond Mallarmé—started to seem, above all, like poetry before Rimbaud.

In short, to readers of 1977, poetry seems to have taken revenge on Valéry for believing himself to be so above it, by station—for treating it like a mistress one is ashamed of being seen with in public.

*

I am always curious to read the reactions (freshly preserved for us) of contemporaries of a major body of work, who speak irreverently of works that will one day make them genuflect. Literary history invariably erases the informal, unseemly testimonies of an infantile promiscuity, just as history plain and simple does not know whether its great men in childhood have exchanged blows with twenty rogues in the course of recreation. This takes nothing away from the solidity of the masterpieces but helps us scrape away the *added value* that time, sheeplike, has mistakenly conceded them.

"I have reread Goethe's *Faust*. It's a mockery of the human species and of all people of science. The Germans find remarkable depth in it. As for me, I find it less worthwhile than *Candide*; it is just as immoral, arid, and mind-deadening, and there is less levity, fewer clever jokes, and much more bad taste" (Benjamin Constant: *Journal*).

Such a judgment does not so much testify to a

deficiency in its author as to the persistence, for years or even decades, of the vulnerable state of every master-piece, before it is cloaked in the carapace of glory that does not completely defend it from blows but almost inevitably skews and deflects them. One might consider this a poor judgment: at least it gives Constant's criticism a cheeky, glancing freshness that is still that of the *polishing*. Consecration will come, the layers of waxy coating of secular veneration will communicate to the work the noble burnishing that is the patina of museums; in order to converse with it, the same partial difficulty will be established as with someone who now only appears in public in uniform.

*

I have never taken great pleasure in reading *Don Quixote*. But if I happen to reopen the book, I am sensitive to the quasi-fabulous remoteness for us of the objects that populate it, its specific furniture that seems to go further back in time and legend than that of Rabelais (for example), older than Cervantes by half a century. Donkeys and donkey-handlers, caravans, mills, jugs of oil, it is not the merchant's life of the countrysides of the Renaissance, already evoked, that emerges here, it is the ageless foundation of the Arabian tales. And the success of the book for many has to do with this time shift. The African backwardness of the steppes of the Castile gives the Knight of La Mancha's exploits a credibility not obtained to the same degree by *Picrochole*, implausibly lost in the economy of the realist and wily market of the countrysides of the Chinonais.

*

There are low density writers one *sees* when they have written three volumes and no longer sees when they have published forty, having wanted to cover too much ground. There is a specific weight to literature, when it is not tyrannically *signature*, which pushes it to enter the anonymous indistinction of one moment of the world and one period of art, just as mimicry in fragile species leads them to blend into their environment to the point of invisibility. Mediocre art is in fact *lifelike*, with a passive tendency toward likeness, not the mastered likeness of the original portrait and its model, but the subjected likeness of the skate's pigment and its sandy depths.

Among these works conceived above all in order to cover all available literary terrain, I would not hesitate to place two or three works by Goethe—in the magisterial category—where the inner need hardly lets you hear its timbre, but where the rigor of a landscape gardener somehow trims in flower beds that might otherwise give the idea of fallow land abandoned to its fate. Just as some flat adjective comes to reupholster a line in a poem as best it can, there are entire books in certain writers that represent the padding in their Complete Works. These are the stopgap works that come with time to punish the artistic imperialism, the will for annexation and conquest applied to territories that belong only in the domain of elective affinities.

*

Huysmans. It is difficult to find a writer whose vocabulary is more extensive, more constantly surprising, more vigorous, and at the same time more exquisitely decadent, more constantly felicitous in discovery and invention. The substance of his language, especially his adjectives, does not emerge multicolored but infused with color in all its mass, with the splendor, material density, and muted fire of cloisonné enamel.

And it is difficult to find a writer whose syntax is more monotonous, hackneyed, indigent, and seemingly dilapidated. The sentence proceeds by flatness juxtaposed with dazzling touches of the palette knife, that no link of relation or subordination seriously cements. Poorer still, almost ataxic, is the progression of the para-

graph, awkwardly scanned by the refrain of *Then . . . Finally . . . And so . . . In short . . .* that return to crush the
text from page to page like blows of a hammer from a
clock figurine. All the linked and supple movement of
the discourse that animates a book, that gives it a slant, a
terracing of levels, a perspective, has been frozen in him;
his books resemble an edifice of rare stones shattered by
an earthquake; luxurious quarry stones and everything
destined to rise loftily in tiers, lie on the ground side by
side, as if dreaming of returning to their original career.
These are sumptuous rock piles of books.

*

In Huysmans, the eventual rejection of naturalism was
inscribed at the outset in his style: in literature, as in politics, the *means* inevitably subvert the ends.

*

I only wanted to reread the belated preface of *Against the
Grain*, but I let myself go and read the whole volume,
carried away by a style (supremely indefensible before
all rhetoric professors) that, at almost every page, leads
me to reopen the Littré with a sort of linguistic licking of
the lips. On top of that, this humorous book, this pot-
pourri of passing fancies, sorts out and reclassifies the

literature of its time as superlatively as Félix Fénéon would do twenty years later with painting.

"Baudelaire had deciphered in the hieroglyphics of the soul the menopause of feelings and thoughts. . . .":[107] how precise this is, and despite the roughness of expression, how perspicacious! I remember an interview I did on the radio in 1968, when a journalist interviewing me, still in the grip of the barricades of the student protest, asked me, as one asks to confirm an obvious fact for the sake of form, if poetry was not in essence linked to youth. My rather curt response was: "And Baudelaire?" And today I would add: "And Mallarmé?"

LITERATURE AND HISTORY

More often than not, the work of Georges Bataille sends one back to the spiritual landscape of Christianity as faithfully as the relief of a medal in the hollow of a mold. If the religion of Jesus—and its affective climate, above all—were to be forgotten, we would still be able to form some idea of it based on the negatives that are his books, just as one can sketch a map of ancient glaciers simply by noting the rising parts of a continent. Post-Christianity could not really begin until after these movements, which geophysicists call *eustatic*,[108] almost as slow as the secular weight they tend to compensate for. Even if Nietzsche is right, a dead God can still reign for a long time through the stabilizing counterattacks of imposed and regulated distribution.

*

For a thousand reasons, Baudelaire mocks Villemain's *conventional* narrative of his evening at the duchesse de Duras's, on a terrace in Saint-Germain-en-Laye, the evening before Chateaubriand's ministerial disgrace. Lord Stuart, Pozzo di Borgo, Capo d'Istria, Humboldt, Rémusat, and Delphine Gay are there. Transpose the scene to 1978: society gossip, the political and literary cancans of *beautifully dressed* Parisians on the shaded lawns of a summer evening, while a ministerial shipwreck without greatness is confirmed in the wings: it is triviality itself. How is it that, by sole virtue of stepping back into the past, this suburban *rout* that nothing, absolutely nothing makes worthy of note or remembrance in Villemain's syrupy prose is suddenly painted for us with a sort of poetry? That is the problem of the irritant, the unfair seduction of the plunge into history that reemerges, plucked, from this diary page of a conceited and unattractive member of the Academy.

I remember a time—so long ago already, it seems—when Sartre triumphantly declared to Mauriac: "Do you want your characters to be alive? Make them free" (no one at the time, by the way, dared mention this high-caliber inconsequence ever again). There are many reasons for prestige to come and adorn even the most marginal figures of History after a few decades, but there is one they share in common with the characters in novels: it is precisely that they are *no longer* free, that any indeterminate future before them has been definitively eclipsed. The imagination cannot cling, or not well, to what is still alive, to what essentially has the vagueness, the fuzziness without the contours, of possibility; the excessive flexibility of the medium resists it; a certain deficit of being constitutes the poetic passive voice of freedom.

*

On the evening of July 29, 1830, when the insurrection had triumphed, Blanqui entered a friendly salon, rifle in hand, and, banging the end of it against the parquet floor, cried: "The romantics have been crushed!" A cry of the heart typical of a country—probably the only one in Europe—where, in feverish moments, literature and politics never fail to join hands.

"It's Voltaire's fault—it's Rousseau's fault": the now bi-secular intellectual reflex of a country where the writer is recruited by parties as needed into its defense corps, like wretched subjects of the Ancien Régime into the king's armies. As for Balzac, who volunteered, but was posthumously transferred by authorities from the white party to the red party, so for Baudelaire and Flaubert. And now poor Mallarmé, with his backpack, promoted to bugler in the troops of metalinguistic progressiveness.

*

If History is as false, as unreal, as viciously distorting as Valéry has said it is, charging it with every sin, it seems to me that personal experience would warn us of it. For if one reaches average longevity—especially in our era, when eras follow and replace each other so quickly— everyone has time to see at least three quarters of what they have experienced become the sediment of history, and nourish an entire library, to which they will turn to spice up the years of their old age. Superimposing the memory of what they saw directly onto what they are reading does not appear to be so great a scandal to them. The experience instead suggests that they generally "find themselves" in it, find themselves perfectly. History's most solid guarantee is not the proud apparatus of its documents, its index cards and testimonies, it is the dissolve that consciously connects each biography to it for most of its duration. To the time when I turned twenty, forty, I could no doubt add nuances, a few personal opinions, the highlight of a significant detail; but what I read about it makes sense, I cannot doubt *what was*, all in all. In the unbroken flow of generations prior to mine that are connected to it and where death has seized the living at every instant without interruption, where can we go to find the rupture—analogous to the passage from waking to dreaming—that, with the wave of a wand, would transform what a mirror showed me all my life, distorting very little, into pure fantasy?

*

The absence of historical memory that makes the Hindu civilization so foreign to us, the fact that only British researchers have restored a definite past for it, and that, with barely fifty years of distance, concrete events and their chronology have already been consumed, dissolved by the fog of myth, would surprise only a European of modern times. The western Middle Ages had a similar conception of its past: Dante testifies to that. The total absence of chronological space and historical perspective that marks *The Divine Comedy* through and through is due, no doubt, to the fact that the lively tide of events turns into the depthless past of transplanted archives. But it is also clear that the distance of the historical gaze has no more reality for Dante than pictorial perspective and the vanishing point, soon to be Leonardo's, had for the frescoes of Giotto, his contemporary. Elapsed time encircles him, and speaks to him less through their succession and interconnection than through the timeless emergence of their most emblematic figures, as Glory delegated illustrious men to Plutarch solely under the criterion of exemplarity.

*

What I sought to do, among other things, in *The Opposing Shore*,[109] rather than tell a timeless tale, was to free a volatile element through distillation, "the spirit-of-History" in the sense that we speak of the spirit-of-wine, and to refine it enough so that it could ignite in contact with the imagination. In History there is an enchantment lying in wait, an element that, though mixed with a considerable amount of inert excipient, still has the virtue of getting you drunk. Of course, it is not a question of isolating it from its support. But the paintings and narratives of the past conceal an extremely unequal tenor, and just as certain minerals are concentrated, fiction is not forbidden from augmenting it.

When History tightens its springs, as it did practically without a moment's respite from 1929 to 1939, it has the same monitoring aggressiveness over the inner hearing that the rising tide has over the ear at the seaside, which I make out so well at night in Sion, from the depths of my bed and in the absence of any notion of time, a specific clamor of alarm, a sound similar to the light buzz of a fever setting in. In English, they say it is "on the move." It is this setting in motion of History, as imperceptible and gripping in its beginnings as the first shudder of a seashell slipping into the sea, that was on my mind when I planned the book. I wanted it to have the lazy majesty of the first distant rumble of a thunderstorm, which does not need to raise its volume to be impressive, prepared as it is by a long, unperceived torpor.

*

What a waste that a literary generation so filled with gifts, so endowed with everything necessary to call itself savvy, so remarkably talented at freedom, Stendhalian mistrust, and even insolence, vying with each other in complete naïveté, should frolic in politics like Little Red Riding Hoods at Grandmother's house—at the very moment she is growing such big teeth!

*

In Solzhenitsyn, what is most striking is not the violent denunciation and rejection in books like the *Gulag Archipelago* and *The First Circle*: it is the almost vegetal growth of a book like *August 1914*, as natural as that of a tree freely sprouting branches and roots in every direction. As if nothing had seriously changed in the rocky soil where it had taken root since Tolstoy—as if sixty years of acculturation to a way of theorizing rather than to a way of feeling had come undone and fallen from this book like a grafted plant where the sap never rose.

*

In Tacitus, there is a beautiful subject for a sword-and-sandal in the manner of Flaubert: Caecina, a commander under Germanicus in the time of Tiberius, finds himself surrounded with his legions by Arminius in the wooded marsh of Long Bridges in Germany. In the middle of the night, Varus appears to him in a dream, covered in blood, emerging from the marsh, and holding out his hand, which he repels, terrified. The Romans, soaked, muddy, devastated, starving, having lost horses and supplies, miraculously escape the encirclement.

Everywhere in *The Annals* we can read between the lines that this border war in Germany, a war beset by bogs, forests, mud, swamps—formless, endless, impossible to win—must have ultimately created the same sort of wretched fatigue in Rome and among the legions as the *dirty war* of Indochina did in France and later in America. Dien Bien Phu, like Varus, was a constant menace and, worse still, the open rebellion of uncertain local "auxiliaries" and even former troops. Only the quarrels of the German tribes finally allowed them to reestablish the frontiers on the Rhine without catastrophe; it was never crossed again; the taboo was placed on the Teutons that ate legions, their unfathomable peat bogs, and their "horrible forests."

What deepens the perspective of a subject like this is that it is not only the tragic phantoms of a recent past reemerging in the guise of Varus: it is the end of Rome appearing to Caecina three centuries in advance. Its death would one day emerge from these marshlands. The forest would recover its silence, the Rhine its somnolent tranquility, at least for long intervals. But it is here, in these lairs impossible to scour, that the great barbarous riot accumulating would one day spring forth. And here we are again, in the familiar precincts of *Marble Cliffs*.

Before this episode, the Roman troops, who wanted to pay their last respects to Varus's army, retraced the steps of its extermination.

"[. . .] they visited the mournful scenes, with their horrible sights and associations. Varus's first camp with its wide circumference and the measurements of its central space clearly indicated the handiwork of three legions. Further on, the partially fallen rampart and the

shallow fosse suggested the inference that it was a shattered remnant of the army which had there taken up a
position. In the centre of the field were the whitening
bones of men, as they had fled, or stood their ground,
strewn everywhere or piled in heaps. Near, lay fragments
of weapons and limbs of horses, and also human heads,
prominently nailed to trunks of trees. In the adjacent
groves were the barbarous altars, on which they had im-
molated tribunes and first-rank centurions."[110]

Here we find the pestilent lighting that bathes the
Rouissage clearing in Jünger, with its dried garlands of
arms and heads, and behind, the lowered curtain of the
forest where the call of the cuckoo echoes mockingly.
Tacitus writes that Tiberius disapproved of Germanicus for this funereal pilgrimage, either out of malevo-
lence, "or because the spectacle of the slain and un-
buried made the army slow to fight and more afraid of
the enemy."[111] Perhaps for an army that revisits the ves-
tiges of an old disaster there is something worse than the
sight of the slain: the image of the *stampede* of the mor-
tally wounded, entrails spilled everywhere confusedly.
Worse than the image of its possible annihilation, which
it must have always imagined: that of the dissolution of
its constitutive link.

*

Joachim Fest: *Hitler*. The only truly expressive words
he quotes from the Führer (but they are!) were uttered in
1941 on the eve of the invasion of Russia: "I feel as if I am
pushing open the door to a dark room never seen before,
without knowing what lies behind the door."[112]

Reading these two compact volumes suddenly resuscitates the old nightmare so brutally that I cannot bring
myself to go to the theater this evening, as I had planned;
I have stayed at home, huddled in a corner, my mind lifeless and shivery, like wet laundry, my brain besieged by
the fluttering of ghosts and specters. I was twenty years
old when the shadow of the manchineel tree began to
spread around us: it was the year that Nazism exploded
and suddenly projected a hundred and ten deputies to
the Reichstag; the significance of the fact was immediately understood and evaluated—which is rare—and its
aura immediately perceptible to almost everyone. The
rise of the storm lasted nine years, a storm so intolerably
slow to burst, so heavy, so livid and so somber at once,
that minds went numb instinctively, and one sensed that
a cloud of apocalypse such as this could no longer resolve itself in hail but only in a rain of blood and toads.

Since we speak (rightly) of the influences that affect writers—they have written of mine as of others'—I offer this one; sometimes on this topic the only thing we do not see is what is right in front of our eyes. There is a potent and multiform poet in History, and most of the time a dark poet, who takes on a new face for the writer in every period but is not marked by a capital letter to alert the unmotivated critic: you must be able to detect him among and beyond so many active memories of reading, which at times may have lasted only one season.

Though less fascinated perhaps than Breton by Achim
von Arnim's *Contes bizarres*, I still enjoy rereading the
best one to my mind: *Les héritiers du majorat*.[113] Because the heady scent of a medieval Germany lingers
there, conserved almost intact in the middle of the eighteenth century, before crumbling suddenly into dust like
the body of Mr. Valdemar. With its outdated *grotesques*,
its feudal remnants, its necromancers, its Jews (not even
in Hoffmann do we find this *sui generis* scent of musty
centuries). But I am even more sensitive to the singularity of the fantastic around which the entire story is built:
an "interior scene, viewed from above, from a window"
that once kept me spellbound on my balcony on rue
Gay-Lussac. The barrier of the street, less symbolic than
footlights, less essentially magic as well, still confers on
the silent scenes that take place in an unknown apartment a fascinating familiarity, revealed by what it leaves
out (silent scenes onto which the heir of Majorat's audio
hallucinations in the story superimposes a sort of arti-

ficial and mechanical dubbing), and a very rare nuance of strangeness, in the sense that, instead of insidiously moving away from the normal, they seem to seek it rather desperately and try in vain to ape it. Watching the five or six inhabitants of the apartment across the way, through their curtainless windows, go from room to room, come together, separate incomprehensibly, or suddenly mime a ghostly, private conversation all alone, I often got the sense that the suppression of one of the constitutive manifestations of life (here, voice and sound) abandoned the human theater to a sort of pathetic drift against which its actors struggled, as one sometimes struggles in a dream, in the vain pursuit of lost rationality, suddenly infinitely more fragile than we imagined collectively. It is this oneiric disarray in quest of an intelligible order beyond reach (contaminated here, unfortunately, by the more traditional procedures of terror) that gives *Les héritiers du majorat* all its glacial pathos: I am made sensitive not to gradually moving away from the coordinated paths of the real, as in the traditional fantastic, but rather to the fact that having barely, accidentally, veered off the main road of normal life, it suddenly seems impossible to find it again.

*

Ideas and the novel: German literature seems to have more trouble than others making this amalgam work. The theoretical reflections of Thomas Mann, in *Tonio Kröger* as well as in *The Magic Mountain*, tear the fictional fabric and expand in the form of ungraceful ruptures—the formalist and demonstrative composition of *Elective Affinities* evokes *The Critique of Pure Reason* more than *The Charterhouse of Parma*. England generally proscribes such an alloy; in Dostoyevsky, a revolutionary reunification of a completely different kind can be sensed: it is the fictional apparatus as a whole that swings to the side of the adventure of ideas unleashed in a brain. The mixture of reflective thought and the imaginative pressure of the novel, a mixture as impossible, in the last analysis, as oil and water, is only displayed in all its variety, in all the subtlety of its problems and solutions, in the French novel. And of these solutions, more than in Balzac and in Flaubert, it is in Stendhal and in Proust that we find the most original.

*

One of the oddities that discourage me in Goethe's novels (with the exception of *Werther*, which I have read seven or eight times) is the abstract quality of the narrative fabric, which almost always treats the external world as a working drawing (one can read *Elective Affinities*, which takes place in the country, almost cover to cover without finding a single touch of color). There are scarcely any great writers worse than he is at the *true little details* of fiction. All the concreteness of occupations, gestures, attitudes melt, barely sketched, in a generalizing and decorative *sfumato*.

I understand that the same could be said of *La Princesse de Clèves* or *Adolphe*. Not entirely, though. In the French psychological novel, the initial convention is to put the material world between parentheses, purely and simply. That much is clear. But *Elective Affinities* comes after Rousseau and recalls him: Goethe's novel is closer to *La Nouvelle Héloïse*, where emotional entanglement is mixed up with domestic economy. All they do is plant, hoe, graft, build, and till, and the passions pitch in as well, as in a Fourierist phalanstery. From now on, I refuse to be left hanging, to be presented with farm hands frenetically fussing with pointillist occupations, and from one end of the book to the other, all I see wriggling in their test tubes—skillfully—are ideas in search of their embodiment. In *Wilhelm Meister*, there is a chapter entitled "Saint Joseph II," and this name seems to be symbolic for so many characters in Goethe's novels:

they lay claim to a carpenter's name, but they never do any carpentry.

Perhaps this deceptive blur that Goethe organizes around the detail of the novel is a defensive reflex against the curious awkwardness he brings to concrete invention, which always has something starchy about it. The lowliest writer of serials often has a lighter touch. Nothing is more absurd or parodic, in *Elective Affinities* (when Goethe takes the exceptional risk of specifying them) than the "fertile activities" (*sic*) to which Edouard and the Captain devote themselves in concert, without ceasing: for example, the charitable organization in the village, with its office giving alms at the entrance and exit, or their plans to develop nature, that make one think of Bouvard and Pécuchet as landscape gardeners.

*

Werther. The effectiveness of the book, like the charming naturalness maintained throughout, has a lot to do with the atmosphere of the *gemütlich* warmth of family Christmases, white balls, and four o'clock teas, where passion develops in an airtight chamber, so far away from anything that might resemble a fatal enchantment. There is barely an object of devotion here besides *the family's eldest daughter*, in whom all decency, gaiety, prudence, benevolence, and modest authority is distilled and concentrated so as to flourish in a gentle and naïve German bourgeois home (she has gotten her fiancé from her mother herself: thus Charlotte's house-shell closes again hermetically around her). The exclusivity of passion does not clash with the overly conventional bond of marriage, as in the classic triangles of romantic dramas, but with something that seems infinitely more entrenched and profound from birth: the tendrils, roots, suckers, and attachments by which the human plant, while growing, clings to its natural supports. It is not only the engagement to Albert that must be broken off for Werther to be fulfilled: it is a whole inextricable tuft of a social nature, that with Charlotte's abduction will find itself uprooted and torn so that none of these cut ties will ever bloom again. For what Werther is in love with is not an ideal and isolated female figure, it is Charlotte-in-the-home, well-lit, well-off, well-fed by the whole natural network of bonds of birth and habit. What drives him to despair is not that she is the elusive female in flight (Goethe takes good care to never show that), it is a fragment of undivided creation that cannot be isolated or appropriated: not the tyranny of social rules resistant to the demands of love, but simply the laws of nature. And this is how the barely concealed naturalist pantheism that creates the mood of the book gives wonderful resonance and depth to this bourgeois triviality in the countryside.

*

Writers and thinkers—Spengler remains the archetype for me—sometimes give the impression that the only ones who have read them are the ones who have pillaged from them, and that their virtue is made known above all in the increased vigor of everything that used them as pasture to graze in. There are vegetal species whose seed only germinates in the evacuations of frugivores that have eaten them.

*

The construction of Thomas Mann's *Tonio Kröger* reproduces that of *The Magic Mountain* in miniature: two segments where narrative life circulates, separated by an ideological stasis of serious dimensions (here, Kröger's monologue on art, there, the endless theoretical discussions of Settembrini and Naphta). There is a Germanic anomaly in the way a narrative is shaped that is no less striking in those of classic temperament like Thomas Mann than in romantics like Jean Paul. In the keen reader, as in the writer, beyond the ultra-sensitive ear that the short rhythms of verse and sentence constantly solicit, there exists a deeper, less vibrant and more dormant ear regulated solely on the cadences of great wavelengths that animate and structure the entire mass of a short story or account. And it's almost as though the gift of a naturally musical ear was compensated for in the Germans by the withdrawal of another: that of the novelistic ear. Even in Jünger, after the marvelous rhythmic precision obtained in *On the Marble Cliffs*, the narrative tempo is bogged down in the dense—but very rich— magma of *Heliopolis*.

*

The continuous decorative imprecision and bourgeois decency used to erase all the sharp angles and anything that might jut out too energetically ruins *Wilhelm Meister's Apprenticeship* for me. The book seems written at a distance from its subject, where distances blend into one another, and where a bluish vapor begins to cloud all the contours. Goethe's tendency to reduce names and all the raw individuality they contain to functions, trades, attributes, or one's order in the social hierarchy, is remarkable: "the old man," "the director," "the count," "the baroness," "the secretary," "the prince," "the inn-keeper," "the magistrate." Mignon, and to some extent Philine, are the only animated beings that break through the gangue in whose rigid crust social commerce has coated and stereotyped each of them, who truly deserve to be called *personages* of the novel—solemn, important, and stiff marionettes whose strings are pulled jerkily by their author, concealing none of their angularity.

O Pedagogue of the Germans! pedagogue that Richard Wagner wanted to be, in turn, three quarters of a century later; Germany's hopeless delay in assembling a territory and a culture cost its greatest artists dearly. Fortunately, for Wagner, the musician's all-powerful instinct was not induced under any circumstances to yield to its didactic outbursts. But nothing stops Goethe for a second—the Jack-of-all-work of German culture in gestation—on the scabrous path that goes from the ultra-sensitive artist of *Werther* to the ponderousness of the last *Meister*, by way of the cold refinement of *Elective Affinities*. A singular case of a genius, who was Napoleon's contemporary, though not a beneficiary as he was of the exceptional conjunction of possibility and immense territory to be occupied, but rather a victim: where the incomparable opportunity for individual expansion incites the conqueror and politician to draw the best, and almost the impossible, from his abilities, the artist, on the contrary, is most often struck with a ruinous insensitivity to his most irreplaceable gifts. It is rarely advantageous when a state of emergency calls a writer to be in two places at once.

*

I am distractedly continuing to read *Wilhelm Meister*, a flimsy novel so excessively decorous it seems to have come into the world already swaddled in the mists of propriety. Everything that is flawed in *Ofterdingen* comes from this book–manchineel tree, which enrages me, and that for decades has injected into the German narrative the Prudhommesque and parodic tone of the Lilliputian courts of the Holy Empire in its final decrepitude. Not to mention the stiff and indigestible legacy of the *bildungsroman* on account of which Flaubert himself suffered (but not Stendhal): one of those cream pies that had to wait for the movies of Mack Sennett in order to be put to good use.

What a beautiful work of literary fiction this would make: the young Goethe precociously afflicted with a chest ailment, and, instead of heading to the icebox of Weimar, going directly to Italy! And—*Werther* and *Goetz* guarantee it—the entire body of work of the Founding Father of German letters would suddenly be rid of its aftertaste of *cold veal in mayonnaise*.

*

In Wagner's attitude toward money there is something of God the Father redescending to earth *to pass the hat*, arguing for an extension to the sixth day. To pull money from pockets where it could be found, the way one taps a barrel, more and more money and ultimately enormous amounts of money, was the rampant form the curse of gold took in him. The taste for robes made of Chinese silk, then furniture and servants, then Venetian palaces, then dramatic "personalized" sanctuaries certainly has its own logic of progression, but one senses that it also has the hidden function of constantly winding up the clock (so Balzacian), of forging ahead, the crazy race that both unleashes mobs of creditors and keeps them at bay. The magical appearance of a king out of a fairy tale does nothing but raise the stakes brutally: money's wounds were not deadly, no doubt because they had every reason in the world to die only with you.

Certainly, nothing in this life is clear, far from it. But the harshest criticisms made against him are the least well established. His musical anti-Semitism, born so long before the Dreyfus affair, was of scarcely any consequence at the time: around 1925, there were composers railing against "negro" music who nevertheless were never banned from the opera. Wagner never separated himself from a collaborator or a friend because he was Jewish: the stubborn choice of Levi to conduct his musical testament, *Parsifal*, a choice maintained in spite of pressures and anonymous letters accusing the conductor of sleeping with Cosima, is rather noble.[114] His guilt *by association* with Hitler, a fan of his work, does not hold up under scrutiny. He was the first to point out, rather imperiously, that genius had the right to formulate certain material demands: who would complain about that? And to raise to unheard-of rates the amount of the demands of glory: infinitely less, in any case, than Picasso.

*

Stuffed with oddities, the *Second Faust* had to incorporate many sublime verses to satisfy a German ear at that point. So what! Filled with life force, misshapen, a bit monstrous, it grows on terrain where it settles alone, where all rivalry moves away from it: not a giant rising up in the middle of a cluster of trees, but rather a baobab isolated on the steppe. Thus those plants do (the flax plant is one), whose root secretes a toxin expelling from the soil the congeneric organisms that fattened them up. Unclassifiable masterpieces that grow to deprive us of any element of comparison, just as they left for adventure without any model. The voice of other great works reverberates over them, in an echo, because they associate with works that are akin; that is when their cry is *reiterated by a thousand sentinels*.[115] But the self-centered voyage of discovery destroys his landmarks behind him and straightens out his broken branches. Paths of literature and poetry, walled off soon after their inauguration, clear-cut forests that no fallow land can repair, where even the grass does not grow back: before *Faust*, *The Divine Comedy*.

The share of inactive, insignificant, neutral filler (the q.s. of distilled water in pharmaceutical preparations)[116] is generally never as great in a painting, a poem, even in a novel, as it is in the cinema, where it reaches its maximum. In the most rigorously composed, most purely significant and pared-down image, the camera's rectangular frame still takes in a swarm of objects—the set designer's bric-a-brac, landscaping details, sparkling waters, cast shadows, clouds, the movements of leaves —which are extra, which are just *there*, and which the sensitive roll of film captures in a state of total non-participation, like Piero della Francesca's supremely unconcerned characters turning their backs on the main scene (color and the recent taste for natural sets considerably increase this lion's share in film, sampled by pure contingency, which seems reduced in a film by Dreyer or Murnau; in this sense, German expressionism with its vigorously simplified and stylized sets—I am thinking, for example, of *The Cabinet of Dr. Caligari*—represents a hopeless but interesting attempt to regain aesthetic premeditation over blind seizure, the blind man's bluff of a snapshot left to chance).

A character in a film is caught in the gelatin of the roll of film like an insect in its piece of amber, suspended pell-mell with leaves, grains of sand, flower petals, fragments of bark. In the constant collision between the ordered line of dramatic action and the inert, incoherent element of raw nature that a film is, nature—fragmented, marginal, and *environmental*—either finds itself reduced to the state of a mediocre foil, to out-of-tune musical accompaniment, or else, on the contrary, to depersonalized heroes camouflaged in greenery and fallen branches, advancing like the forest at Dunsinane.[117]

This is not a matter of arguing—ridiculously—against the cinema in which I have taken and continue to take such great pleasure. The corrections of reading, an instinctive elision, the eye's habit of automatically rejoining the various components of a heterogeneous image into a single unit, come to mask the fundamental contradiction of film—as art—which is to set in motion a predetermined human action (more rigidly than any other art) in an objective environment and against a natural background which are neither; or, if you prefer, to juxtapose constantly and to entangle in each image two sequences with no affinities between them: that of natural contingency and that of the cohesion implied by art. Film, which is movement, mixes these two sequences, as difficult to combine as oil and water, and in an unstable way keeps them united in a state of emulsion. But this union is never a unity, and from time to time, even in the most successful films, it is ruptured for a few moments, each time an image reaches a remarked and remarkable summit, which signifies not so much a successful shoot as the cameraman's ephemeral victory over the director. Because for an instant the current of the narrative is fixed (in a novel, images can never, *ever* be fixed on the retina, least of all in descriptive passages), and it is the singularity of the world, suddenly captured, that emerges foreign and all-powerful, interjecting a pause in the dynamic of the narrative, a break that is less brutally dissonant but just as inharmonious as the famous pistol shot at a concert.[118]

*

In one of his books, Malraux wonders if a culture might one day exist that is based on the film archive, the way traditional culture has been on the library. The answer to this question probably depends on a single problem: can—could—one's memory of a film blend naturally as commentary, stimulant, or counterpoint into our "inner lives," our reveries, our fantasies, our private theater, in the infinitely supple form of allusion, excerpt, or *compression*? The deep affinity one has for a film is translated by the need to see it again, but that which one has for a book is not linked, or only episodically, to the need to read it again. With a great book much more than a great film, the part (even a small part) evokes the whole, and the whole is present in the part, as far as affective memory. For style in writing is a voice, while style in film is a certain personal constant in the conception and then assemblage (there is no single element in this art, whether visual, auditory, or rhythmic, that the filmmaker is master of *to the first degree*, the way the writer is master of his words, or the musician master of his notes).

Every film, however magnificent, thus retains the character of a manufactured object at the end of its chain of production, to take or leave as a whole; not soluble in memory or reverie, defined by the clear and isolating contour of its peremptory images and its rigid framing, it is—if I dare use this expression—*non-psychodegradable*, a "unit" that can certainly be enclosed in the memory but that does not dissolve, or penetrate, or sow seed there. Can there be a culture where there is only a kaleidoscope of memory, and not the active work of the mind upon the object that required it—active work, which is to say, digestion, assimilation, and, ultimately, incorporation?

*

The cinematic transcription of a novel brutally imposes on the reader, and even on the author, the largely arbitrary incarnations it has chosen for each of the characters; only with time will the text eliminate the too-specific faces that the film superimposes on it and that are not of its substance. How fragile the defenses are that the written fiction sets up against these substituted images that violate it—and how their resistance, in order to organize, must first, very broadly, give way! The rights of the cinematic image in relation to the literary text are a bit like those that the present, which "will not be robbed of its daemonic right," exerts in life at the expense of the at once vague and tenacious intangibles that are anticipation, regret, and memory.[119] Then, once the film has taken its leave, the multitude of words gradually comes, antlike, to eat away at and digest the peremptory and perishable images that offended it. I remember once seeing *The Red and the Black* and *The Charterhouse of Parma* at the movie theater. Gérard Philipe acted in both adaptations, and for several weeks, in spite of myself, in spite of Stendhal's genius and the films' mediocrity, his image came to superimpose itself on the text, unexpellable. Then, little by little, a separation occurred; from time to time, I will still distractedly conjure Gérard Philipe "in *The Charterhouse*," but I only see him now as a dismounted jockey, before the scales, symbolically and a bit ridiculously holding his stirrups and saddle in his hands. The book shook him off, and, unburdened, galloped far away.

*

When we compare a film based on a novel to the novel itself, the quasi-infinite sum of instant data that the image delivers, in contrast to the parsimony, the poverty itself, of the notations of the corresponding sentence in the novel, allows us to see how closely fiction's effectiveness parallels the methods of acupuncture. Indeed, the novelist is not meant to instantly saturate perception, as the image does, and thereby obtain a state of fascinated passiveness in the viewer, but only to pinpoint a few nerve centers capable of irradiating and energizing all the stagnant intermediary zones.

*

The transposition of a novel to the screen, when it is exceptionally, meticulously faithful, might one day be one of literary criticism's sharpest scalpels for its dissection, almost on a par with the X ray of a painter's canvases for painting. All the effects that I would call "exaggeration by omission," so frequent in the novel (for example, the text's focused attention on one or two protagonists in a scene of multiple characters) are brought out, by contrast, with microscopic magnification. Because the camera, too, centers the viewer's attention and circumscribes it like a circle of light from a lamp, but within this circle, or rather this rectangle, it elides nothing, while, at the writer's whim, the pen casts one of those pointed spots of concentrated light that product demonstrators use to underscore a significant detail or feature of an image on a screen.

On another level, transposition to the screen may allow a tighter grasp on the multiform role that description plays in a novel. There is a straightforward candor in the photographic image (it does not *erase* anything) that proscribes—and thereby betrays—one of fiction's craftiest descriptive processes, which is the allusive or revelatory detail slipped furtively into description like a trick card by a conjurer's hand. If you film *The Fall of the House of Usher*, the fissure streaking the edifice from top to bottom will be displayed as innocently on the screen as a nose on a face, while Poe's pen casually lets it zigzag along, trailing at the end of the sentence: it is no longer an observation of decrepitude, it is a parting shot, a stinging nettle embedded in the mind.

All the signs that appear in an image speak directly and clearly, arranged as they are on the same level at the outset; by contrast, they reveal all the more clearly in the language of the novelist not only the use of various keys, as in musical language, but also a constant chromaticism, as well as the sharps, flats, and naturals for each separate sign that syntax distributes at will. There is a musicality of the text—the visual art that cinema is proves this by default—but it does not consist of a struggle with the wealth and incomparable plenitude of the art of sounds and timbres; rather it exists in a latent state in its aptitude for complex harmonies among various levels of writing that, though successive instead of simultaneous, are nevertheless layered on top of one another, like a sonic construction.

It is the nonexistence of formal simultaneousness in the text, where everything is successive, that usually discourages a comparison of this sort between music and writing; but that is to sell short a remarkable property of the written word. The possibility of literature, and of poetry and fiction in particular, rests on a persistence in the mind of the images and impressions set in motion by words, a persistence infinitely superior in duration to that of luminous impressions on the retina, or sonic impressions on the eardrum. At times I have dreamt of a machine that could measure the persistence of a strong image *hitting its stride* in a reader's mind: it would no doubt reveal that the reader kept some of them "stored in the cellars of his mind, where they could improve" until the end.[120]

In the novel reader's mind, a whole stratification of memory is created while reading, a process perhaps like folding linear sequences of material in layers, like a piece of fabric. Even the voices and gestures of two interlocutors in dialogue, so naturally inseparable on screen, are the object of a reassemblage in reading, a synchronization *a posteriori* that is a complex operation of the mind, and that moreover, unlike what passes for description here, makes the novel yield to film in all matters of dramatic efficiency.

When I see a story unfold on screen that I know first from reading, what is clearest to me is that the images, unlike those born of words and sentences, are never given coefficients of value or intensity: centered and circumscribed by the screen so that the rays of light they emit strike the eye perpendicularly, the rule that presides over their sensory distribution is strictly egalitarian. To grasp this singularity, just imagine a cinema where, alongside a scene unfolding right in the optical field, other scenes or landscapes, related or different, would be vaguely and simultaneously perceived, in secret or in lost profile, from the corner of the eye—now anticipating the future, now revisiting the past, and always qualifying, coloring, contesting, neutralizing, or reinforcing the scenes being played out on the main screen. This domain of margins distractedly but effectively perceived, this domain of *the corner of the eye*—in order to compensate for other inferiorities, such as less direct dramatic efficiency, less of a sense of the present, the elastic vagueness proper to images born of literature—accounts for almost all the superiority of written fiction. The screen knows neither the *plus* sign nor the *minus* sign; it only uses the *elsewhere* sign, awkwardly, through abrupt ruptures in camera angles, and is less skilled than literature at weighting the images it unfolds with the sign of *infinity*.

*

When I reread *Les Chouans*, aside from the many other glories that reemerge intact from this reading, I am more sensitive than ever to the absolutely singular panoramic quality that distinguishes the book. While reading it, one frequently gets the impression that one is observing an entire district, with its towns and its network of roads, vertically, from the heights of one of those helicopters that survey traffic flow on Sundays. The whole first part unfolds like an aerial, spacious traveling shot where, in perpetual motion, one goes from Couësnon's washbasin, over the ridge of La Pèlerine, to another compartment of vast and isolated terrain where—the visual field coupled with a particularly expressive sonorous reverse shot—the ancient coach announces itself down the road, in the distance, coming from Ernée, while the drums of the national guard returning to Fougères resonate behind La Pèlerine. Often, the overhanging point of view where Balzac almost always positions himself allows him to seize and bring to life in their simultaneity the coordinated or thwarted movements that make up the ebb and flow of the war of the hedges, and to animate this corner of the Bocage as intensely as the vicinities of an ant hill. The panoptical singularity of the open air scenes offers almost no exceptions: whether it is the road from Fougères to Ernée of the beginning, which seems to be observed from the height of a captive balloon anchored to the summit of La Pèlerine, the assault of Fougères surveyed by Marie de Verneuil from the top of the cliffs of Saint-Sulpice, or the final episode, not only totally surrounded by the author's circular gaze, but observed from top to bottom and from bottom to top (once again, the high-angle shot and the low-angle shot!), almost everything in the book announces a prescience, and an efficient literary use, of the mechanical ubiquity of points of view that will be one of the contributions of cinema alone. Landscapes contemplated from a high place are, as we know, one of Stendhal's obsessions, but with him it is only a matter of motionless observatories: as for the aerial-panoramic traveling shot, Balzac must be credited with inventing it, in *Les Chouans*.

*

Everything is blocked, completely inhibited, in terms of my mechanisms of acceptance and assimilation, my mental and emotional self-regulation, when I see a film: my passiveness as a consumer reaches its maximum. I cannot be spared either the tiniest detail of the most fleeting image or some shortcut, even if it is a few seconds, in the rhythm according to which the film is administered to me. In order to measure the total refusal of collaboration I feel when I enter a dark theater, one would have to imagine a piece of music that could only be heard in a single recording (and music is by far the art where the listener's required passiveness reaches its apex). This freedom, so essential in bringing to life the art lover's relationship to the work of art: the freedom to choose, then to vary at will the angle of attack of a work based on a sensibility, the seventh art, the last to arrive, lets nothing survive. All the delicately active and adjustable apparatuses through which I am used to apprehending the external world, film authoritatively positions in a fixed point, immobilizing my eye and the pavilion of my ear alike, blocking me in my seat: the viewer in a dark theater is a man amputated from all his physical and mental mechanisms of accommodation. In cinema's intimation to its followers—*Stare at the screen, we'll take care of the rest*—there is an excess of disdainful and alienating kindness that comes to meet the user four-fifths of the way.

Of all works of art, a film is the one that gives the least free play to the talent of its consumers (the principal difference it tolerates among them is the relative ease of reading brought to its elliptical writing—a purely mechanical ability, born of habit, like reading stenography).

A great novel or poem, like an alpine pass in a cycling race, narrows the pack of its audience to start with (but eventually latecomers catch up), while a film assembles its audience from the start (only to slim it down a little). The phenomenon of the audience's gradual access to the masterpiece, over time, which is standard in literature, hardly applies in the cinema: for it, neither paperbacks nor hardcover libraries of classics: the years that pass bring no new points of view, bring no unperceived potential to light; they just make it unfashionable; what a film archive resembles most is certainly a library, on the one hand, but also a car museum. In such a museum, one admires wonderful models here and there whose shapes and technical advancements at times even seem able to stride over the years and predict the future, but the admiration we accord them remains bound to chronology: what comes next, even if it is less successful, formally demotes them; settling in behind the wheel is a kind of travesty and parody: everything about them aggressively resuscitates their era, different from our own and forever dated, whereas the reader of a good novel erases these anachronisms automatically in reading it. In 1977, one can certainly admire *The Battleship Potemkin*, *Nosferatu*, or *The Street of Sorrow* (and oh how I admire them!) —yet no one can deny that the charm—potent—that they dispense has something of a little world from another time with its old-fashioned dresses. No one can

claim to have the same access to them today that is accorded us each time we reopen one of the great novels of
the last century. And that we also find in an art museum
before a primitive.

*

The literary massif of the nineteenth century, as its
panorama is disclosed in 1978, with its three snowy summits, Balzac—Stendhal—Flaubert, and, a bit lower in al-
titude, the Zola peak, did not have exactly the same
configuration when I was a student (Stendhal only took
his place there for the trained eye and Daudet was barely
discernible). It is not impossible, far from impossible,
that it will change markedly in appearance again in the
twenty years to come. The establishment today of Tolkien, as well as Simenon, in the tableau of contemporary
literature, achieved by suddenly broadening the limits of
the "noble" novel, would retroactively bring the promotion of Dumas in the nineteenth century as it brought
that of Jules Verne (though almost as unthinkable in its
own way, thirty years ago, as Sade's reintegration into
eighteenth-century literature in the last century). This
sudden and massive promotion in literature of all the
variants of its marginality is one of the new aspects of the
contemporary critical eye: the equalizing power of the

cinema, which borrows its scripts haphazardly from either category with equal results, has played more than a minor role in this. The popular novel that finds its way into film or television does not exactly earn its letters of nobility, of course; but it does acquire the sort of promotion that occasionally warrants equal relationships with *the upper crust*. With the screen, a terrain now exists where, in an unexpected uniform, genres that never *spoke* to each other address each other casually, and literature has been profoundly changed as a result, just as society found itself to be the day compulsory service sent all the French to the barracks.

For adaptation to the screen always does a disservice to great books, but pure ingenuity in a novel, not supported in the written work by a style and an original vision of the world, sometimes acquires a decisive vigor in its transposition into images, that regenerates the reading of it after the fact: more than once, the good fairy of the camera, simply by getting rid of the writing, has led Cinderella to the ball. And the cinema, which devours books without sifting through them, somewhat changes our approach to written fiction, no matter what we might say, through its indiscriminate bulimia: the effectiveness of a durable structure that loses nothing by slipping from the world of words to that of images, on the contrary, shortens the time in purgatory to which literary taste condemned *The Three Musketeers* and gives new glamour to somewhat plain but *solidly built* works that can change elements without ceasing to function. In our era, when every artistic concept is solicited by a double, triple, and perhaps someday soon even quadruple incarnation (Mme Marguerite Duras has currently derived a novel, a play, and a film from a single subject), I sometimes think I can see a time coming when a decisive *plus* will be attached to migrant works, to those that a single form of expression will no longer suffice to contain. *El Burlador de Sevilla*, the initial model for *Don Juan*, conceived in the time of film, would have preserved for Tirso de Molina the eminent paternity of which he was wholly stripped by Molière and Mozart. In classic literature, there is an excessive plundering of the inventor by the accomplished artist who sets himself up as his usufructuary: in the time of the seventh art, this plundering is no longer allowed.

SURREALISM

Dream and memory. The volatile nature of dreams
makes them like electricity: no sooner are they produced
than consumed; their life expectancy on waking barely
exceeds the image of an incandescent wire on the retina
when the lights have been switched off. If a true oneiric
memory existed, it would have a major function in our
life; it would focus attention on the emotions, establish
the dominant tone on waking from day to day, like an all-
powerful musical key. But this memory does not exist
except as the blackened carcass of a spent firework;
dream narratives, which early surrealism made much
use of, and an estimable compendium of which Marguerite Yourcenar once offered in *Dreams and Destinies*,[121] describe from the outside a chain of *conductors*
that the current no longer passes through, its voltage
fantastically unstable. Surrealism was only able to take
dreams as guides because, without saying so, it always
considered memory highly suspect: an obstacle to the
total availability of being, which it wanted to open wide
at all times; from moment to moment, everything had to
be burned, even the furniture, *especially the furniture.*

*

History-and-Geography: early on, in high school, this pair was linked for me almost as solidly as time and space (sometimes a simple, ready-made alliance of words, stereotypical to the point of becoming invisible, tells you something about yourself). They were, to me, the true moving content of time and space, the only content that prepared me to dream, endlessly. Freed from any true chronology and any orthodox geographic morphology, their purified *continuum*, reduced to its pure dramatic lineaments, served as a substratum to *The Opposing Shore*, just as it imprisoned "La Route." Aside from the many ways of feeling we share in common, the demand for true "a priori forms of sensibility" distanced me completely from the world of Breton, for whom Earth was a Noah's ark teeming with natural wonders, for whom history "fell outside like snow."[122] The Earth and History mattered little to Breton, Gide, Valéry, or Proust—to say nothing of Claudel, who only acknowledged the unwrinkled planet of Genesis and politics derived from Holy Scripture! Only with Malraux, whom I don't even really like that much, can one find oneself on solid ground on this topic.

*

What was vibrant—to use his vocabulary—about Breton's refusals, came, I often got the sense, from the fact that they were often based on a secret complaisance, not entirely abolished, toward what he refused, or, rather, refused himself. More than Valéry, his opposite, so disdainfully estranged from what he rejected, he had a wealth (like most good governments in combat) of useful, secret intelligence with the enemy.

*

At André Breton's house. The two rooms, separated by a short staircase, always seemed dark to me, even on sunny days and in spite of the studio's high windows. The overall tone, dark green and chocolate brown, was that of a very old provincial museum—more than a collector's treasure-trove, the jumble of angular, light, impossible to dust objects—masks, tikis, indigenous dolls made of feathers, cork, and wisps of straw—with its glass cabinets enclosing a collection of tropical birds in semi-darkness, at first glance recall both a naturalist's study and a disorderly storage room in an ethnographic museum. The profusion of art objects crammed against the walls gradually limited the available space; you could only walk around using specific paths established by habit, while avoiding the branches, vines, and thorns of

forest footpath along the way. Only certain rooms of the
Museum, or even the ageless premises that housed the
Geography department at the old university in Caen,
have given me this impression of a rainy and invariable
day, of light seemingly aged by the piles and dateless an-
cientness of wild objects.

Nothing has changed here since his death: ten years
already! When I came to see him, I came in through the
door on the other landing that led into the high room.
He would sit down, a pipe in his mouth, behind the
heavy, counter-shaped table already overflowing with a
hodgepodge of objects—to his right, on the wall, De
Chirico's *Child's Brain*—barely alive himself, scarcely
mobile, almost woody, with the large, heavy, lifeless eyes
of a tired lion, in dim light seemingly darkened by winter's fallen branches—an ancient and almost ageless
figure, seated before his gold-plated, money-changer's
table that seemed to call around it the heavy, fur-lined
coats filling the half-light of Rembrandt's paintings, or
the judge's robe of Doctor Faust: a Doctor Faust still listening in fascination for the sound of youth, but only until the pact—impossible—and retiring every evening to
his paintings, books, and pipe, after *coffee*, in the magic
capharnaum[123] which was his true element, in the middle of the accumulated and motionless sediment of his

entire life. For everything in this *interior*—and a single
visit suggested the word in its fullest sense—of this fa-
natic of the new spoke of immobility, accumulation, fine
layers of dust, and the maniacal and immutable arrange-
ments that a maid would be reluctant to disturb. At
times, out of curiosity, I have tried to imagine Breton at
home, in the evening, in the morning, Breton alone—the
lamp lit, the door closed, the curtain drawn on the theater of *my friends and me* (but Elisa Breton, the only one
who could do so, never lifted that veil). Many reasons allow me to believe (most recently, a little notebook con-
taining drawings, self-portraits, whimsical letters, sentences jotted down on waking) that it was at these
supposed hours of solitary work that he preferred to
welcome life's charming nothings—doodling, musing,
gathering nectar in the copse of his museum, and always
ready to delay in sovereign fashion the unsavory moment of writing. This taste he had for immediate life
down to its slenderest gifts, down to its crumbs—a taste
always new and renewed, always dazzled, even in old
age—is what brought him closest to me; nothing was
more likely than this inexhaustible attention to *the daily
pleasures* to truly make friendship with him flower at any
moment. I think of the ferocious and arid concoctions of
those who came after him, ridiculously occupied with

refashioning on concepts—as one buys on spec—a world already drained of its sap and that they already began to desiccate, thereby summoning Nietzsche's words: "The desert grows: woe unto him that harbors deserts in himself!"[124] It is when the luxuriance of life is diminished that emboldened planners and technicians with sketches poke their heads in; after that, the moment comes when all that is left is to diminish life even more, in order to free up the planning of it. There was a refuge here against all the world's mechanicalism.

*

The violent antinomy between the nature of Breton's intellectual and literary means and the content of his aesthetic is often what makes the power of his books. In Péret, where the *surrealist voice* does not collide with any established structure, and seems to speak in its native tongue, this voice does not focus one's attention, but Breton's preaching, paradoxically, has this supplement of imperious and almost anxious vigor that is usually added to the voice of the converted. In his intransigence, his excessiveness, in the fulminating rigidity of his orthodoxy, he often comes across as the Saint Paul of surrealism rather than its founder. And he never lets you forget that, in life, there is the fundamental caesura of a

Before and After—an "old man" to be conjured, always reappearing, always present in his readings, tastes, friendships. His way of being, so ostensibly of a piece, had to do with a supercilious and constantly renewed reconquest: "If, from a system in which I believe, to which I slowly adapt myself, like Surrealism, there remains [. . .] enough for me to immerse myself in, there will nonetheless never be enough to make me what I would like to be. . . ."[125]

*

Past the period of the revelation and enthusiasm of its beginnings, surrealism was ineluctably destined to blend in with preexisting ways of feeling, ways of living, and ways of writing, because its initial stakes were entirely placed on exceptionally rare conjunctions, almost as slow to reproduce themselves as the conjunctions of stars, and which it could not ultimately claim to read in the book of life in the faint glow of a flash of lightning (the singular merit of *Nadja* is to almost convince you, through the potent charm of the writing, that such conjunctions could be rather frequent and form the fabric of a life). But blending in was what Breton could not accept, could never accept. In wanting to establish surrealism as an autonomous and closed way of living, the problem was making a lifestyle work full time that in the last analysis relied only on miracles, intermittent by definition. Hence, with the passage of time, everything in the surrealism of the group, depending on whether one is well disposed to it or not, appears to us either as ingenious substitutes or makeshift activities: games, surveys, scandals, varied experiences, punitive expeditions, addresses, leaflets, exquisite corpses, etc. In this sense, the entrance of "the Revolution" around 1925 into surrealist life seemed inevitable after the fact: in a stable way, and in the interval of miracles, it alone could sustain the temperature of exaltation and the illusion, with which Breton lulled himself for a long time, that it was of the same nature, and perhaps the same, as that provoked by the lights of the surrealist Grail, when they were revealed. In fact, surrealism was never placed in the service of the Revolution (here, the Communist party was not mistaken); it was the reverse: the political Revolution remained a substitute for the days *without*, for the weekdays, and deep down it would always remain perfectly clear to Breton that it would never be able to encroach on the true Sundays of life.

LANGUAGE

I sometimes get the sense that, if the French language continues to evolve in a natural way (which I think is unlikely because of the ever-increasing Anglo-Saxon contamination), it would tend vocally to be *r-ified*. The *r* is its most original consonant, and, perhaps, of all its register, the sound secretly preferred by its users. No other letter gives the uttered sentence more solid emphasis and support—no other consolidates the articulation of French better: the desire comes to us instinctively from using it. I am often struck by Claudel's preferred use of it, for example, in the sorting of his vocabulary ("Et le fleuve ... n'arrose pas une contrée moins déserte que lorsque l'homme, ayant perforé une corne de bœuf, fit retentir pour la première fois son cri rude et amer dans les campagnes sans écho"—*Connaissance de l'Est*).[126] I get more pleasure saying *tartre* than *tarte*, *martre* than Marthe. And Père Ubu—great expert on the spontaneous distortion of language—would not contradict me.

*

When I write, I have always had a tendency to use the elastic construction of the Latin sentence, only concerned in a very cavalier way, for example, with the proximity of the relative pronoun and the substantive to which it refers. And scarcely more concerned with the identity papers demanded of the personal pronoun *he* or *she*, in the strictly grammatical sense. It is the free movement of the sentence that guides me, and not the solid sutures of French syntax, which always require both edges to be closely joined before they can be sewn together. The purist has the right to grimace, but the reader seems to manage to find his way around. For some, the genius of our language is to button up its sentences and track down the amphibology above all as *carelessness*. But what if my natural inclination is to give each proposition, each member of the sentence, the maximum autonomy, as the increasing use of dashes suggests to me, suspending syntactical constriction and forcing the sentence to stop pulling at the reins for a moment? Proust has done a lot for us here, by working toward a *continuum* of prose, rid of the obsession with sutures, more soluble in the mind, where the difference in value and even in meaning between punctuation signs tends to diminish. But his marvelous crochet work—each stitch linked fluidly not only to the preceding and following, in the order of fabrication, but also transversally, above and below it, to the entire texture of the fabric as a whole—also detracts from the dramatic temporality, the flow of no return of the prose, which gradually casts the *just said* into inert solidification, and approaches all things with the decisive point of his homing device.

*

Language: an antediluvian vehicle, especially in its abstract vocables, never completely overhauled, simply patched through the ages with odds and ends, filled with imported spare parts that do not quite fit its overall structure. Because of the antiquity of its usage, the enormous—irreplaceable—artistic potential of the multiple internal connections and delicate anastomoses of nerves, awakened at the slightest, somewhat sensitive touch, make it a fundamentally vibrant texture, a harmonic instrument: a knowledge of its handling, produced after long use, an inveterate passion, and an instinct alert to its hidden automaticisms, its *hushed-up liaisons*, has more than a thing or two to do with the slow and patient erotic science, the slow and patient medical science of China. I was not really concerned with its theoretical questions, contrary to almost all the beautiful airs of today's literature, not that I believe in the slightest in the validity of its fine-tuning of the real, but for the pragmatic reason that this is a "problem" that promises no "solution" of any consequence to the user that I am. Why give flight to yet another metaphysical crane? There is no conceivable means of communication other than the language that is given me—except perhaps, one day, through the slow erosion, upheaval, and sedimentation of time—that does not increase the mental cacophony and at the same time deprive itself (like Esperanto) of the whimsicality and richness of its harmonics for lack of long-term use: I make do with what I have.

*

What controls the effectiveness of a writer's use of words is not the capacity to clasp the meaning tightly, it is an almost tactile knowledge of the layout of their property lines, and, even more, their litigations over common ownership. For the writer, almost everything in the word is a border, and almost nothing is contained.

*

I have never forgotten my first French class, when I started rhetoric. Our professor, whose name was Legras —tall and skinny as a vine, enamored of poetry, as one said at the time, and skilled at getting it across—gave us a sentence of La Bruyère's to husk for a good half an hour, to cut our teeth on, and that remains in my memory: "A mesure que la faveur et les grands biens se retirent d'un homme, ils laissent voir en lui le ridicule qu'ils couvraient, et qui y était sans que personne s'en aperçût."[127] We gnawed on it like puppies without laying bare the underlying image of a tide, successively concealing and revealing, lying in wait like a riddle hunter in the foliage of words. From what was then a small revelation, I was left with a sense and taste for the latent image, which a single dynamic indication (As . . .) sets in motion, with nothing, however small, coming to specify or define it. Benjamin Constant's style is full of these images, both visible and invisible, depending on the angle of reading, that communicate to prose what moiré gives to a fabric: a more economical sense of movement.

*

Of all punctuation signs, one is not exactly like the others: the *colon*. Neither wholly punctuation nor wholly conjunction, it has long posed a problem for me in writing. All the other signs, more or less, mark breaks in the rhythm or inflections in tone of voice; there is no sign except the colon that reading aloud cannot render acceptably. But in the colon another function lies in wait, an active function of elimination; it marks the place of a mini-breakdown in speech, a breakdown where a superfluous conjunction has disappeared life and limb in order to assure the two members of the sentence that it connected a more dynamic, seemingly electric contact: in the use of the colon there is always the trace of a small short-circuit. It also marks the beginning, within the connected discourses, of the transgression of the telegraphic style; a statistical study would no doubt reveal the scant use ancient writers made of it (how far back does it go, anyway?) as well as its growing frequency in modern texts. Any impatient style preoccupied with swiftness, any style that tends to explode intermediary links, is especially attached to it, as to a carburetor, peremptory and expeditious.

"I shudder at the thought that, later on, some Taine will judge our society according to the plays of Bernstein and Bataille, according to the Malvy and Steinheil trials, etc." (Gide: *Journal*).[128] Of course not! They will judge it according to Gide, Proust, and Valéry and the merciful principle *De mortuis nil nisi bonum*. And even if they think ill of them, the fact remains that the slightest mediocrity is removed from every era that has become historic, like wine that is allowed to rest—the fact remains that a strange transparency, the color of drunkenness or color of poison, is established in every period whose only lighting is that of memory. If only by the automatic elision of everything trivial in an era: the everyday, monotonous elements that paint life gray. All this erosion of the interstitial and conjunctive matter that makes Time the poet of events.

*

The retrospective glance a writer casts over his books has little value: their content, too ruminated over in the course of preparation, no longer means anything; what is sharpened, on the contrary, in an exaggerated way over the years, is a sensitivity to the mutations of form ("I would not write like that today"). All the signs of maturity, or aging, that a simple interval of a few years brings, are perceived and registered with a subtlety on alert.

The reader, however, has the opposite tendency to bring back the successive parts of the work under a uniform and timeless light; he prefers the repeated observation of sameness, yielding delightedly to the unifying tyranny of the signature ("this is definitely *his!*"). The writer before his books is sensitive above all to his evolution, the reader to his constants. An author is always naïvely surprised, it seems to me, when he observes how easily a reader without particular critical experience can detect him behind a fragment of a few lines taken randomly from his books. He did not realize how much he resembled himself, since his own books were never really able to hold out a mirror to him. If he opens them again, he sees only what is clouded, scratched, or chipped in them, not what they reflect that is lasting and shapely.

*

Malraux's mythomania chills me, less because it is mythomania than because it is calculated gravity, and sometimes profitable speculation, because it has written other checks besides literary checks: think of the incredible Chinese bluff, which even Trotsky was taken in by, and that allows him to deal with Russia as an equal (in Chateaubriand, even when he recounts his fake visit to Washington, his mythomania always remains good-natured, a wink to the reader, but alas! when Malraux spins his yarns, he rarely seems to enjoy himself).

Reacting against my own irritation, I accuse myself of biographical pettiness and tell myself that, all in all, Malraux only fleshed out his life with *addenda* to which it seemed entitled, that expanded it organically, and of which it had been pruned by the too narrow confines of individual existence in the twentieth century. The Orient fascinated him, as it fascinated Napoleon, not because Europe had become a molehill, but because Asia remained the continent where, contrary to our archival civilization, history became legend when the event was scarcely completed (always Alexander! how captivated he was by Bucephalus's tomb and the bronze cavalries turning green on the Turanian steppes! how bizarre that he could mold his life's project for a moment on abstract Marxist schemas, when it was more like the Macedonian's before Achilles's tomb!). Why didn't personal history become a legend itself before ending (distance in space replacing stepping back in time)? The soft focus of the core of *Antimemoirs* marks the formal rejection at the end of his life of registry offices and reference numbers, a more systematic rejection than in *Mémoires d'outre-tombe*, in which Chateaubriand only retouches the details of his biography, while Malraux in his writings boldly treats his entire life like an inflatable structure, capable of indefinite expansion, but always according to its hallmark form. Why reproach him, after all, for having introduced, successfully overall, a bit of play, freer play, between existence as it is privately lived—that is, half-led, half-dreamed—and the trivial *curriculum vitae* that corresponds to him in official documents and police records? He protests in his own way, which is not illegitimate, against a reduction of man— corseted in a stifling armature of objective data—which the twentieth century makes unbearable for all those who live by the imagination. There was a time, not so long ago, when man's representation of his life floated chronologically in an indeterminate realm between the date of his birth and that of his death, and was bound spatially only by the elastic and displaceable limits of eclipsed memories and individual fantasies. It was less difficult, then, to satisfy Rimbaud's words—and we made his word law without concern for ourselves: "To each being it seemed to me that several *other* lives were due."[129]

*

Nine-tenths of the pleasures we owe to art over a lifetime are conveyed not by direct contact with the work but by memory alone. How little we have preoccupied ourselves, however, with the different nature, fidelity, and intensity of forms cloaked in memory, depending on whether it is a painting, a piece of music, or a poem! Only for a poem is memory absolute presence, complete resurrection, and perhaps even—rather oddly—something else: the only truly authentic contact, since its capacity for memorization through meter and rhyme is an essential component of the poem, so that even if it is heard for the first time, regulated as it is on the rhythm and refrains of mnemonic sounds, it already takes on the tonality proper to recollection: that is why all poetry, alone among the productions of the muses, may be called the *daughter of memory*. The memory of a painting is the memory of an emotion, a surprise, or a sensual pleasure, brought back mechanically but not linked affectively to the persistence in the mind of a vague distribution of masses and colors within a frame. Almost as deprived of life as one's memory of the furnishings in a room. Musical memory has some of the precision of the memory of a poem, but conserves neither the volume and sonorous intensity, nor the vigor of the instrumental or vocal timbres inseparable from the performance.

It is odd that an art exists—poetry—whose substance is entirely soluble in the memory, and only really resides in it, to which no production, performance, or materialization can add anything. For the poem, being read by an actor on a stage has something necessarily uncouth about it, and even caricatural, because it is superfluous (to read a poem is already to half-mime it, it is to leave the *medium* that is proper to it completely); the poem, which is already purified and gains the power of suggestion if it comes out of the anonymous, shadowy mouth of the radio, only attains all its expressive plenitude when it goes back to the consciousness borne by the voice—not murmured, not even silently mimed by the throat, but abstract and as though rid of any carnal constraint—of memory alone.

There are consequences to this inequality of the various arts before memorization. It would take away any real consistency in a culture based primarily on the plastic arts. A purely musical culture, on the contrary, seems possible, without large windows on the exterior, closely bound and tied to an aural imagination that is rarely bestowed—hence, the almost complete closing off to the profane in true musicians' circles. The predominantly "literary" key, fundamental in all modern cultures of the western type, probably has to do with the fact that language is the favored vehicle of thought, but almost as much perhaps with the eminently internalized and entirely portable character of its base production, which was first lyric, epic, or gnomic poetry, learned by heart.

I could only make out a corner of the wall of the château de Ferney, through the wire mesh of the foliage: visits are only allowed on Saturday afternoons. Between two of the centennial elms on the avenue leading there, Mont Blanc is framed spectacularly, illuminated by the setting sun: King Voltaire borrowed Jean-Jacques's domestic landscape, which bears no resemblance to him.

Here lived, somewhat paradoxically, a *Nobel* in a class of his own acting as village squire and charity office, the most voluminous man of letters of all time, but there is no great writer with whom the word "genius," as we understand it, clashes more. Voltaire's situation is singular; it is that of a container whose strange dimensions are epoch-making, and that releases shards of works, none of which have weight (I am including *Candide*, which owes too much to France's stylistic adulation for the accomplishments of the *elegant pen*). His flaw was to believe in his tragedies: alas! Mérope place, at Ferney, makes one smile: what small fry, for so phenomenal a name! But, after all, a shoal of sardines could perhaps weigh as much as *Moby Dick*.

What distances us from him so much is that everything he wrote, outside of his stillborn tragedies, was current, was made to be current, to be consumed, in immediate, complete communication: pure transparency that leaves no room for any resurgence, any posthumous reinterpretation, and which is journalism raised to its most excellent degree. "I call 'journalism' everything that will be less interesting tomorrow than today," Gide said.[130] The remark hits the bull's-eye in Voltaire.

*

From the window of my kitchen, which is flooded with sun in the afternoon and the most cheerful part of my little Parisian apartment, you can look down on the courtyard of the Fontaine des Quatre-Saisons.[131] To the left and right of this courtyard are the narrow, two-story ornamental houses, without thickness, leaning against the gables of the neighboring buildings overhanging them; blocking the back of the paved courtyard, the unassuming house that the poet of *Nights* inhabited with his parents for years in middle-age: a provincial construction, also two stories, coated in ocher and, until recently,

crested with tiles. This is where Musset received clandestine visits in the very early hours from Aimée d'Alton:

> *Petit moinillon blanc et rose . . .*
> [Little monk white and pink . . .]

A letter from the poet, preserved, tells his lover what pre-
cautions to take so as not to wake his parents, whose
room had to be crossed. I can scarcely pass the high,
vaulted porch that offers the only access to the courtyard
without the white-hooded silhouette (so bold, and, I
imagine, charming) floating there for an instant—a sylph
in early morning under rough wool, wet as a meadow—
a light image of a romantic folly where nothing is fraught,
gliding over cobblestones made for the fracas of carriages like an April morning.

*

Milly-Lamartine is a dying hamlet of about twenty traffic lights, trellised on the slope of the Mâconnais mountains, and connected less by streets than by a network of
narrow, paved roads. Half the houses are abandoned, or
semi-dilapidated, as in an "end of the world" of Cor-
bières, but the masonry of the beautiful limestone, warm
and golden, unconcealed by plaster, still ennobles them;
the dry heat, the crisp and curled vegetation of the Midi,

slide along this narrow balcony of scorched stone, to which only a steep, small road gives access, like inhabited niches one sees on the south-facing slopes of high mountain pastures. It is an apiary taking in the sun, basking in and awakening to the vibration of heat on the rocks long after the swarm has left. Embedded in the middle of the hamlet and its stony dryness, behind a gate, at the back of a cool, green, shaded garden, the home of the swan of Saint-Point,[132] a square family house, solidly and comfortably built in the beautiful stone of the Mâconnais: one of those good bourgeois properties, in retreat behind their shades, lowered like eyelashes, that do not like to be stared at from the street: a discreet plaque of notarial opulence, unafraid of alerting the tax department, would not come as a surprise at the gate of this residence where nothing speaks of the gentleman. It is the house of an esquire, very Balzacian, a moneyed enclave, born after the tax and the tithe, in the time of the three percent, that does not care about dovecotes, kennels, and turrets. It is the village that is noble, not the house; the poet did not take flight in this plush house in the country that dryly dismisses romanticism: what you imagine—if anything can be imagined here— is a deputy of the Temperate Monarchy.

*

I visit *Roche*, taking a brief detour from my route at Attigny.[133] Nothing remains of the farm where *A Season in Hell* was written, except part of a wall. But for everything else, "this is certainly the same countryside."[134] A washing house overrun by algae, where the laundry must have been beaten well before the author of "The Seekers of Lice" came into the world. Five or six rural homes or farms, studded loosely around an intersection of local roads, caught in a network of orchards and hedges. Nothing marks this totally insignificant *divergence*, this landscape of boredom and thick, rural sleep: not a hillside, or a river, or a forest. How could he have come back here, again and again, to rejoin the familial figures so obstinately? It is here, and not in Harrar, that the eagerness to die explodes; it is here that he returned—"a ferocious invalid, back from the torrid countries"—with his leg cut off and his belt full of gold, not *to die in barbarous rivers*, but, really, *to go where the cows drink.*[135]

*

Roche, again, which struck me so much that, weeks later, its image still obsesses me. "The man with wind at his

heels" is too easily said. Even in deepest Ethiopia, he remained moored by a very long rope to this *dead body*, to
this wallow in the country in the form of a family vault,
to this never-changing tenure, and to his serfs: *mère
Rimbe*, the bus driver, the birdbrained Vitalie, whom,
one imagines, he must have protected like an invalid.[136]
And, beyond this meager delegation, it would seem that
he cherished the burden, the hereditary cross, the iron
rod of the *increasingly ferocious* ancestors.

> *Nous sommes tes grands parents*
> *Les Grands . . .*
> [We are your grandparents
> Grown-ups . . .][137]

In truth, never has a child prodigy been more burdened
by family, as one is burdened by malediction, than this
intractable convict, this escapee thirsty for his penal col-
ony. At Roche, the perspective shifts, and, in a way, it is
Lawrence of Arabia who becomes Rimbaud's brother
via the Red Sea: a free man fascinated by hair shirts and
discipline, and like him, a frantic inventor of atonements.

*

Enfance au bord d'un lac! Angélique tendresse
D'un azur dilaté, qui sourit, qui caresse...
[Childhood at the edge of a lake! Angelic tenderness
Of extended azure, that smiles, that strokes...][138]

These bare unremarkable lines are all that remains in my memory from reading in high school the *Selected Works* of the comtesse de Noailles, whose property in Amphion I walked alongside last year, between Evian and Thonon, planted like a fruit tree above the Léman. In fact, after the first, heavenly impression of the interpolated sky created from the appearance of the mountain lake, a sense of confinement eventually takes over: a cozy, quilted, protected confinement, that almost always speaks to me at once of convalescence, retreat, and exile; more than anywhere else, the shadow cast by passing time is materially incorporated into the stagnant water, like that surrounding Poe's "Island of the Fay." It is this intimate complicity of the landscape and the pitch of emotion that—alone, but effectively—establishes the power of Lamartine's mediocre "Lake," just as its absence detracts a good deal of the realism from the Waldensian peasant stories of Ramuz, allegories rather than images of work, plastered in trompe l'oeil onto the vaporous emptiness of a Chinese wash.

All slopes lead to this idle, unlined eye of water, as to a central and final perfect calm that wipes everything away. It is truly here that the soul bends toward the tomb "as thirsty oxen bend toward a lake."[139] The public gardens of Vevey and Montreux, on the edge of the Léman, their banks painted white, so tidy against the green grass, their clusters of pensioners, sitting with their elbows on their knees, so motionless they already seem to be holding their offering between their teeth, the slow waterwheel of little old paddle steamers, the color of ambulances, that ceaselessly, at each embarcadero, pass silently to load shadows. In a brief tale by Patrick Modiano called *Villa Triste*, I found this meditative, tranquil mood of white mourning—these cool malls raked each morning of their dead leaves, these lime trees, these hotels made of whipped cream: Bellerive or Beaurivage, with the flat water against the mountain's muted blue-green wall, these phantom thermal towns in autumn where passersby seem both lighter and less boisterous than elsewhere. And it's a beautiful book.

*

What never appears in *These Jaundiced Loves* by Corbière,[140] which I love so much, is the mildness specific to Roscoff; rarely has the empty dinner hour on evacuated beaches, while the sun still shines fairly high in the sky, seemed as delicious, as intimate for the late stroller, as tender in color and silence, between the sky turning yellow at the edge of the horizon and the already slate-blue color of the sea. And tender, too, along its paths, the sea grass and bushes of faded green, fuzzy as the hull of an almond. I walked there in the evening along the narrow, pale sea meadow, between the blue green of the ocean, cottony with white at all the lovely coastal reefs, and the curled, chiseled greenery, delicate as acanthus, of the artichoke fields. The evening was so calm at the end of the season in a resort barely frequented at the time, that, wherever I was, I heard the *angelus* ring at the pretty, low-lying church where Brittany, for an instant, Italianizes itself. I skirted the giant fig tree, the thick granite buildings of the square, buildings of lawyers, woeful and opulent, located between the garden and the sea, whose waves came from behind at high tide to crash against the service entrance. I never passed the modest and appealing marine biology laboratory without thinking jealously that the naturalists at the Ecole Normale, where I was at the time, had the opportunity to break away for a year in this blue grotto; it seemed to me that, assigned here, captive once and for all to this sea of sirens, I would have pitched my tent forever between the aquarium and the artichokes.

Only at Saint-Cast, around the point of La Garde, did I find this mordant clarity of line, as in a garden after a watering in the evening, that Japanese chiseled quality where the wetness of the foliage and rock is not misted by even a particle of haze, that certain mornings in Roscoff have after a night of rain.

But what regret not to have known the Roscoff of Tristan Corbière! Roscoff before the cauliflower and the artichoke, and before this bourgeoisie of wholesale distributors, nurserymen and seedsmen, suppliers of Les Halles and merchants of fertilizer, thickening the streets of Saint-Pol, and already colonizing the little leonine port. At times I dream of the beautiful name *Coatcongar*, near Morlaix, where Corbière was born: in this countryside, razed today by horticulture, there must have already been the stately manors of Saint-Malo paid for by the pillage of the seas, lying low in the hollow of rippled oak groves, soaked by November rains, where Breton captains with no lips, old leather faces between side whiskers of pig bristle, ruminated over their last beaching, before a glass of rum, watching the downpour of the *dark months* through the broth on the pane. Through

Corbière's verse, we get a glimpse of a vanished Roscoff, half pirate and still populated with old sailors of seas large and small, Cape Horners or *skippers of fishing boats*

> *Tu dors sous les panais, capitaine Bambine*
> *Du remorqueur havrais l'Aimable-Prosperine*
> [You rest beneath the parsnips, Captain Bambine
> from towing *The Amiable Proserpine* to harbor][141]

that land disables and that we see behind their seaside shacks, spitting tobacco juice on potato plants, or else, in some dark little apartment in town, *burying themselves*, as Montesquieu said, *in a whore.*

A few days ago, I reread "La Rapsode foraine," the only long poem by Corbière that is admirable from end to end. Particularly admirable in that its subject is only a "genre scene," a fantasy in the manner of Callot, a subject for a Dutch or Flemish dandy, and in that the material, throughout its fifty strophes, is distilled, transmuted, and re-crystallized into a substance that tolerates no slag. It is perhaps the sole example that I know of in our poetry of a wholesale sublimation of the *picturesque.*

How can one understand or get along with these Ph.D.s in music who speak Greek to my comprehension of sounds lying fallow, who idolize Mozart, Bach, and Beethoven, and smile disdainfully at Wagner? Whereas, for me, the Titan of music, who is also the Victor Hugo of music, was as clearly and brutally demoted by Bayreuth (which takes away none of his glory) as the sublime grandfather found himself to be by the *Flowers of Evil* (and Wagner is not only Baudelaire—the Baudelaire of *Against the Grain*—he is a Baudelaire who is also a Claudel, which is to say, the power of the collar joined to the timbre of a musical language that is unmistakable as soon as one hears three measures). It doesn't matter to me who is "greater": what I am sure of is that in Wagner there is a beyond Beethoven (still formally anchored to the symphony, moreover, whereas Hugo himself in his maturity had already gone beyond the odes of his youth) as obviously as there is a *Sunbeams and Shadows*[142] in *Illuminations*. While there is not a literary handbook in use today in France that does not spontaneously historicize the work of Chénier or Lamartine, there exists in the regressive structure of the musical Pantheon of my period something that clashes both indirectly with my idea of the development of art, and directly with my sensibility.

Certainly, there is no reason to believe in "progress" in art. And if we go back in time a few centuries, it seems no one ever really believed in it at all, except in a not very serious and very ephemeral way (on the other hand, for long periods, and with all his soul, mankind believed in the reality and almost in the inevitability of its regression). Only there is this: in the long history of aesthetic creation, a period is inserted to which no other can be compared, a period just short of a century, that extends from approximately 1800 to 1880. There follows, particularly in poetry, at very brief intervals, a series of major creators in whom, from one to the other—all questions of supremacy aside—an added benefit that can no longer be squandered, a stored *surplus* almost without counterpart, is perceptible each time. This *surplus* consists, not in extra genius liberally accorded, but in an at least partially transmissible acquisition of means: specifically, a very rapid increase of the resolving power of the artist's eye and ear, a sensitivity to nuance, timbre, the most extenuated modulation, in short a continuous and victorious moving back of the threshold of the infinitely small, resolvable and *realizable*. (Moreover, for me at least, it is not without significance that the ultra-subtle positional touch which is that of a modern-day chess champion, through rapid and continual progress, was acquired entirely in this same period, between Philidor and Lasker, which is to say, between 1780 and 1895.) Who can deny that, from Parny to Lamartine, from Lamartine to Hugo, from Hugo to Baudelaire, from Baudelaire to Rimbaud and Mallarmé, a type of artistic succession was established, entirely different from that of centuries past: no longer a calm and linear passing of the scepter, but a cumulative mode of transmission where the capital received in inheritance each time seemed to snowball exemplarily in the hands of the legatee?

So it is for me in music from Beethoven to Wagner, whose real and new superiority Nietzsche perspicaciously located not in the "breath" and the aptitude for *great machines*, but in musical miniaturism: the capacity to "sustain an infinity of nostalgia or suffering in a few measures."[143] And so it was, and almost had to be, from Wagner to Debussy, whose overly modest format seems to mark in stippling the place of Rimbaud or late Mallarmé, which he could have been, which he wasn't, and which Proust would be a bit later for the novel. After Debussy, as after Mallarmé (and after Cézanne in painting), the conquering line that was the most continuous and strongly elevatory of all of modern time is ruptured at a capital caesura: another era begins, a disorientation supplants deepening; an artistic, composite intermixing invades the West: a *third world* is already incorporated in the music of Stravinsky, as in the cubism of Apollinaire and Picasso.

*

There has never existed a more terrifying waffle iron in literature than the classic tragedy in five acts. In order to distinguish by style the successive rehashings of various disciples of Corneille and Racine, one would need a professional flair as refined as that of those old jurists capable at times of identifying a writer behind the liturgical jargon of a ruling from the Court of Cassation.

Certainly, the rules of the genre were persnickety. But, though strict in terms of construction and the "unities," in principle, they gave free play to the writing, they did not involve the stereotype that freezes the alexandrine of tragedy from the beginning, and that makes the most prized literary genre of the era a tedious one, an endless *in the manner of* that never stops dying. The masterstroke of the founders, Corneille and Racine, does not explain everything. In reality, tragedy, the *fancy dress* ball of literature, established at the same time as the ceremonial of the Sun King, is the only case in the modern age where rigid etiquette is imposed on the writing right away, dictating the low bows of style, its genuflections, its metaphors, its periphrases, its circumlocutions, phrasing itself and the rhythm linking parts of speech. It is not only the schedule, place, and costume that are fixed here by protocol, it is carriage itself, the bearing of the head and inflections of the voice, the manner of inquiring or responding, caught in the implacable gaze of a master of ceremonies.

*

The focus of our era that fixed all eyes on the eighteenth century of *Dangerous Liaisons* for several decades at the same time turned them away from *Manon Lescaut*, a forgotten star, no less representative of the elegant cynicism of the age, but mingled with sentimentality and thereby distanced from the *type* that fascinates us in literature, a type whose absolute purity a writer like Beckett today attempts to realize in his domain, through a process of elimination.

The immediate, readily sought-after reduction to type accounts for much of the authority with which the existentialist works emerged right after the war. It might make them wince a bit today; the emergence of a pure metaphysical novel in 1947, on the contrary, validated their passport to glory. Similarly, the meager attributes of Camus's *The Stranger* assured the swiftness of its punch, making it a barely fictionalized manifesto of the philosophy of the absurd. Newness, which was coming into the world for the first time and which was not even accepted, which dragged around fragments of its broken eggshell still stuck to it, only seems to emerge today if it rejects everything that is not of its space and its domain and manages to reach its crystallized form on the first try. And we project this demand retrospectively into the history of literature, favoring—to the detriment of works in transition and works unconsciously pregnant with the future—all the clearly aggressive forms of rupture.

*

"The literary tableau of an era describes not only a present of creation, but a present of culture," Jakobson wrote —pertinently.[144] And every literary school is certainly characterized as much by its creative contribution as by its new filtering of works of the past (Surrealism, which seems to have discerned and employed more clearly than others the means of power by which a "movement"

emerges, took great care, almost before producing anything, to publish its Index: *Lisez—Ne lisez pas*,[145] and its
ideal genealogy: *Nouveau is surrealist in the kiss*, etc.).
But the proportion of what each school brings that is
new and what it is bound to demote and reclassify as
earlier work is not constant. If one considers the great
movements that have marked French literature for four
centuries: the classicism of the seventeenth century—
the philosophical movement of the eighteenth—the romanticism of the nineteenth—the surrealism of the
twentieth, it is clear that each time the reordering of the
past thrives at the expense of the original contribution
(Boileau placidly liquidates all that precedes Malherbe
—Surrealism finds a place in literary history no doubt as
much for its works as for having completely overturned
the old poetic library in its light). As if a principle of en-
tropy was at work in the gradual decline of a civilization's creative powers, and as if, for every new change, a
balance for recovering energy became more and more
necessary.

*

What set the tone of a period of art until now was fundamentally the combination of a poetry, a music, and a
painting: Racine—Lulli—Le Brun are an example, as are

Hugo—Delacroix—Berlioz, or even Baudelaire—Manet
—Wagner.

Since 1940, and practically since 1930, if you look
closely, poetry and music have often been absent from
the domain of creativity—and, for the past two or three
decades, so has painting. Every artistic metamorphosis
has been eclipsed: the era attempts to capture itself as it
is, directly, through the essay, the testimony, applied philosophy, the novel of reportage. The eras to come that
will try to recapture this subtle essence, which for ours
was "the spirit of the time," will only have raw materials
at their disposal, or, at the most, partially worked materials. Nothing but a direct look at ourselves, not really
followed by any expressive transmutation. Not even a
portrait of our artists and our writers: nothing but photographs.

For a long time in universities there have been de-
partments of comparative literature. What is missing is a
department of the relationship between the arts, a department of the Nine Muses, whose goal, for each age,
would be to study not only the reciprocal influences of
literature, music, sculpture, painting, architecture, and
today, cinema, but the secret hierarchy that presided in
the mind of the artists and the public over these respec-

tive influences. For, in every era, there is a rarely admitted but effective hegemony that passes from one art to another at whim, just as political hegemony in Europe is due in turn to a half a dozen powers. It is difficult, for example, with the compartmentalization of education, to have a definite idea of the dominant musical key that presided over romanticism, not only because of Beethoven, Weber, Chopin, Liszt, and Berlioz, but because of the saturation of social life by opera, with which the works of Stendhal remain thoroughly obsessed. It is just as difficult to clearly feel the blistering rise, in influence and prestige, of painting in the time of Apollinaire, whereas, twenty years before, Wagner had literally crushed symbolism beneath his sonic mass. And the building mania of Louis XIV had far from given up center stage without a fight (as we tend to think) to classical literature, which the enormous complex of Versailles counterbalanced as a realization in and of itself.

*

The quality of a writer's production is impossible to evaluate objectively, not only because each isolated reader will judge it in his own way but because each of the following eras in the history of literature will, too.

What is established with the help of time, however, is a sort of accord that leaves room for only limited variations.

There is also the writer's "volume" in his time, during his lifetime and even noticeably beyond it, that interferes with this notion of quality in a complex way. Affecting this volume, sometimes in very large proportion, are the quantity of his output, his rhythm, the scope of his immediate audience, and the overall image this audience has of the writer, which often depends largely on extra-literary factors: physical or moral prestige, membership in a group, friends, lovers, a sparkling biography, a historical or political role.

This volume, insofar as it is linked to factors that are not directly artistic, is diminished with time: in different ways, the posthumous fate of Voltaire or Lamartine, Edmond Rostand or Béranger, testifies to this. But, during a writer's lifetime, no one is in a position to evaluate, and possibly remove, this "not-applicable" part of the situation. Neither his friends, nor his enemies, nor his readers, nor the writer himself. Either he tries honestly, as Camus tried during his lifetime, to reduce the exceptional credit of extra-literary circumstances, or, much more frequently, considering himself to be unrecognized, tries on his own, more or less arrogantly, to reevaluate what he considers to be his true place. I do not think for a second that Nerval ever believed posterity would one day negate the divide between Hugo and himself regarding poetic quality, and I do not even think he would have found it legitimate. Nor do I think Hugo could have seriously imagined a (soon felicitous) rival in the marginal and confidential Baudelaire. The objective hierarchy into which a writer is inserted is imposed on him willingly or unwillingly during his lifetime: he can only make relative corrections, as a swimmer caught in a river's current swims against it without really making headway. In every era, even when the order of its preferences must be entirely overturned, the rejected consent more readily than we think to the hierarchy that penalizes them: Baudelaire and Nerval—to use this example again—no doubt complained (and, for Nerval, it's far from certain) but complained less than we do of the situation to which their era relegated them. They knew themselves, of course. But, like all other artists, they also saw themselves through the eyes of their time.

*

What is most interesting to me in the history of literature are the cleavages, seams, and fractured lines that cross it, diagonally or in zigzags, in contempt of schools, "influences," and official filiations: the oft-broken chain of singular literary talents that follow one another or appear discontinuously but return, as different from one another and yet as mysteriously linked as those feminine faces, that reemerge unforeseeably each time, that reveal the exclusive love certain men devote to them and make clear the hidden conformity to a type.

*

When the young Hugo cries, "To be Chateaubriand or nothing!" he is completely unaware at the time (and for good reason) of *Mémoires d'outre-tombe* and *Vie de Rancé*. What he is striving for is the "surface" that brilliance sometimes gives, even more than its substance. All recognized geniuses of the period, Goethe in Germany, Byron throughout Europe, and Chateaubriand in France, enjoyed an immense position, in which literature was far from occupying all the space; and the magnificent minister of Foreign Affairs was no doubt the most ravenous of the three and the least solidly established. All three gave the image of poets who had "arrived" via literature, but not—not by a long shot—literature alone. There is no conceivable royalty of letters in 1820 without the contribution and exploitation of great birth, great duty, or intimate relationships with *royalties*, and this is already true for Voltaire. Oddly: it was Hugo, precisely, with his Balzacian ambition, who at twenty would not have dreamt for a second of being Rousseau in his hermitage, who would be the first literary person to rise to the level of one of this world's powerful by the exclusive virtue of his pen, without ever trading literary glory for other values. But, while his means are different, it is the same image of great success that he has before his eyes, and that he will make material: to topple the image of the *majestic* genius, one would have to wait until after Baudelaire, Flaubert, Rimbaud, and Mallarmé.

*

It is remarkable that, at the end of this twentieth century, we nourish ourselves, often by preference, with what the great writers of the past would have regarded as the crumbs of their table. In Gide, his *Journal* rather than everything else, and very often in Hugo, his *Things Seen*. *Conversations with Eckermann* more than *Elective Affinities*, and today Flaubert's *Letters* more often than *Sentimental Education*. It was Barrès's posthumous *Cahiers*, more than any other book, that prolonged his presence among us. And who could say that Chateaubriand himself did not rely more on *Génie* and *Les Martyrs* than on his *Mémoires* to live beyond posterity? As if the bulk of a body of work, hallowed and with time somewhat abandoned, served today, above all, as a free pass for the personal indiscretion, the run-of-the-mill, the impulsiveness of the first draft? What we want is literature that moves, seized at the very moment it still seems to be moving, just as we prefer a sketch by Corot or Delacroix to their finished paintings. What we no longer want is literature-as-monument, everything that felt the need to acquire and abide by the building permits of its age.

Thus, in literature, we can verify the forceful return of the marginality of all its forms, which mark our era much more than the novelty or vigor of its contribution. A re-enthronement at the heart of literature of all its former rejects. Relinquishment of the *masterpiece* in favor of everything by the writer that still babbles and prattles freely around him (to prove this, it would suffice to weigh all the great writers' published or reprinted *Notes*, *Notebooks*, *Journals*, *Memoirs*, or *Letters*, and the *Recollections* gleaned from them, against the parsimonious reprints of their key books). What I write here should not be taken at all as a disavowal of my era: as I constantly notice when choosing what to read, I have the same inclination.

*

There was a myth of Paris, a myth with a tenacious life, but it collapsed brutally in the past thirty years. It was born after 1789 and especially after 1830 (before 1789, "the City" was but a shadow cast by Versailles and "the Court") in a political and bellicose form, that of Paris-as-light-of-the-revolutions: in that period, it was the *cobblestone*, the burning cobblestone of Paris, always ready to rise up in barricades, that was the dynamic, explosive symbol of the city. The Commune prolonged this myth until The Third Republic; its recurrence would again impel, as belated parody, the barricades of 1968. Starting with the Second Empire, and coexisting with it for a moment, the Paris of *Parisian Life* takes over, the Paris of little theaters and little women, bordello of the world and mecca of haute couture, with its nickname à la Goldoni: *Paname*, the city of *cheeky urchins* (the passage from Hugo's Gavroche to the Parisian street kid excellently illustrates the change in the myth's content), of card players in cafés, of the well-to-do in gaiters, and of white wine. Its *Marseillaises* are now sung in the Moulin Rouge: "Paris reine du monde," "J'ai deux amours," "Tu reverras Paname," "Paris sera toujours Paris" (we're already trying to reassure ourselves).[146] After 1940, it's over: Paris, which made itself provincial on a global scale and stopped dazzling the provinces, now becomes a problem of city planning and demographics.

This would be an interesting topic for university study (but since it has come to mind, it must already be in progress, or done)—the passage from the first myth to the second, from the Paris of the barricades to the Paris of the Moulin Rouge. Its causes, its modalities. It is singular that this myth, which, in its first form, occupies so much room in Hugo's *Les Misérables*, occupies none in *La Comédie Humaine*, perhaps (but not only) because of the author's monarchic convictions. All the hyperbole to which the shadowy gigantism of the city gives rise is, in Balzac, purely psychological and material: in contrast to what Hugo and Michelet (and even Rimbaud) sense instinctively, there is for him no *numen* of Paris, nothing but a social Behemoth, a spineless and abulic monster, for which knowledge of its secret and complicated forces, and sometimes certain magic practices, allow putting on the bit, with Rastignac as well as Vautrin or Ferragus.

It would be instructive, moreover, to examine more closely the figure of Paris as depicted in the great novelists. In Zola: a catoblepas with no muscles and no skeleton (there is no longer a trace of the revolutionary myth of Paris remaining in this leftist novelist), all viscera, all gobbling and digesting, defecating and copulating. In Stendhal, "the City" of the eighteenth century reappears, a pleiad of salons where one glitters, solicits, or schemes, all equipped with a communicating door that leads directly to the theater, as in Hoffmann's *Don Juan*. In Flaubert, there is no *vision* of the capital (one is struck by it, rereading *Sentimental Education*), nothing of this enormous and magnifying echo chamber that exalts the voice and timbre of all of Balzac's Parisian characters, and that alone makes up half of Hugo's novel. A bit like Einstein's space, Flaubert's Paris is a neutral, all-encompassing social space whose volume is shaped only by the displacements of the fictional figures inhabiting it.

*

It is extremely curious that the Revolution of 1789 took place in a quasi-absolute literary void, when all the great writers of the century without exception had disappeared, while their successors were still being bottle-fed (Chateaubriand was only twenty and saw almost nothing; as for Sade, the Revolution was only a brief interlude separating the solitary confinement of the psychiatric ward). From 1789 to 1799, there is not a single reliable *great witness* working, not the slightest "chief contemporary." The only remarks of any scope, endowed with loftiness and detachment, that one can cite of a contemporary of '92, must be sought in Goethe.

Of course, the great ancestors might have gained in prestige there. Imagine Saint-Simon—or even simply Barrès—listening to the sessions of the Convention. . . .

*

What I find tedious in the Marxist reading of history, in spite of the sparkling brochures by the master, written in the thick of things (*Class Struggles in France, The 18th Brumaire of Louis Bonaparte*) is the sense of seeing the curtain rise on a thesis play instead of on Shakespeare, however good the quality of it—let's say a play by Ibsen. Barely is the curtain raised, the three knocks are drawn out endlessly;[147] from the depths of the ages we hear the proletariat mobilizing in their big clogs: so much for *suspense*.

Mozart: how can we not read in his music—so polished, so measured, of such tender and elegant company—the war in laced costume of the eighteenth century, when companies were still led with the sound of the violin, when officers in jabots drew a pinch of tobacco from their musical snuffboxes, just as they were engaging in their business? Wagner, born in Leipzig the very year of the "Battle of the Nations": the somber battles of peoples of the nineteenth century and of the twentieth century to come, even more, are the sound of the rising ocean, as well as the first chords of the overture, from the bottom of his *mystical abyss*; what separates him from Mozart is also, primarily, a brutal break with scale and volume, it is the end of the nice, bland, facile music of History. It also separates Laclos from Balzac, but not from Stendhal, who was in Moscow, and who experienced this end more intimately than anyone, but who never really recognized it or understood it.

*

What elevated rates of mortality among works considered masterpieces during their authors' lifetimes! Quite often, those books that remain alive for us seem to be arranged, like a crater's edge, around a central collapse. O tragedies of Voltaire, o *Natchez* and *Martyrs*, *Nights* of Musset, *Girondins* of Lamartine, you have barely outlived the snows of yesteryear! O *Burgraves*, *Hernani*, *Cromwell* and *Ruy Blas*, you still exist, of course, but not like Racine in the theater, more like *The Three Musketeers* in the novel. It is here, perhaps, that the classics give

proof not of their superiority but of greater stability: neither Racine, nor Corneille, nor Molière changed horses
in the relay of the centuries.

The full and lasting vitality of a literary genre of defined and established form (seventeenth-century tragedy), and not the superiority of the taste of the era, must
no doubt be the reason why the same *performances* considered best in each classical author by their contemporaries have remained so for us: a judgment of excellence
based on definite norms involving academic ranking,
and even, deep down, athletic competition. Periods of
accelerated literary mutation, on the contrary, make us
take into account the "who loses wins" that can so often
be observed in great writers: this is because it is impossible, in the moment, to judge the power of the ascen-
dant movement, still in a nascent state, that bear the
works that will capture the future, while a delay in taste,
a phenomenon of inevitable inertia, still favors works
born in the wake of the day before yesterday: *Mérope*, for
example, or *Les Martyrs*, at the expense of *Zadig* or *La
Vie de Rancé*.

*

Le Voyage de Gratz à La Haye by Montesquieu[149] is a
dry, anecdotal, and technical memento, all encoded with

distances, charts, statistics, and budgets, and that might have been the travel diary of a matter-of-fact Anglo-Saxon such as the second half of the century would see: Arthur Young or Benjamin Franklin. The commissariat no longer follows, it marches in the front line, and the quintessential legislator seems here without much pleasure, in the lurching of post-stages, to lay open Europe's accounts in a cook's notebook.

In the West of the first half of the century, already bathed in the glow of the Enlightenment, there are no passports, almost no police barriers, at least for people of quality, and no conscription. But to read these travel diaries, which are most often reduced to a flat inventory of fixtures in the countries traversed, one is reminded of what one tends to forget in favor of the age's overly vaunted *sweetness of living*: these are entire towns that are now barracks, corseted by bastions, regaled with drums, bristling with artillery, and that each evening as night falls they bolt their doors twice. The city remained encamped like a Roman legion; the ditch, the drawbridge, and the fortification remained the besetting backdrop of life, more symbolic than functional, certainly, but always present, like the sword at a gentleman's side, and Europe, where the feudal lord of La Brède feasts and strolls, counting with sordid avarice its store-

houses and powder magazines, battalions and de-
milunes, it is much less the Europe of Voltaire than the
Europe of the Sergeant-King.[150]

*

There is more than boredom, more than restless, exiled
sadness in the somnolent chatter of the Russian provinces in Turgenev or Chekhov; there is a presentiment
of nothingness, doubled by a strange absence of echoes:
like mouths slowly being silenced by a pillow. Nothing,
absolutely nothing of the sort transpires in even a page
of our eighteenth-century literature, where pleasure remains free of aftertaste or disappointment until the last
minute, where affluent society, whatever we might say,
never seems to have felt the end coming. Is this because
of a complete lack of useful historical reference? It is
difficult in 1978 to imagine that two centuries ago the
idea of social revolution not only roused no distant or
recent memory, but not even an intelligible image in
three thousand years of culture taking root: nothing but
Juvenal's verse: *Quis tulerit Gracchos de seditione quer-
entes,*[151] and the insignificant phantom of a stillborn
agrarian reform.

"If the word *love* is spoken between them, I am lost,"
Count Mosca says somewhere in *The Charterhouse*. It

has been somewhat the same for the word *revolution*. Prosperous France, which had never heard it or had completely forgotten it, slept soundly until the last moment. The belatedness of the term over the event on the eve of 1789 was found to be as remarkable as its omnipresent antecedence in the years of this postwar period.

*

A great writer never allows himself be completely obscured, even when asleep, even when asleep for good. In *Beyond Good and Evil*, Nietzsche's unspectacular, not very incisive work, in addition to being more clearly proto-Nazi than permissible at times, suddenly there are two serene pages, relaxed and as though unlocked by a bright likability, pages where he examines in one stroke, without regret and without blot, the bizarre season of the soul that opens for Europe with Rousseau and closes with Beethoven (a season in which Novalis, on the poetic level, and Saint-Just, on the political level, for me, pretty much represent the solstice, and to which the work of Goethe in its entirety, as complex as it is, owes the sun-filled succulence of its maturation). A season already pathetically behind, the summer of Saint-Martin, blossoming in opposition to the calendar just as History approached its most merciless turning point—a sunset experienced as a dawn, with Fourier at the very end representing its *green flash*.

History has no doubt known these nervous gestations of the golden age more than once, these visions of celestial strikes of "white joyous nations."[152] The only one somewhat familiar to us in the past is the century of Augustus, that of Virgilian predictions: *Jam redit et Virgo, redeunt Saturnia regna*.[153] While strictly speaking a vision of the return of the seasons, it is also a return of the ages, a fantasy of the affluent and holders of lifelong pensions: the arrested world, fixed boundaries, immutable laws, and pleasure without trouble of the *modicum et bonum*.[154] More mocked than the Rousseauist utopia, it is in truth founded differently in its historical moment. The Roman world, in the head of a few of its intellectuals tired of the upheaval of civil wars, imagined that it was finally going to sit down, really sit down, really retreat after so many war projects, and for a century or two it really did, the regular return of its monthly salary placed under the protection of the constellations. The intimate accord of a society running its course and of a personal, still-smiling world-weariness, which hasten a world's final sclerosis, indulges and entrusts it with its repose: Virgil's golden verses are only the millenarian and sumptuous draping of a still-green caducity that prophesizes easily, because the aging of souls is, for an exceptional, enduring moment, in step with the fatigue of a civilization guarding its beautiful remains. Almost young again, the pensioners of Augustus and Maecenas guessed that they belonged to the only civilization that would have the chance to die at a hundred: that is what makes the unique tone of their poetry, smiling but already half illuminated by the sun of the dead, like those summer afternoons when the ghost of a white moon does not leave the vault of the sky and where we pass imperceptibly from one light to the other. There is no more future: nothing more than the Chinese recurrence of the cycling seasons and years; all events are now in the past; nothing more ahead of oneself but the monotony of a blank void, punctuated only by the toga praetextas of consuls and earthly projects; nothing more than a gradual dozing off: how could every inclination of the heart not go to *eternal return*, which the world, unburdened of the eventual, became the transparent figure of? For a while, for a strange pause in Time, this was a truth. Christianity prospered on this vacation of a dismantled time that history abandoned on the shore: the whole scene of a drama that was still possible was relegated to the conscience.

Rousseau's dream, with which he inoculates France, and soon Europe, a dream of a Man springing virtuous from the baptismal breast of Nature, is something else entirely. While Virgil's circle draws from its fatigue of historical events the presentiment, which is verified, of a world ejected from History to the point of becoming almost abstract, the Rousseaus and the Schillers, Novalises and Saint-Justs, dream of an abstract Man, of a freedom bathed in virtue, autocratic and solitary, and that exemplarily escapes the servitudes of temporality ... at the very moment room is being made for them. Man who emerged immaculate from the hands of nature is raised up by them, in the most untimely fashion, his votive status on the point of departure of what will soon become History-as-god and History-as-nightmare. Saint-Just's silence at 9 Thermidor is perhaps the affidavit of this blatant discordance: it is that of a devout and timeless believer in innate Virtue who brutally discovers ("The Republic is lost, the brigands have triumphed!") what the torrent of History in madness makes of man, all men. The guillotine's blade was already being sharpened in the idyllic vision of the Noble Savage that appeared so singularly at the very threshold of a Time of Troubles: what to do with a Man finally perfected and immediately becoming the broken plaything and the puppet in this thorny melee? if not, from vexation, to "shorten" him.

*

The enigmatic, and mind-irritating, case of writers that bookstores, in the long run, imposed on literature: Simenon or Jules Verne, Dashiell Hammett or Tolkien.

They lay bare the arbitrariness of the changing rules that preside over enthronement in the *belles lettres*. At first glance, one seemed left aside because of a stubborn ambition to entertain, one because of his audience's age group, another because of the total absence of inclination and necessity in his talent. But in art there is nothing that violates the rules of qualification, however numerous they may be, that an isolated breakthrough into excellence, even one in a yet uncategorized direction, does not redeem. We do not know what elements the future will incorporate into contemporary literature that today seem marginal and perfectly incongruous. The capricious beam of the dark lantern that pulls the *beau monde* of writing from the shadows shifts with time. Let's remember that for centuries when the eloquence of the flesh and the Apologetics were engulfed as though by right in literature, Sade found himself banned, almost as much as *The Letters of a Portuguese Nun*.

*

Coming from the heart of a forest to its edges, the last trees can be seen silhouetted, isolated, against the empty sky, already bathed in a completely different light, already incorporated in the white daylight of the naked plain. Retreating, the traveler glancing back reincorporates them into an indistinct whole. More than once, in the history of art or literature, only the distance of years can judge false novelty: Leconte de Lisle reintegrates the Hugolian forest, Lamartine, the sentimental pseudo-classicism, the à la Delille periphrases of the eighteenth century expire. Only the luck of being born in a hinge-era, near the threshold separating two violently contrasting periods of sensibility and technique, can at times gratify an artist with this overly advantageous effect of *backlighting*.

*

No immunity in literature—even by reason of universal glory—is ever acquired forever (which is perhaps what the expression "resting on ones' laurels" is meant to signify). In 1942, the "cultural" directives of the government of the virtuous Maréchal banned *Phèdre* and *Tartuffe* for immorality.

There are two cases in France when a narrow minority that social evolution condemned as hopeless—fundamentally reactionary, but intellectually influential—was propelled *back* into power by a national catastrophe: in 1814 and 1940.

The first had a model of reference, the second did not: this abstract reaction regressed toward an ectoplasmic Salente that never took place, just as its thinker, Maurras, passed it the recipe for an agnostic Catholicism and a kingless monarchy. Its anchoring points were an ellipsis, its antecedents, academic and literary, its regime was called the French State.

*

In the past few years, a change in climate has desensitized our era to certain aspects of life and art, and sensitized it, on the contrary, to certain others. Romantic passion, for example, the depiction of which reigned for several centuries in literature, and that not long ago held such place in adolescent reverie, has returned to the marginal position it occupied, according to Denis de Rougemont, before *Tristan*. If one still tolerates its representation, it is only, most often, for the sake of excusing a deviant sexual practice. The fictional production of a writer like Mauriac may be considered symptomatic from this point of view: all the "problems" that haunt his books—and not only that of "sins of the flesh"—are almost without exception those that the following era erased or ignored systematically. Today where would we find a Christian youth still sensitive to the physical torments of *The River of Fire*, or even a familial cocoon that could help us understand *The Frontenac Mystery*?

It is too easy to attach such a change to the simple decline of a few bourgeois and Christian values. Sixty years after the October revolution, it is clear that Solzhenitsyn today (and no doubt many Russians before him) reads Dostoyevsky again exactly as one read him before Lenin (which Mayakovsky, placed in eclipse, could no longer do). Rather than a demystifying progress of enlightenment, I tend to believe that the opaque *mask* that every society casts over a part of its activities, obsessions, and fantasies, was shifted once again without expanding or contracting much. Shifted in what sense? One dictated by a new sensitization to the meaning of *original sin*, resuscitated under a new social travesty. In the refusal born in 1968, and even before, of a fundamentally corrupted and "alienated" art and life, there is something of the harshness of the first Christians against art and against the "world." "Tant que l'eau du nouveau bapteme n'aura pas passe sur eux . . ."

*

The history of ancient Greece, which has weighed so heavily on our literature, somewhat corresponds (as it comes up in the mind of the high school student finishing his classes) to what the history of England would be if it were stopped after the Wars of the Roses, which is to say, precisely the moment it truly began. As soon as the confused massacres between urban Lilliputian feudalities stop, everything beyond no longer counts. The conquest of the civilized world, the giant *dominions* of the Epigones, and the profoundly Hellenized America of the Far East, are like a sort of epilogue, in truth already outside the text. For once, there was a noticeable time lag between the culmination of a civilization's art and the culmination of its power and influence. And art, sanctified, imposed its point of reference and chronology.

*

Aside from individual differences, is there a specific way of dreaming proper to each era—dominant themes, style, material obsessions? Is the oneiric style of an era (if it exists) modified to the same rhythm as the style of its concrete and calculated realizations?

Our age is the first in which this question may be raised, because of its increased attempts to record and write down its dreams. And it is also the last to remain incapable of resolving it, for lack of elements of comparison passed down by vanished eras (where dreams only slipped into writing as stereotypical adornment or prophetic subterfuge).

Breton perfectly saw, and said, in the *First Manifesto*, that the marvelous proper to each era proceeded from a sort of "general revelation." Given his mind's inclination, it is singular that he did not seek to unite this "general revelation" to a collective oneiric emergence and, consequently, to some vast inquiry on dreams, which at the time would have been so natural for him.

*

It was during Voltaire's lifetime that *men-of-letterism* knew its most provocative forms, just as sycophantism found its own in the times of Tiberius and Nero. Three quarters of the writers in France in the mid eighteenth century only aspired, it would seem, to being literary thugs, swordsmen, or seconds. Around the hermit of Ferney, one always catches a glimpse of the lives of the hack writers who, from one end to the other, between the blackmail and the plagiarism, the mendacity, adulation, venality, espionage, false testimony, swings of the censer and blows of the cudgel, flowed limpidly from the gutter of the rue du Bac. And, it must be recognized, through and through, that it is the fake hermit himself who sets the *tone*.

It is clear, in any case, that the first royalty conferred by literature, Voltaire's, was only imposed so quickly because he inextricably combined the unction of the Spirit and the court jester. In the end, Voltaire's universal companionship with crowned heads, by whom he was so duped, signified less the sublimation of the plebeian by genius than a not very costly confirmation of divine birthright by the daily and dismissable commerce of the Holy Spirit.

*

"It is true that French intelligence is incomparable. There is none more powerful, more acute, more profound. If one must accuse me of effrontery, I will follow my thoughts through to the end: it is the only one that exists in the world today. We alone have been able to preserve an intellectual tradition, we alone have been able to preserve ourselves somewhat from pragmatic dumbing down; we alone have continued to believe in the principle of identity; we are the only ones in the world, I repeat coldly, who still know how to think. In philosophical, literary, and artistic matters, all that counts is what we say."

These strange lines are Jacques Rivière's (*Le parti de l'intelligence*) and date from 1921.[156] Through them, today, we can still see that in France after 1918 there was a brief transport that rose from the saber to the brain, a drunkenness of Gallic *Kultur* not totally incomparable to the cuvée after 1871 of the pan-Germanist and Wagnerian vapors in the Germany of Bismarck and William II. One could find other traces in Maurras, Massis, in the postwar Barrès. This *sunstroke* hardly lasted more than two or three years: not only (as everyone knows deep down) was the "victory" hollow, vitality extinguished, and the slope slippery, but the affair was fluttering from the beginning: twice alienated in its deep sources, with Marx, then with Lenin, the French left was forbidden from contributing to such triumphalism. After Combism—whose mental luxuriance, despite Alain's efforts, was not meant to dazzle—the left in France no longer received a national intellectual influx, and that weighed heavily: on it, and on us.

*

My century in the past is the nineteenth, which began with Chateaubriand and extended until Proust, who comes to complete it somewhat beyond its historical frontiers, just as Wagner came to complete an off-limits

Romanticism. I don't like the eighteenth century, except perhaps for one or two books by Rousseau: the books, not the man (*Rêveries, La Nouvelle Héloïse*, certain parts of *Confessions*). Also, a few pages of Sade, who otherwise bores me in the extreme: I like *Philosophy in the Bedroom* and the Revolution discussed during breaks in the screwing ("Yet another effort, Frenchmen, if you would become republicans!"). To me, the best of the spirit of the age is concentrated there, more nervously still than in *Liaisons*. Perhaps there was an art of living in this century, as we are assured: we no longer have a knack for it; there was also enlightenment for the public good: we have had too much of a knack for it. The nineteenth century is of a pythic and prophetic nature: it reaches divinatory depths that the eighteenth century had no idea of, for it enlightened everything and guessed nothing; its humanitarian tune on the flute was that of the rat catcher of Hamelin, but it didn't know it.

1. André Malraux, *L'homme précaire et la littérature* (Paris: Gallimard, 1977). A *fata morgana* is a "fairy mirage" (Italian).

2. "Tel qu'en Lui-même enfin l'éternité le change"; the first line of Stéphane Mallarmé's "Tombeau d'Edgar Poe," *Oeuvres complètes* (1945; Paris: Gallimard, Bibliothèque de la Pléiade, 1956), p. 70.

3. A reference to Charles Baudelaire's "Don Juan in Hell," in *The Flowers of Evil*.

4. "Such was the apothecary's name for a small room under the eaves, filled with pharmaceutical utensils and supplies. He often spent long hours there alone, labeling, decanting, repackaging. He considered it not a mere storeroom, but a veritable sanctuary, birthplace of all kinds of pills, boluses, tisanes, lotions and potions [. . .]"; Gustave Flaubert, *Madame Bovary*, trans. Francis Steegmuller (New York: Knopf, 1993), p. 234.

5. *ut pictura poesis*: Painting resembles poetry (Horace, *Ars poetica*, v. 361).

6. Suit of lights: the glittering, embroidered clothing of a bull-fighter.

7. Gracq paraphrases this passage of Marcel Proust's *Swann's Way*.

8. Flaubert's *Sentimental Education*.

9. Balzac's *Le Pere Goriot*.

10. Both English novelists, Margaret Moore Kennedy (1896–1967) wrote *The Constant Nymph* (1924) and Rosamond Lehmann (1903–1990) wrote *Weather in the Streets* (1936).

11. Gracq was a student of Alain (Emile Auguste Chartier, 1868–1951), a noted French philosopher, journalist, and teacher.

12. *Men of Good Will* (*Les hommes de bonne volonté*) is by Jules Romains.

13. *Le Charivari*, founded in Paris in 1832, was an illustrated newspaper that led an anti-monarchial campaign.

14. Willy was the pen name of Colette's first husband, Henry Gauthier-Villars (1859–1931).

15. Constantin Guys (1802–1892) was a draftsman and watercolorist. Honoré Daumier (1808–1879), caricaturist and painter, and Paul Gavarni (1804–1866), painter, lithographer, and draftsman, both produced caricatures for *Le Charivari*.

16. The journal *Le National* was founded in 1830 by Adolphe Thiers.

17. Marie-Henri Beyle (1783–1842) wrote under the pen name of Stendhal.

18. *Quid*, Latin for "what."

19. "To usher us in": Gracq uses the expression *frapper les trois coups* (to sound the three knocks), a signal for the curtain to rise in the French theater.

20. Gracq refers to passages in André Breton's *Poisson soluble* [*Soluble Fish*] and *Vases communicants* [*Communicating Vessels*].

21. Paul Valéry (1871–1945) preferred Nicholas Edme Restif de La Bretonne (1734–1806) to Stendhal.

22. "Dime-store success": "réussite dans l'épicerie," a reference to Stendhal's job at an import-export company. Gracq takes this phrase from Breton's *Les pas perdus* (1924).

23. Novelists Eugène Sue (1804–1857), Emile Zola (1840–1902), Pierre Alexis Ponson du Terrail (1829–1871), and Michel Zévaco (1860–1918); the latter specialized in cloak-and-dagger novels.

24. Honoré de Balzac, *A Woman of Thirty*, trans. George Burnham Ives (Boston: Little, Brown, 1909), pp. 175–76.

25. *Les Diaboliques (The She-Devils)* (1874), a collection of short stories by Jules Amédée Barbey d'Aurevilly (1808–1889).

26. *ex abrupto*: without preparation.

27. Louis-Ferdinand Céline, *Journey to the End of the Night*, trans. Ralph Manheim (New York: New Directions, 1983), p. 172.

28. Henry de Montherlant, *La Marée du soir, Carnets 1968–1971*, "Année 1970" (Paris: Gallimard, 1972), pp. 88–89.

29. Henry de Montherlant, *Desert Love [La rose de sable]*, trans. Alec Brown (New York: Noonday Press, 1957).

30. Honoré de Balzac (1799–1850), *The Country Doctor [Le médecin de campagne]*; *The Country Parson [Le curé de village]*; and *The Wrong Side of Paris* (also translated as *The Seamy Side of History*) *[L'envers de l'histoire contemporaine]*.

31. Balzac, *The Peasantry [Les paysans]*.

32. Balzac, *The Country Doctor*, chap. 1.

33. *The Embarkation for Cythera* [*L'embarcation pour Cythère*], a painting by Antoine Watteau (1684–1721).

34. *parfait défini*: the aorist or passé simple tense.

35. Hector Berlioz (1803–1869), *The Memoirs of Hector Berlioz*, trans. and ed. David Cairns (New York: Knopf, 2002).

36. Stendhal, *Rome, Naples, and Florence* (1826; New York: Braziller, 1960).

37. *lazzaroni*: homeless idlers of Naples who live by chance work or begging, named for St. Lazarus hospital, where they loiter.

38. *sediola*: a one- or two-person horse-drawn carriage.

39. *intelligenti pauca*: For he who understands, a few words suffice.

40. An eclectic anti-German and pro-monarchical political movement centered on General Georges Boulanger (1837–1891).

41. *vert paradis*: "But the green Paradise of childhood loves . . . ," from "Grieving and Wandering" ("Moesta et errabunda"), in *The Flowers of Evil*, trans. William Aggeler (1857; Fresno, Calif.: Academy Library Guild, 1954).

42. *egregore*: a "group spirit."

43. Dulcinea was Don Quixote's idealized beloved.

44. "returning upstream": "*retours amont*," a reference to René Char, *Retour amant* (Paris: Gallimard, 1966).

45. Degas's phrase is "se mettre en espalier."

46. *M.L.F.*: Mouvement de libération des femmes, the French women's liberation movement.

47. grand-guignolesque: The Grand Guignol was a theater of the macabre in Montmartre that operated from 1897 to 1962.

48. Paradou: the wild, enchanted garden in Zola's *La faute de l'abbé Mouret* (*Abbé Mouret's Transgression*, 1875); La Lison: a character in Zola's *La bête humaine* (*The Human Beast*, 1890).

49. *The Kill*: *La Curée* (1871).

50. *Worth*: the House of Worth, founded by the fashion designer Charles Frederic Worth (1826–1895); *Ladies's Delight*: the fictional department store in Zola's *Au bonheur des dames* (*The Ladies' Delight*, 1883).

51. "The broad country . . .": "*Les grands pays muets longuement s'étendront . . .*"—a line from Alfred de Vigny (1797–1863), "La maison du berger" ["The Shepherd's House"] in *Les destinées* (1864).

52. *New Heloise*: Rousseau's *Julie, or the New Heloise* [*Julie, ou la nouvelle Héloïse*] (1761).

53. André Le Nôtre (1613–1700), landscape architect for the park at Versailles; François Mansart (1598–1666), classical French architect.

54. *falling asleep*: in French, the more awkward word *endormissement*.

55. Valéry, *La jeune Parque* [*The Young Fates*] (1896).

56. *Bitter Victory*: Louis Guilloux, *Le sang noir* (1935).

57. *Locus solus*: a novel (1914) by Raymond Roussel (1877–1933).

58. *résurrectine*: a fluid invented in the novel *Locus solus* capable of reviving the dead.

59. Works by Gérard de Nerval, pen name of Gérard Labrunie

(1808–1855): *Petits châteaux de Bohème* [*Small Castles of Bo-hemia*] (1853); *Les nuits d'octobre* [*October Nights*] (1852); *Chansons et légendes du Valois* [*Songs and Legends of Valois*] (1854).

60. *Mobilis in mobile*: "Mobile within a mobile element," Captain Nemo's motto for the *Nautilus* in Jules Verne (1828–1905), *Twenty Thousand Leagues Under the Sea* [*Vingt mille lieues sous les mers*] (1869).

61. *Dilettas* and *Unicas*: "delights" and "unique things" (Italian); used here as women's names.

62. *conjure up horrors before me*: *dresser des épouvantes devant moi*, from Arthur Rimbaud (1854–1891), "Delirium II," "The Alchemy of the Word," in *A Season in Hell* [*Une saison en enfer*] (1873).

63. Paul Bourget (1852–1935), *Le danseur mondain* [*The Worldly Dancer*] (Paris: Plon-Nourrit, 1926).

64. From "Literature," in Paul Valéry, *Cahiers/Notebooks*, trans. Rachel Killick and Brian Stimpson (Frankfurt am Main: Peter Lang, 2000), vol. 2, p. 262.

65. The "(*sic*)" is Gracq's. Valéry's exact text reads:

"Novels. Arbitrariness—

"The countess caught the 8 o'clock train.}

"ad lib

"The marchioness caught the 9 o'clock train.}

"Yet what I can vary indefinitely in this way, so malleably—any fool can do it in my stead,—the reader. My concern, however—is with the things that cannot be substituted—that are crucial to me" (Valéry, *Cahiers*).

66. *exquisite*: "exquise" in French.

67. third floor: "deuxième étage" in the original denotes "third floor" in American English.

68. "Outil!": literally, "Tool!"

69. Porto-Riche and Bataille: Georges de Porto-Riche (1849–1930), and Henry Bataille (1872–1922), both playwrights.

70. *natura naturata*: passive, created nature.

71. A play on the phrase "mariage de la main gauche" or "left-handed marriage," a morganatic or common-law marriage.

72. Thomas Mann (1875–1955), "L'artiste et la société," in *L'artiste et la société: portraits, études, souvenirs*, trans. from German to French by Louise Servicen (Paris: Grasset, 1973).

73. *L'Assiette au Beurre*: a satirical journal of cartoons.

74. Baudelaire, first line of "Spleen" in *The Flowers of Evil*, trans. William Aggeler (1857; Fresno, Calif.: Academy Library Guild, 1954).

75. Charles-Albert Cingria (1883–1954), *Bois sec, bois vert* [*Dry Wood, Green Wood*] (1948; Paris: Gallimard, 1983).

76. A phrase from Paul Valéry, *The Graveyard by the Sea* [*Le cimetière marin*].

77. Edgar Allan Poe, *The Fall of the House of Usher*; Paul Claudel, *Knowing the East* [*Connaissance de l'Est*].

78. *dark flights scattered in the future*: an abridged line from Mallarmé's "Tomb of Edgar Poe" ("dark flights of Blasphemy scattered in the future").

79. his *I* . . . an other: an allusion to Rimbaud's statement "I is another," in a letter of May 13, 1871, in *Collected Poems*, ed. Oliver Bernard (1962).

80. Etienne Bonnot de Condillac (1715–1780), in *Traité des sensations* [*Treatise on the Sensations*] (1754), following Locke's empiricism, posits a statue like a man being introduced to the senses, beginning with the sense of smell.

81. Pierre Beaumarchais (1732–1799) based the character Don Guzman in *The Marriage of Figaro* on the magistrate Goezman, whose help in overturning a court ruling contributed to Beaumarchais's financial ruin; the character of the critic Claude Vignon in Balzac's novel *Béatrix* is based on Gustave Planche (1808–1857), who wrote critically of Balzac; and Charles Péguy (1873–1914) criticized Fernand Laudet in *Un nouveau théologien, M. Fernand Laudet* (1911).

82. Rimbaud, "First Communions," in *Complete Works*, trans. Wallace Fowlie (Chicago: University of Chicago Press, 1966), p. 97.

83. Victor Hugo (1802–1885), "Booz endormi," *La Légende des siècles*; "Boaz Asleep" from *Legend of the Ages*, in *Selected Poems of Victor Hugo: A Bilingual Edition*, trans. E. H. and A. M. Blackmore (Chicago: University of Chicago Press, 2001), p. 337.

84. Gérard de Nerval, "Delfica," in *Les Chimères*, trans. William Stone (London: Menard Press, 1999), p. 37.

85. Guillaume Apollinaire (1880–1918), "Marie," in *Alcools*, trans. Donald Revell (Hanover: Wesleyan University Press, 1995).

86. "A Throw of the Dice" ["Un coup de dés"], by Mallarmé.

87. *Les chimères*: *The Chimeras*.

88. Chambre Introuvable: the ultra-reactionary French Chamber of Deputies in 1815–1816.

89. Pierre-Jean de Béranger (1780–1857), "Le vieux céli-bataire" ["The Old Bachelor"], in *Chansons* [*Songs*] (Paris: Perrotin-Guillaumin-Bigot, 1829).

90. "the winegrower of La Chavonnière" ["vigneron de La Chavonnière"]: the political writer Paul-Louis Courier (1773–1825).

91. Emile Combes (1835–1921), a radical socialist politician, argued for the separation of church and state.

92. *Above the Battle*: *Au-dessus de la mêlée* (1915), antiwar essay by Romain Rolland (1866–1944).

93. the "good master" of La Béchellerie: Anatole France.

94. the school of Pigier: a secretarial and trade school.

95. *The Cathedral*: *La cathédrale* (1898), by Joris-Karl Huysmans (1848–1907).

96. *Bugatti*: luxury and race cars produced by Ettore Bugatti (1881–1947).

97. *espagnolades*: picturesque works of art or literature.

98. lex *Julia de maritandis ordinibus*: strict marriage laws introduced in 18–17 B.C.E. by emperor Augustus, intended to encourage marriage and childbearing.

99. Yves Bonnefoy, *Rimbaud par lui-même* [*Rimbaud by Himself*] (Paris: Seuil, 1961).

100. "Parents, you have made me a slave of my baptism": Rimbaud actually wrote: "I am a slave to my baptism. Parents, you have caused my misfortune and your own"; from "Night of Hell," in *A Season in Hell*.

101. Poems by Rimbaud: "Le pauvre songe" ["The Poor Man

Dreams"]; "Bonne pensée du matin" ["A Good Thought in the Morning"]; "Comédie de la soif" ["Comedy of Thirst"]; "Larme" ["Tear"]; "Eternité" ["Eternity"]; and "Jeune ménage" ["Young Couple"].

102. Poems by Musset: "A Saint Blaise, à la Zuecca . . ."; "La chanson de Barberine" ["The Song of Barberine"].

103. Poems by Apollinaire, in *Alcools* (1913): "Chanson du Mal Aimé" ["Song of the Poorly Loved"]; "Adieu" ["The Farewell"]; "Marizibill"; "Colchiques" ["Saffrons"]; "Clotilde"; and "Marie."

104. *L'Intermédiaire des chercheurs et des curieux* [*The Intermediary for Researchers and the Curious*]: a monthly journal that reports on the questions and responses of its readers for a wide variety of subjects, similar to the English *Notes and Queries*.

105. "To die and finally know irresistible eternity...": "Mourir et savoir enfin l'irrésistible éternité . . ."; "Lou" is Louise de Colligny-Chatillon, whom Apollinaire addressed in his *Calligrammes* (1918).

106. *The Rotting Magician*: *L'enchanteur pourrissant* (1904).

107. "Baudelaire . . . feelings and thoughts": "Baudelaire avait déchiffré dans les hiéroglyphes de l'âme le retour d'âge des sentiments et des idées . . ."; from Huysmans, *Au rebours* [*Against the Grain*].

108. *eustatic*: relating to a worldwide change in sea level as a result of melting glaciers or earth movements.

109. *The Opposing Shore*: *Le rivage des Syrtes* (1951), for which Gracq refused the Prix Goncourt.

110. Tacitus, *The Annals*, book 1, chap. 61, trans. Alfred John Church and William Jackson Brodribb (New York: Modern Library, 2003), p. 35.

111. Ibid., chap. 62, p. 36.

112. Joachim Fest, *Hitler*, trans. Richard and Clara Winston (New York: Vintage Books, 1975), p. 647.

113. *Contes bizarres* [*Strange Tales*]: three tales by Ludwig Achim von Arnim, translated from German into French by Théophile Gautier, with a introduction by André Breton. *Les héritiers du majorat* [*The Inheritors*].

114. Hermann Levi (1839–1900) conducted Wagner's *Parsifal* at its first performance.

115. *reiterated by a thousand sentinels*: *répété par mille sentinelles*; from Baudelaire, "Beacons" ["Les phares"], in *The Flowers of Evil*.

116. q.s.: *quantum sufficit*, a sufficient quantity.

117. the forest of Dunsinane: "Macbeth shall never vanquish'd be until / Great Birnam wood to high Dunsinane hill / shall come against him"; Shakespeare, *Macbeth*, act 4, scene 1, lines 92–94.

118. pistol shot at a concert: a reference to Stendhal's *The Red and the Black*.

119. "will not be robbed of its daemonic right": "And yet the present will not be robbed of its daemonic right," from J. W. Goethe, *Elective Affinities*, trans. R. J. Hollingdale (Harmondsworth, Eng.: Penguin, 1971), p. 106.

120. "stored in the cellars . . .": an allusion to a line in Valéry's *Notebooks*.

121. *Dreams and Destinies*: Marguerite Yourcenar, *Les songes et les sortes*.

122. "fell outside like snow": in A. Breton, "Avis au lecteur pour *La Femme 100 têtes* de Max Ernst."

123. *capharnaum*: See note 4 above.

124. "The desert grows: woe unto him that harbors deserts in himself!": from Friedrich Nietzsche, *Thus Spoke Zarathustra*.

125. "If, from a system in which I believe, . . .": from André Breton, "Preface for a Reprint of the Manifesto" (1929), in *Manifestoes of Surrealism*, trans. Richard Seaver and Helen Lane (Ann Arbor: University of Michigan Press, 1972), p. x.

126. "Et le fleuve . . .": "And the river [. . .] waters a region no less deserted than [. . .] when man first pierced a bullock's horn and blew a rude and bitter note in the unechoing countryside" (*Knowing the East*); Paul Claudel, "The River" (March 1897), in *Knowing the East*, trans. James Lawler (Princeton, N.J.: Princeton University Press, 2004), p. 47.

127. "A mesure . . . ": "As a man's favor and wealth recede, they reveal the ridiculous aspects of his character that they concealed, and that were always there without anyone noticing.": Jean de La Bruyère (1645–1696), "Des biens de fortune" ["Of Worldly Goods"], in *Les caractères* [*The Characters*].

128. *The Journals of André Gide*, vol. 2 (1914–1927), trans. Justin O'Brien (New York: Knopf, 1948), p. 234.

129. "To each being . . . ": Rimbaud, "Delirium II," in *A Season in Hell*.

130. *The Journals of André Gide*, vol. 2 (1914–1927), trans. Justin O'Brien (New York: Knopf, 1948), p. 289.

131. Fontaine des Quatre-Saisons: Fountain of the Four Seasons, by Edme Bouchardon (1698–1762).

132. the swan of Saint-Point: the poet Alphonse de Lamartine (1790–1869).

133. *Roche*: the village where Rimbaud's family farm was located.

134. "this is certainly the same countryside": from Rimbaud, "Deserts of Love."

135. "ferocious invalid, back from the torrid countries": from Rimbaud, "Bad Blood"; "to die in barbarous rivers" and "to go where the cows drink": from "Comedy of Thirst."

136. *mère Rimbe*: Rimbaud's mother, née Vitalie Cuif.

137. *Nous sommes tes grands parents* . . . : Rimbaud, "The Parents" from "Comedy of Thirst."

138. *Enfance au bord d'un lac!*: from "La Savoie" in *Comtesse de Noailles* (Paris: G. Crès, 1922).

139. "as thirsty oxen bend toward a lake": Victor Hugo, "Boaz Asleep" in *Selected Poems of Victor Hugo*, trans. E. H. and A. M. Blackmore (Chicago: University of Chicago Press, 2001), p. 341.

140. Tristan Corbière, *Les Amours Jaunes*.

141. *Tu dors* . . . : first line of "Bambine" by Tristan Corbière, in *Amours Jaunes*.

142. *Sunbeams and Shadows*: *Les Rayons et les ombres*, by Victor Hugo.

143. Nietzsche, *Le cas Wagner* [*The Case of Wagner*], in *Œuvres philosophiques complètes* (Paris: Gallimard, 1974), vol. 8, p. 34.

144. Roman Jakobson (1896–1982), Russian linguist, cited by

Gérard Genette in "Structuralisme et critique littéraire [Structuralism and literary criticism]," *Figures I* (Paris: Seuil, 1966), p. 168, translated as *Figures of Literary Discourse* by Alan Sheridan (New York: Columbia University Press, 1982).

145. *Lisez—Ne lisez pas*: a list of authors titled *Read—Do not read*, published in various Surrealist publications.

146. "Paris reine du monde": "Paris, Queen of the World"; "J'ai deux amours": "I Have Two Loves"; "Tu reverras Paname": "You'll See Paname Again"; "Paris sera toujours Paris": "Paris Will Always Be Paris."

147. See note 19 above.

148. catoblepas: mythological creature with a long neck and low head.

149. Charles-Louis de Secondat, baron de La Brède et de Montesquieu (1689–1755), *Voyage de Gratz à La Haye*, *Œuvres Complètes*, ed. Roger Caillois (Paris: Gallimard, Bibliothèque de la Pléiade, 1949), 2 vols., vol. 1, pp. 544–800.

150. demilune: a work in the shape of a half-moon built to defend an entrance of a fortification; Sergeant-King: Roi-Sergent, the Prussian King Frederick William I (1688–1740)].

151. *Quis tulerit Gracchos* . . . : "Who could endure the Gracchi railing at sedition?" from Juvenal, *Satires* 2.

152. "white joyous nations": Rimbaud, "Adieu," in *A Season in Hell*: "Sometimes I see in the sky endless beaches covered with white joyous nations."

153. *Jam redit et Virgo, redeunt Saturnia regna*: "Justice returns, returns old Saturn's reign"; Virgil, *Bucolics*, book 4, v. 8.

154. *modicum et bonum*: moderate and good.

155. "Tant que l'eau . . .": As long as the water of new baptism has not passed over them . . . ; a reference to John 3:5: "Except a man be born of water and of the spirit, he cannot enter into the kingdom of God."

156. Jacques Rivière, *Le parti de l'intelligence* (1921) in *La Nouvelle Revue Française* 72 (September 1, 1919), p. 615.